21世纪国际商务教材教辅系列

编写委员会

21世纪国际商务教材教辅系列

总 主 编　余世明
副总主编　袁绍岐　张彬祥　何　静

DOCUMENTS & CREDIT FOR INTERNATIONAL BUSINESS

国际商务单证实务练习册

（第二版）

主编　余世明　　副主编　张少辉　张小彤

暨南大學出版社
JINAN UNIVERSITY PRESS

中国·广州

图书在版编目（CIP）数据

国际商务单证实务练习册/余世明主编；张少辉，张小彤副主编．—2 版．—广州：暨南大学出版社，2013.8（2018.8 重印）
（21 世纪国际商务教材教辅系列）
ISBN 978－7－5668－0542－3

Ⅰ.①国…　Ⅱ.①余…②张…③张…　Ⅲ.①国际贸易—票据—高等学校—习题集
Ⅳ.①F740.44－44

中国版本图书馆 CIP 数据核字(2013)第 084066 号

国际商务单证实务练习册
GUOJI SHANGWU DANZHENG SHIWU LIANXICE
主　编：余世明　副主编：张少辉　张小彤

出 版 人：徐义雄
责任编辑：张仲玲　冯　琳
责任校对：王嘉涵
责任印制：汤慧君　周一丹

出版发行：暨南大学出版社（510630）
电　　话：总编室（8620）85221601
营销部（8620）85225284　85228291　85228292（邮购）
传　　真：（8620）85221583（办公室）　85223774（营销部）
网　　址：http：//www.jnupress.com
排　　版：广州市天河星辰文化发展部照排中心
印　　刷：佛山市浩文彩色印刷有限公司
开　　本：787mm×1092mm　1/16
印　　张：14.25
字　　数：340 千
版　　次：2009 年 10 月第 1 版　2013 年 8 月第 2 版
印　　次：2018 年 8 月第 11 次
印　　数：30001—33000 册
定　　价：33.00 元

目　　录

编写说明

国际商务单证实务是一门实践性相当强的课程。虽然近年来全国推行国际商务单证员和国际商务操作员的培训认证，但有关的实训材料较少。本书作为《国际商务单证实务》教材的配套练习册，力求使学生在学好教材的同时有针对性地进行训练，达到巩固、强化的目的。本书的编写具有如下特点：

（1）内容新。以最新的国际贸易惯例（如《UCP600》、《2010 年通则》等）进行解释，采用的单证材料和案例也是近几年外贸公司的实际业务资料，力求贴近实际。

（2）题型全。练习题中包括了中英文术语、短语互译，单项选择题，多项选择题，判断题，阅读理解，单据填制，单据改错和案例分析等，保证学生能得到全面的训练。

（3）单证真。书中的单证大多数来自公司的实例，除客户名等资料有所改动外，其他全部保留，力求给学生更直观的感觉。

（4）针对性强。本书以国际商务单证员、国际商务操作员、外销员、报关员和国际货运代理从业人员等统考的内容和题型为基础，有助于学生顺利通过上述各种认证考试。

本书的编写分工如下：第一章、第二章的第三节和第五节、第三章的第三节和第四节由余世明编写，第二章的第四节和第六节、第三章的第一节和第二节由张少辉编写，第二章的第一节和第二节、第六章、第七章由张小彤编写，第四章、第八章由杨子电编写，第五章由陈夏鹏编写，第九章由余世明、邓棣嫦编写。全书由余世明负责总纂和修审。

本书不仅可作为高职高专和中等职业技术学校国际商务专业和其他相关财经类专业学生学习《国际商务单证实务》的配套用书，而且可作为涉外各类考证和各类干部培训国际商务基本知识的实训用书。

本书在编写中参考了大量的资料，特别是现行国际商务单证各版本的教材，还引用了很多外贸公司的实际单证，在此谨向各位作者和外贸公司的经理、业务员、单证员表示衷心的感谢！由于水平有限，错误之处敬请批评指正。

编　者

2013 年 6 月

第一章
信 用 证

一、中英文术语、短语互译

（一）中译英

（1）不可撤销信用证________

（2）开证日期________

（3）电汇索偿________

（4）一切银行费用________

（5）佣金________

（6）出票根据________

（7）正本单据________

（8）通知行________

（9）账户________

（10）保兑行________

（二）英译中

（1）Applicant ________

（2）Beneficiary ________

（3）Negotiation Bank ________

（4）Drawee Bank ________

（5）Expiry Date ________

（6）Documentary Credit ________

（7）Documents Required ________

（8）Special Conditions ________

（9）Up to an Aggregate Amount of ________

（10）The Full Name and Address of the Openers ________

二、单项选择题

1. 不可撤销信用证在信用证的有效期内，未经（　　）的同意，开证行或开证人不得撤销或修改。

A. 受益人　　　　B. 开证人

C. 开证行　　　　D. 受益人、开证人以及有关银行

2. 根据《UCP600》的规定，若信用证没有注明（ ）字样，则认为该信用证为不保兑信用证。

A. Confirmed B. Revocable

C. Revolving D. Transferable

3. 在进料加工贸易中，经常先向外商购买原材料或配件，我方加工成品后再卖给该外商。为了避免上当受骗，我方应采用（ ）比较稳妥。

A. 保兑信用证 B. 可转让信用证

C. 预支信用证 D. 对开信用证

4. 下列对信用证有效期的描述，属于直接写明具体日期的是（ ）。

A. Documents must be presented for negotiation within 10 days after the on board date of bill of lading

B. Negotiation must be on or before the 15th day of shipment

C. This L/C is valid for negotiation in China until Oct. 1, 2002

D. Documents to be presented to negotiation bank within 15 days after shipment

5. 根据《UCP600》的规定，如使用"于或约于"之类词语限定装运日期，银行将视为在所述日期前后各（ ）内装运，起讫日包括在内。

A. 3 天 B. 5 天

C. 7 天 D. 10 天

6. "Transshipment permitted, part shipments allowed, but part shipment of each item not allowed" 的中文意思是（ ）。

A. 转运允许，分运允许，但每个品种的货物不得分运

B. 转运不允许，分运允许，但每个品种的货物不得分运

C. 转运允许，分运允许，但每个品种的货物必须分运

D. 转运允许，分运不允许，但每个品种的货物不得分运

7. 下列信用证有关费用的条款，要求卖方负担有关费用的是（ ）。

A. All banking charges for seller's account

B. Port congestion surcharges, if any, at the time of shipment is for opener's account

C. All banking charges outside Hongkong are for account of accountee

D. Drawee bank's charges and acceptance commission are for buyer's account

8. 下列属于信用证条款中开证行保证文句的是（ ）。

A. Letter of guarantee and discrepancies are not acceptable

B. We hereby undertake to honour all drafts drawn in accordance with terms of this credit

C. One copy of commercial invoice and packing list should be sent to the credit openers 15 days before shipment

D. Drafts to be drawn for full CIF value less 5% commission, invoice to show full CIF value

9. 下列英文词组中，表示"议付行"的是（ ）。

A. Confirming Bank B. Opening Bank

C. Negotiation Bank D. Advising Bank

10. 根据《UCP600》的规定，若信用证没有特别说明，则信用证（ ）。

A. 未注明“Transferable”字样或条款，即为可转让信用证

B. 未注明“Irrevocable”字样，即为可撤销信用证

C. 未注明“Confirmed”字样，即为不保兑信用证

D. 未注明是否即期付款，即为远期付款信用证

三、多项选择题

1. 信用证中，表示开证人的常见词或词组有（　　）。

A. Principal　　B. Opener

C. Applicant　　D. account of...

E. Accountee

2. 信用证中，表示受益人的常见词或词组有（　　）。

A. Beneficiary　　B. in favour of...

C. Opener　　D. in your favour

3. 对于保兑信用证，承担第一性付款责任的有（　　）。

A. 通知行　　B. 议付行

C. 开证行　　D. 保兑行

4. 下列信用证条款中，属于佣金条款的是（　　）。

A. Port congestion surcharges, if any, at the time of shipment is for opener's account

B. Signed invoices must show 5% commission

C. 5% commission to be deducted from the invoice value

D. Beneficiary's drafts are to be made out for 95% of invoice value, being 5% commission payable to credit opener

5. 对 SWIFT，下列表述正确的是（　　）。

A. 使用 SWIFT 系统的银行必须加入该协会，方可使用 SWIFT 系统

B. 使用 SWIFT 信用证，必须遵守 SWIFT 使用手册的规定，使用 SWIFT 手册规定的代号

C. SWIFT 信用证必须按国际商会制定的《UCP600》的规定处理

D. SWIFT 系统具有自动收发储存信息、自动加押和核押等功能

E. SWIFT 系统可每周 7 天、每天 24 小时连续不停地运转

四、判断题

1. 2005 年 6 月 18 日在 SWIFT 电文中表示为 180605。（　　）

2. 在 SWIFT 信用证中，数字“2584678.36”表示为“2584678,36”。（　　）

3. 信用证不准分批，又没有数量增减条款，则实际装运数量允许有 5% 的增减幅度。（　　）

4. 信用证规定起运港为 CHINA PORTS，若信用证禁止分批，则信用证中装运港 CHINA PORTS 的实际意义与 CHINA PORT 相同。（　　）

5. 信用证没有规定有效期或装运期，则该信用证为无效信用证。（　　）

6．信用证修改通知书的内容，受益人可根据实际情况，接受其中的一部分，拒绝其中的另一部分。(　　)

7．信用证修改通知书必须由原通知行转递或通知。(　　)

8．信用证的性质是银行信用，因此，信用证项下使用的汇票必定是银行汇票。(　　)

9．背对背信用证是指交易的一方开出第一张信用证，但暂不生效，须在对方开来一定金额的回头信用证经受益人表示接受时，才通知对方银行两证同时生效。(　　)

10．对于不可撤销信用证，如果开证人提出申请，开证行可随时撤销该信用证。(　　)

五、案例分析

1．某公司从国外某商行进口一批钢材，货物分两批装运，支付方式为不可撤销即期信用证，每批分别由中国银行开立一份信用证。第一批货物装运后，卖方在有效期内向银行交单议付，议付行审单后，即向该商行议付货款，随后中国银行对议付行作了偿付。我方在收到第一批货物后，发现货物品质与合同不符，因而要求开证行对第二份信用证项下的单据拒绝付款，但遭开证行拒绝。问：开证行这样做是否合理？为什么？

2．我某轻工业进出口公司向国外客户出口某商品一批，合同中规定以即期不可撤销信用证为付款方式，信用证的到期地点规定在我国。为保证款项的收回，应议付行的要求，我方商请香港某银行对中东某银行（开证行）开立的信用证加以保兑。在合同规定的开证时间内，我方收到通知银行（即议付行）转来的一张即期不可撤销保兑信用证。我出口公司在货物装运后，将有关单据交议付银行议付。不久接保兑行通知：“由于开证行已破产，我行将不承担该信用证的付款责任。”问：(1) 保兑行的做法是否正确？为什么？(2) 对此情况，我方应如何处理？

六、阅读理解

（一）阅读理解一

*KRUNG THAI BANK PUBLIC COMPANY
*LIMITED
*BANGKOK

User Header	Service Code	103:	
	Bank. Priority	113:	
	Msg User Ref.	108:	
	Info. from CI	115:	
Sequence of Total	*27	:	1 / 1
Form of Doc. Credit	*40 A	:	IRREVOCABLE
Doc. Credit Number	*20	:	BL 120197
Date of Issue	31 C	:	010123
Expiry	*31 D	:	Date 010422 Place CHINA
Applicant Bank	51 D	:	KRUNG THAI BANK PCL., SUANMALI IBC.
Applicant	*50	:	METCH THAI CHEMICAL COMPANY LIMITED 45-7 MAITRICHITR RD., BANGKOK, THAILAND.
Beneficiary	*59	:	SINOCHEM GUANGDONG IMPORT AND EXPORT CORPORATION 58 ZHANQIAN ROAD. GUANGZHOU, CHINA
Amount	*32 B	:	Currency USD Amount 16,264
Available with/by	*41 D	:	ANY BANK BY NEGOTIATION
Drafts at ...	42 C	:	SIGHT
Drawee	42 D	:	KRUNG THAI BANK PCL., SUANMALI IBC.
Partial Shipments	43 P	:	PROHIBITED
Transshipment	43 T	:	ALLOWED
Loading in Charge	44 A	:	GUANGZHOU, CHINA
For Transport to ...	44 B	:	BANGKOK, THAILAND
Latest Date of Ship.	44 C	:	010412
Descript. of Goods	45 A	:	42.80 MT LITHOPONE 30PCT ARROW BRAND USD380.- PER MT DETAILS AS PER PROFORMA INVOICE NO.01TH44GD176A3-032 DATED JAN.22,2001. C.I.F. BANGKOK, THAILAND
Documents required	46 A	:	

+ SIGNED COMMERCIAL INVOICE IN 10 COPIES SHOWING SEPARATELY F.O.B.VALUE, FREIGHT CHARGE, INSURANCE PREMIUM, C.I.F.VALUE AND COUNTRY OF ORIGIN.
+ FULL SET OF CLEAN ON BOARD OCEAN BILLS OF LADING TO ORDER OF KRUNG THAI BANK PUBLIC COMPANY LIMITED MARKED FREIGHT PREPAID PLUS TWO NON-NEGOTIABLE COPIES, NOTIFY : APPLICANT
+ MARINE INSURANCE POLICY OR CERTIFICATE IN DUPLICATE, ENDORSED IN BLANK, FOR FULL INVOICE VALUE PLUS 10 PERCENT STATING CLAIM PAYABLE IN THAILAND COVERING INSTITUTE CARGO CLAUSES (A) AND WAR RISKS.
+ PACKING LIST IN 5 COPIES.
+ CERTIFICATE OF ANALYSIS IN 5 COPIES.
+ ONE FULL SET OF NON-NEGOTIABLE SHIPPING DOCUMENTS MUST BE SENT TO THE APPLICANT BY AIR COURIER WITHIN 3 DAYS AFTER SHIPMENT AND BENEFICIARY'S CERTIFICATE TO THIS EFFECT IS REQUIRED.
+ BENEFICIARY'S CERTIFICATE CERTIFYING THAT ONE COPY EACH OF INVOICE, N/N B/L HAVE BEEN FAXED TO BUYER TO FAX NO.662-225 WITHIN 3 DAYS AFTER SHIPMENT.

JAN31 07:19:37　　　　　　　　　　　　　　　　Logical Terminal GDPF
S700　　　　　　Issue of a Documentary Credit　　　　　　Page 00002
　　　　　　　　　　　　　　　　　　　　　　　　　　Func JSRVPR1

Addtional Cond.　　47 A :
+ ALL DOCUMENTS MENTIONING THIS L/C NO.
+ BOTH AMOUNT AND QUANTITY PLUS OR MINUS 5PCT ACCEPTABLE.
+ IF ANY DISCREPANCY,WE SHALL DEDUCT USD50.- BEING OUR FEE FROM THE PROCESS.
+ THE NAME, ADDRESS, TELEPHONE NUMBER OF SHIPPING AGENT IN BANGKOK MUST BE MENTIONED ON B/L.

Details of Charges　　71 B : ALL BANK CHARGES OUTSIDE THAILAND INCLUDING COST OF WIRE AND REIM.CHARGE ARE FOR BENEFICIARY'S ACCOUNT.

Confirmation　　*49　: WITHOUT

Instructions　　78　:
+ UPON RECEIPT OF SHIPPING DOCUMENTS IN STRICT CONFORMITY WITH L/C TERMS,WE WILL COVER YOUR ACCOUNT AND LESS OUR COST OF WIRE IF ANY ACCORDING TO YOUR INSTRUCTION.
+ DRAFT(S) AND DOCUMENTS TO BE SENT TO US BY COURIER SERVICE MAILING ADDRESS(SUANMALI IBC.,20 YUKHON 2 RD.,POMPRAB,BANGKOK 10100,THAILAND.)
+ THIS ADVICE IS OPERATIVE WITH NO CONFIRMATION TO FOLLOW AND SUBJECT TO ICC 1993 REVISION PUB 500.

Send. to Rec. Info.　72　: KINDLY ACKNOWLEDGE RECEIPT THIS CREDIT BY RETURN SWIFT WILL BE MUCH APPRECIATED.

Trailer　　Order is <MAC:> <PAC:> <ENC:> <CHK:> <THG:> <PDE:>
MAC:642A77D3
CHK:4111579499C7

请从上面信用证中找出以下内容：

（1）开证人：

（2）受益人：

（3）信用证号码：

（4）开证日期：

（5）信用证有效期及到期地点：

（6）装运港：

（7）目的港：

（8）装运期限：

（9）分批和转船的要求：

（10）商品数量及名称：

（11）要求单据：

（12）交单期限：

（13）信用证金额：

（14）信用证数量和金额增减百分比：

（15）信用证特殊条款：

（16）单据不符点扣费额：

（17）形式发票号码及日期：

（18）贸易术语：

（二）阅读理解二

```
980CT22   17:15:23                                          Logical Terminal P5A7
MT S700                  Issue of a Documentary Credit              Page 00001
                                                                    Func GZPRQ
MSSACK  DWS765I Auth OK, key B1980419F862E4A3, BKCHCNBJ SAIBJPJT record652333
Basic Header          F  01 BKCHCNBJA400 8954 778732
Application Header    O 700 1624 981022 SAIBJPJTCXXX 4970 776422 981022 1524 N
                                        *ASAHI BANK LTD. THE (FORMERLY.THE
                                        *KYOWA SAITAMA BANK, LTD.)
                                        *TOKYO
User Header           Service Code     103:
                      Bank. Priority   113:
                      Msg User Ref.    108:
                      Info. from CI    115:
Sequence of Total     *27    : 1 / 1
Form of Doc. Credit   *40 A  : IRREVOCABLE
Doc. Credit Number    *20    : LC-410-046405
Date of Issue          31 C  : 981022
Expiry                *31 D  : Date 990115 Place CHINA
Applicant             *50    : SUMITOMO CORPORATION
Beneficiary           *59    : GUANGDONG YUEFENG TRADING CO.
                               NO.31 ZHEN'AN ROAD GUANGZHOU,
                               CHINA.
Amount                *32 B  :          Currency USD Amount 98.000,00
Pos. / Neg. Tol.(%)    39 A  : 5  / 5
Available with/by     *41 D  : ANY BANK
                               BY NEGOTIATION
Drafts at ...          42 C  : DRAFTS AT SIGHT FOR FULL INVOICE
                               VALUE
Drawee                 42 A  : SAIBJPJT
                              *ASAHI BANK LTD, THE (FORMERLY THE
                              *KYOWA SAITAMA BANK, LTD.)
                              *TOKYO
Partial Shipments      43 P  : ALLOWED
Transshipment          43 T  : ALLOWED
Loading in Charge      44 A  :
           SHIPMENT FROM CHINESE MAIN PORT
For Transport to       44 B  :
              OSAKA, JAPAN
Latest Date of Ship.   44 C  : 981231
Descript. of Goods     45 A  :
           HALF DRIED PRUNE 1998CROP
           GRADE    SPEC                  QNTY      UNIT PRICE               SHIPMENT
                                          (CASE)    (USD/CASE)
             B    L:700CASE   M:700CASE  1,400     21.0   C AND F OSAKA    NOV.,1998
             A    L:700CASE   M:700CASE  1,400     26.0   C AND F OSAKA    DEC.,1998
             B    L:700CASE   M:700CASE  1,400     21.0   C AND F OSAKA    DEC.,1998
           PACKING:IN WOODEN CASE, 12KGS PER CASE
           TRADE TERMS: C AND F OSAKA
Documents required     46 A  :
           +2/3 SET OF CLEAN ON BOARD OCEAN BILLS OF LADING MADE OUT TO
           ORDER OF SHIPPER AND BLANK ENDORSED AND MARKED ''FREIGHT
           PREPAID'' AND ''NOTIFY SUMITOMO CORPORATION OSAKA.''
           +MANUALLY SIGNED COMMERCIAL INVOICE IN TRIPLICATE(3) INDICATING
           APPLICANT'S REF. NO. SCLI-98-0474.
           +PACKING LIST IN TRIPLICATE(3).
           +MANUALLY SIGNED CERTIFICATE OF ORIGIN IN TRIPLICATE(3).
           +BENEFICIARY'S CERTIFICATE STATING THAT CERTIFICATE OF
           MANUFACTURING PROCESS AND OF THE INGREDIENTS ISSUED BY GUANGDONG
           YUE FENG TRADING CO., SHOULD BE SENT TO SUMITOMO CORP ESCLZ
           SECTION.
           +CERTIFICATE OF WEIGHT AND QUALITY IN TRIPLICATE.
Additional Cond.       47 A  :
           1. INSURANCE TO BE EFFECTED BY BUYER.
           2. TELEGRAPHIC REIMBURSEMENT CLAIM PROHIBITED.
```

98OCT22　17:15:44　　　　　　　　　　　　　Logical Terminal P5A7
MT S700　　　Issue of a Documentary Credit　　　Page 00002
Func GZPRQ

3. 1/3 ORIGINAL B/L AND OTHER SHIPPING DOCUMENTS MUST BE SENT DIRECTLY TO APPLICANT SUMITOMO CORP ESCLZ SECTION IN 3 DAYS AFTER B/L DATE. AND SENT BY FAX.
4. AMOUNT AND QNTY 5PCT MORE OR LESS ALLOWED.
5. THIS COMMODITY FREE FROM RESIN.

Details of Charges　71 B : ALL BANKING CHARGES OUTSIDE JAPAN ARE FOR ACCOUNT OF ~~BENEFICIARY.~~

Presentation Period　48 : DOCUMENTS TO BE PRESENTED WITHIN 15 DAYS AFTER THE DATE OF SHIPMENT, BUT WITHIN THE VALIDITY OF THE CREDIT.

Confirmation　*49 : WITHOUT

Instructions　78 :
THE NEGOTIATING BANK MUST FORWARD THE DRAFTS AND ALL DOCUMENTS BY REGISTERED AIRMAIL DIRECT TO US (INT'L OPERATIONS OFFICE MAIL ADDRESS: C.P.O.BOX NO.800 TOKYO 100-8691 JAPAN) IN TWO CONSECUTIVE LOTS. UPON RECEIPT OF THE DRAFTS AND DOCUMENTS IN ORDER, WE WILL REMIT THE PROCEEDS AS INSTRUCTED BY THE NEGOTIATING BANK.

Trailer　Order is <MAC:> <PAC:> <ENC:> <CHK:> <TNG:> <PDE
MAC:9E9080D4
CHK:AEFC879GF339

请从上面信用证中找出以下内容：

（1）开证人：

（2）受益人：

（3）信用证号码：

（4）开证日期：

（5）信用证有效期及到期地点：

（6）装运港：

（7）目的港：

（8）装运期限：

（9）分批和转船的要求：

（10）商品数量及名称：

（11）要求单据：

（12）交单期限：

（13）信用证金额：

（14）信用证数量和金额增减百分比：

（15）信用证特殊条款：

七、信用证审核

（一）信用证审核一

根据下面的合同审核信用证：

售　货　合　同
SALES CONTRACT

卖　方：　GUANGDONG LIGHT ELECTRICAL
Sellers：　APPLIANCES CO.，LTD.　　　　Contract No.：　98SGQ468001
　　　　Date：　APR. 22，1998
地　址：　　　　Signed at：　GUANGZHOU
Address：　52 DEZHENG ROAD SOUTH，GUANGZHOU，CHINA　　　　Telex：　0835
　　　　Fax：　83556688
Buyers：　ABC CORP.　　　　Telex：
Address：　AKEDSANTERINK AUTO P. O. BOX　9，FINLAND　　　　Fax：

This Sales Contract is made by and between the Sellers and the Buyers，whereby the Sellers agree to sell and the Buyers agree to buy the under-mentioned goods according to the terms and conditions stipulated below：

（1）货号、品名及规格 Name of Commodity and Specifications	（2）数量 Quantity	（3）单位 Unit	（4）单价 Unit Price	（5）金额 Amount
HALOGEN FITTING W500	9,600PCS	PC	CIF HELSINKI USD3. 80/PC	USD 36,480. 00
10% more or less both in amount and quantity allowed	Total Amount			USD 36,480. 00

（6） Packing：　12PCS IN A CARTON　（7） Delivery from GUANGZHOU to HELSINKI （8） Shipping Marks：

（9） Time of Shipment：

Within 30 days after receipt of L/C allowing transshipment and partial shipment.

（10） Terms of Payment：

By 100% Confirmed irrevocable Letter of Credit in favor of the Sellers to be available by sight draft to be opened and to reach China before MAY　1，1998 and to remain valid for negotiation in China until the 15th day after the foresaid Time of Shipment. L/C must mention this contract number. L/C advised by BANK OF CHINA，GUANGZHOU BRANCH. TLX：444U4K GZBC CN. All banking Charges outside China（the mainland of China）are for account of the Drawee.

（11） Insurance：

To be effected by Sellers for 110% of full invoice value covering　FPA　up to　HELSINKI　.

~~To be effected by the buyers~~

（12） Arbitration：

All dispute arising from the execution of or in connection with this contract shall be settled amicably by negotiation. In case of settlement can be reached through negotiation the case shall then be submit China International Economic & Trade Arbitration Commision. In Shenzhen（or in Beijing）for arbitration in act with its sure of procedures. The arbitral award is final and binding upon both parties for setting the Disputes. The fee，for arbitration shall be borne by the losing party unless otherwise awarded.

The Seller　张三　　　　The Buyer　**PAUL**

Issue of Documentary Credit

Issuing Bank	:	METITA BANK LTD. , FINLAND
Form of Doc. Credit	:	REVOCABLE
Credit Number	:	LRT9802457
Date of Issue	:	980428
Expiry	:	Date 980416 Place FINLAND
Applicant	:	ABC CO. AKEKSANTERINK AUTO P. O. BOX 9, FINLAND
Beneficiary	:	GUANGDONG LIGHT ELECTRICAL CO. , LTD. 52 DEZHENG ROAD SOUTH, GUANGZHOU, CHINA
Amount	:	USD 3,648.00 (SAY US DOLLARS THIRTY SIX THOUSAND FOUR HUNDRED AND EIGHT ONLY)
Pos. / Neg. Tol. (%)	:	5/5
Available with/by	:	ANY BANK IN ADVISING COUNTRY BY NEGOTIATION
Draft at...	:	DRAFTS AT 20 DAYS' SIGHT FOR FULL INVOICE VALUE
Partial Shipments	:	NOT ALLOWED
Transshipment	:	Allowed
Loading in Charge	:	Guangzhou
For Transport to	:	HELSINKI
Shipment Period	:	AT THE LATEST MAY 30, 1998
Descript. of Goods	:	960PCS OF HALOGEN FITTING W500, USD6.80 PER PC AS PER SALES CONTRACT 98SG468001 DD 22, 04, 98 CIF HESINKI
Documents Required	:	* COMMERCIAL INVOICE 1 SIGNED ORIGINAL AND 5 COPIES * PACKING LIST 1 SIGNED ORIGINAL AND 5 COPIES * FULL SET OF CLEAN ON BOARD MARINE BILLS OF LADING, MADE OUT TO ORDER , MARKED "FREIGHT PREPAID" AND NOTIFY APPLICANT (AS INDICATE ABOVE) * GSP CERTIFICATE OF ORIGIN FORM A, CERTIFYING GOODS OF ORIGIN IN CHINA, ISSUED BY COMPETENT AUTHORITIES * INSURANCE POLICY/CERTIFICATE COVERING ALL RISKS AND WAR RISKS OF PICC. INCLUDING WAREHOUSE TO WAREHOUSE CLAUSE UP TO FINAL DESTINATION AT HELSINKI, FOR AT LEAST 120 PCT OF CIF-VALUE. * SHIPPING ADVICES MUST BE SENT TO APPLICANT WITHIN 2 DAYS AFTER SHIPMENT, ADVISING NUMBER OF PACKAGES, GROSS & NET WEIGHT, VESSEL NAME, B/L NO. AND DATE, CONTRACT NO. , VALUE.
Presentation Period	:	3 DAYS AFTER ISSUANCE DATE OF SHIPPING DOCUMENT
Confirmation	:	WITHOUT
INSTRUCTIONS	:	THE NEGOTIATION BANK MUST FORWARD THE DRAFTS AND ALL DOCUMENTS BY REGISTERED AIRMAIL DIRECT TO US IN TWO CONSECUTIVE LOTS, UPON RECEIPT OF THE DRAFTS AND DOCUMENTS IN ORDER, WE WILL REMIT THE PROCEEDS AS INSTRUCTED BY THE NEGOTIATING BANK.

不符点描述及改正：

(1)

(2)

(3)

(4)

(5)

(6)

(7)

(8)

(9)

(10)

(11)

(12)

(13)

(14)

(15)

(16)

(17)

（二）信用证审核二

根据下面的销货确认书审核信用证：

卖　方
SICHUAN CHANGHONG
ELECTRIC CO., LTD.
35 EAST MIANXING ROAD,
HIGH - TECH PARK,
MIANYANG, SICHUAN,
CHINA

销 货 确 认 书
SALES CONFIRMATION

号码：
No. 800678
日期：
Date: 13 - 02 - 2005
签约地点：
Signed at: MIANYANG, CHINA
电报挂号：
Cable:
TELEX:
FAX: 86 - 760 - 3138616

买　方
Buyers: ABC CORPORATION LIMITED
地　址
Address:

电报挂号：
Cable Address:
TELEX:
FAX:

兹 经 买 卖 双 方 同 意 按 下 列 条 款 成 交：

The undersigned Sellers and Buyers have agreed to close the following transactions according to the terms and conditions stipulated below:

1.

货　号 Art. No.	品名及规格 Description	数　量 Quantity	单　价 Unit Price	金　额 Amount
80230019	AIR CONDITIONER KFR - 35GW/NL, MODEL, R407C, 220V	10,000SETS	CIF VALENCIA @ USD160.00	USD1,600,000.00

数量及总值均得有 3 %的增减，由卖方决定。

With 3 % more or less both in amount and quantity allowed at the Sellers' option.

2. 总　值

Total Value: USD1,600,000.00（US Dollars ONE MILLION SIX HUNDRED THOUSAND ONLY.）

3. 包　装

Packing: ONE SET IN TWO CARTONS, TOTAL 20,000 CARTONS

4. 装运期

Time of Shipment: 3,000 SETS BY 31ST, MARCH 2005, 7,000 SETS BY 15TH, APRIL 2005

5. 装运口岸和目的地

Loading port & Destination: FROM SHENZHENG TO VALENCIA SPAIN

6. 保　险　由卖方按发票全部金额110%投保至＿＿＿＿为止的＿＿＿＿＿＿险。

Insurance: To be effected by Sellers for 110% of full invoice value covering FPA ＿＿＿＿＿＿ up to VALENCIA SPAIN only.

7. 付款条件：　买方须于　年　月　日将不可撤销的见票30天付款的信用证开到卖方，议付有效期延至上列装运期后15天在中国到期，该信用证中必须注明允许分运及转运。

Terms of payment:

By Irrevocable Letter of Credit to be available by 30 DAYS' AFTER sight draft to reach the Sellers before MAR. 13, 2005 and to remain valid for negotiation in China until the 15th day after the aforesaid Time of Shipment. The L/C must specify that transshipment and partial shipments are allowed.

8. 装船标记

Shipping Mark: N/M

9. 开立信用证时请注明我们的成交确认书号码。

When opening L/C, Please mention our S/C number.

10. 备　注

Remarks:

卖　方
THE SELLERS
张明华

买　方
THE BUYERS
MARRY

希 将 本 确 认 书 一 份 签 署 后 寄 回 本 公 司

Please sign and one copy of this sales confirmation to us at your earliest convenience.

2005FEB20				Logical Terminal GDPF
MT S700	**Issue of a Documentary Credit**			Page 00001
				Func JSRVP
User Header	Service Code	103:		
	Bank Priority	113:		
	Msg User Ref.	108:		
	Info. From CI	115:		
Sequence of Total	*27	:	1 / 1	
Form of Doc. Credit	*40 A	:	IRREVOCABLE	
Doc. Credit Number	*20	:	C20050226	
Date of Issue	31 C	:	050220	
Expiry	*31 D	:	050430	
Applicant	*50	:	ABC CORPORATION LTD., SPAIN	
Beneficiary	*59	:	SICHUAN CHANGHONG ELECTRIC CO., LTD. 35 EST MIANXING ROAD, HIGH-TECH PARK MIANYANG, SICHUAN, CHINA	
Amount	*32 B	:	Currency Amount 1,600,000.00	
Pos. / Neg. Tol. (%)	39 A	:	05/05	
Available with/by	*41 D	:	ANY BANK BY NEGOTIATION	
Draft at ...	42 C	:	30 DAYS' AFTER SIGHT	
Drawee	42 D	:	OURSELVES	
Partial Shipments	43 P	:	ALLOWED	
Transshipment	43 T	:	ALLOWED	
Loading in Charge	44 A	:	ANY CHINESE PORTS	
For Transport to...	44 B	:	VALENCIA PORT	
Shipment Period	44 C	:	LATEST MAR. 30, 2005	
Descript. of Goods	45 A	:		

AIR CONDITIONER
KFR-35GW/NL, MODEL, R407C, 220V, 10,000SETS, @USD160.00, CIF VALENCIA
3,000SETS SHIPMENT BY 31ST, MARCH 2005, 7,000SETS SHIPMENT BY 15TH, APRIL 2005, OTHER DETAILES AS PER S/C

Documents Required 46 A :

+COMMERCIAL INVOICE IN 3 COPIES

+PACKING LIST IN 3 COPIES

+2/3 ORIGINAL CLEAN SHIPPED ON BOARD B/L, MADE OUT TO ORDER, MARKED "FREIGHT PREPAID" AND NOTIFY APPLICANT

+GSP CERTIFICATE OF ORIGIN FORM A, CERTIFYING GOODS OF ORIGIN IN CHINA, ISSUED BY COMPETENT AUTHORITIES

+INSURANCE POLICY/CERTIFICATE COVERING RISKS FPA OF PICC. INCLUDING WAREHOUSE TO WAREHOUSE CLAUSE, FOR AT LEAST 110 PCT OF CIF-VALUE.

+SHIPPING ADVICES MUST BE SENT TO APPLICANT WITHIN 2 DAYS AFTERSHIPMENT ADVISING NUMBER OF PACKAGES, GROSS & NET WEIGHT, VESSEL NAME, BILL OF LADING NO. AND DATE, CONTRACT NO., VALUE.

2005FEB20 Logical Terminal GDPF

MT S700 **Issue of a Documentary Credit** Page 00001

Func JSRVP

Addition Cond. 47 A :

1. 1/3 ORIGINAL B/L MUST BE SENT DIRECTLY TO APPLICANT IN 3 DAYS AFTER B/L DATE AND SENT BY FAX.
2. QUANTITY 3PCT MORE OR LESS ALLOWED.
3. ALL DOCUMENTS MUST BE MADE OUT IN ENGLISH LANGUAGE.
4. ALL DOCUMENTS MUST BEAR OUR LETTER OF CREDIT NUMBER.
5. DISCREPANCY FEE OF USD 80.00(OR EQUIVALENT)WILL BE DEDUCTED FROM THE PROCEEDS OF ANY DRAWING IF DOCUMENTS ARE PRESENTED WITH DISCREPANCY (IES) UNDER THIS DOCUMENTARY CREDIT. NOT WITH STANDING ANY INSTRUCTIONS TO THE CONTRARY, THIS CHARGE SHALL BE FOR THE ACCOUNT OF BENEFICIARY.

Details of Charges 71 B : ALL BANK CHARGES EXCLUDING ISSUING BANKS ARE FOR ACCOUNT OF BENEFICIARY.

Presentation Period 48 : DOCUMENTS TO BE PRESENTED WITHIN 15 DAYS FROM SHIPMENT DATE.

Confirmation *49 : WITHOUT

Instructions 78 :

DISCREPANT DOCUMENTS, IF ACCEPTABLE, WILL BE SUBJECT TO A DISCREPANCY HANDLING FEE OF USD50.00 OR EQUIVALENT WHICH WILL BE FOR ACCOUNT OF BENEFICIARY. ON RECEIPT OF COMPLETE SET OF DOCUMENTS IN CONFORMITY WITH THE TERMS OF THIS CREDIT, WE WILL BE DULY HONOURED ON PRESENTATION IF THE DRAFT(S) ACCEPTED BY APPLICANT.

Send To Rec. Info. 72 : THIS CREDIT IS ISSUED SUBJECT TO 1993 REVISION, I. C. C. PUBLICATIONS NO. 500

Trailer Order is <MAC: ><PAC: ><ENC: ><CHK: ><THG: ><PDE: >

MAC: AD9A4F07

CHK: E2069EEF189A

不符点描述及更正：

（1）

（2）

（3）

（4）

（5）

（6）

第二章
常用结汇单证

第一节　发　票

一、中英文术语、短语互译

（一）中译英

（1）商业发票______

（2）海关发票______

（3）运费______

（4）保险费______

（5）佣金______

（6）折扣______

（7）付款方式______

（8）生产国别______

（9）运输方式______

（10）一式三份______

（二）英译中

（1）Invoice No. ______

（2）Date ______

（3）Marks & Nos. ______

（4）Contract No. ______

（5）Shipped from... to... ______

（6）Description of Goods ______

（7）Quantity ______

（8）Unit Price ______

（9）Amount Total ______

（10）Currency of Settlement ______

二、单项选择题

1．信用证的货物名称错把 BLACK TEA（红茶）写作 BLACK TEE，审证时没留意到这个问题，那么制作单据时应（　　）。

A. 改作“BLACK TEA”

B. 按原文写作“BLACK TEE”

C. 按原文写作“BLACK TEE”，然后在后面加上（BLACK TEA）

D. 把“信用证”改成“托收”收款

2. 根据《UCP600》的规定，商业发票中货物的描述（　　）。

A. 可以使用统称，不得与信用证中有关货物的描述有抵触

B. 可以使用统称，并可与信用证中有关货物的描述有所不同

C. 必须完全符合信用证中的描述

D. 必须与合同的描述完全一致

3. 一般情况下，发票金额应与（　　）一致。

A. 合同金额　　B. 信用证金额

C. 保险金额　　D. 汇票金额

4. 来证规定“COMMERCIAL INVOICE IN TRIPLICATE CERTIFYING THAT THE GOODS HEREIN ARE IN ACCORDANCE WITH THOSE SPECIFIED IN THE S/C NO. 9857”，制作发票时应（　　）。

A. 商业发票一式两份，然后在发票上注明“COMMERCIAL INVOICE IN TRIPLICATE CERTIFYING THAT THE GOODS HEREIN ARE IN ACCORDANCE WITH THOSE SPECIFIED IN THE S/C NO. 9857”

B. 商业发票一式三份，然后在发票上注明“COMMERCIAL INVOICE IN TRIPLICATE CERTIFYING THAT THE GOODS HEREIN ARE IN ACCORDANCE WITH THOSE SPECIFIED IN THE S/C NO. 9857”

C. 商业发票一式三份，然后在发票上注明“WE CERTIFY THAT THE GOODS HEREIN ARE IN ACCORDANCE WITH THOSE SPECIFIED IN THE S/C NO. 9857”

D. 商业发票一式两份，然后在发票上注明“WE CERTIFY THAT THE GOODS HEREIN ARE IN ACCORDANCE WITH THOSE SPECIFIED IN THE S/C NO. 9857”

5. 如来证没有申请人（或付款人）一栏，而是直接指明汇票付款人，如“WE OPEN CREDIT NO. PS8803 AVAILABLE BY DRAFTS DRAWN ON EEC CO., LTD.”，那么发票的抬头人应做成（　　）。

A. 不填　　B. 开证行

C. DRAWN ON EEC CO., LTD.　　D. EEC CO., LTD.

6. 合同规定按 CIF 价成交，已知总 CIF 价为 USD17,200，运费为 USD2,528，保险费为3%，来证要求分别注明 FOB 价、运费、保险费，那么制作发票时填写正确的是（　　）。

A.

TOTAL FOB VALUE	USD14,156.00
FREIGHT	USD2,528.00
INSURANCE	USD516.00
TOTAL CIF VALUE	USD17,200.00

B. TOTAL CIF VALUE	USD17, 200. 00
C. TOTAL FOB VALUE	USD13, 956. 00
FREIGHT	USD2, 528. 00
INSURANCE	USD716. 00
TOTAL CIF VALUE	USD17, 200. 00
D. TOTAL FOB VALUE	USD13, 956. 00
FREIGHT	USD2, 528. 00
INSURANCE	USD716. 00

7. 假如信用证的价格条款规定，商品的价格为STG4. 00，CIFC5 London ，且商品数量为6, 145PCS，信用证的金额为扣除佣金的净值，那么在发票总值栏中的金额应填写（　　）。

A. CIFC5 London	STG24, 580. 00
– C5	STG1, 229. 00
CIF London	STG23, 351. 00
B. CIFC5 London	STG24, 580. 00
– C5	STG2, 229. 00
CIF London	STG22, 351. 00
C. CIFC5 London	STG24, 580. 00
– C5	STG1, 299. 00
CIF London	STG23, 281. 00
D. CIFC5 London	STG24, 580. 00
– C5	STG1, 339. 00
CIF London	STG23, 241. 00

8. 海关发票是由（　　）制定的一种特殊发票格式。

A. 出口方　　B. 进口方

C. 出口国海关　　D. 进口国海关

9. 根据《UCP600》的规定，信用证金额前有“大约”、“大概”或类似的词语，交货时允许总值有（　　）的增减幅度。

A. 5%　　B. 3%

C. 10%　　D. 20%

10. 海关发票的抬头一般应该是（　　）。

A. 开证申请人　　B. 受益人

C. 进口国海关　　D. 进口地的收货人

三、多项选择题

1. 商业发票的作用主要有（　　）。

A. 进出口报关完税必不可少的单据　　B. 是全套单据的中心

C. 是结算货款的依据　　D. 是物权凭证

2. 发票的抬头人应是（　　）。

A. 托收项下的卖方　　B. 托收项下的买方
C. 信用证项下的受益人　　D. 信用证项下的开证申请人

3. 某来证规定："ABOUT 20 MT CITRIC ACID MONO BP80 AT USD1, 180. 00/MT CFR HAIFA PORT", "PCT credit amount tolerance : 10/10", "CURRENCY CODE AMOUNT: USD23, 600. 00", 那么以下发票的数量和金额可以符合规定的是（　　）。

A. 20 MT, USD23, 600. 00　　B. 25 MT, USD29, 500. 00
C. 22 MT, USD25, 960. 00　　D. 18 MT, USD21, 240. 00

4. 海关发票的主要内容包括（　　）。

A. 商品数量　　B. 商品成本价值
C. 商品的生产国家　　D. 商品的品质

5. 海关发票的主要作用是（　　）。

A. 作为进口货物估价完税的依据　　B. 是买卖双方收付货款的依据
C. 核定货物原产地的依据　　D. 进口国海关统计资料的依据

四、判断题

1. 商业发票日期应早于提单日期。(　　)

2. 商业发票是由买方开给卖方的价目清单，是出口交易中最重要的单据之一。(　　)

3. 信用证规定：FROM CHINA PORT TO LONDON，则发票上应严格按照信用证要求填上"FROM CHINA PORT TO LONDON"。(　　)

4. 按照《UCP600》规定，无论信用证有无规定，商业发票必须签章才能生效。(　　)

5. 除非信用证另有规定，银行将不接受出单日期早于信用证开立日期的单据。(　　)

6. 除非信用证另有规定，商业发票必须由信用证的受益人开立。(　　)

7. 商业发票的主要内容包括货物名称、数量、单价、总价等。(　　)

8. 海关发票是由进口国海关制定并由进口方填制的一种特殊发票格式的书面单据。(　　)

9. 海关发票中"出口国国内价格"一栏，应以出口国货币填写 CIF 价格，同时应注意价格不得低于该出口商品在国内的价格，否则将被进口国视为低价倾销。(　　)

10. 有的来证要求在发票上加注"证明所列内容真实无误"，我们为避免麻烦应一律拒绝。(　　)

五、案例分析

1. 有一份信用证对货物的描述如下：7, 000PCS OF 100% COTTON SHIRTS AT USD9. 60 PER PCS AS PER CONTRACT NO. 02AB120 FOB QINGDAO。开证行收到单据后经审核发现商业发票未注明 FOB QINGDAO，因此认为单证不符而拒绝付款。而受益人认为价格术语并不是货物描述的一部分，而且其已经在提单中注明了"FREIGHT COLLECT"，表明价格术语就是 FOB 价，因此单证是相符的。请问哪一方有理？

2. 某轻工业品进出口公司出口一批商品，于 3 月 4 日收到信用证，信用证中条款规定：“... Amount：USD616, 000. 00... Quantity：400M/T（quantity 5% more or less allowed），Price：@ USD1, 540. 00 per M/T net，CIF Hamburg. Shipments to Hamburg immediately. Partial shipments are not allowed.”（……总金额 616, 000. 00 美元。……某商品 400 公吨，数量允许增减 5%。价格：每公吨净重 1, 540. 00 美元，CIF 汉堡。立即装运至汉堡。不许分批装运。）轻工业品进出口公司根据信用证条款，在接到信用证后立即安排装运出口。轻工业品进出口公司于 4 月 7 日将货装运出口，取得 4 月 7 日签发的已装船的提单，并备妥信用证项下所需的其他单据向议付行交单办理议付。议付行经审单发现单证不符，不同意议付，因信用证规定总金额为 USD616, 000. 00，而发票和汇票金额却为 USD634, 480. 00，议付金额比信用证规定总金额超出 USD18, 480. 00。轻工业品进出口公司认为其不符点不成立，即向议付行申述：信用证规定 400 公吨货物的数量，又规定装运数量可允许增减 5%。按 400 公吨的增减 5% 计算，即最高可以装 420 公吨，最低可以装 380 公吨。我们实际只装了 412 公吨，仅增装 3%，不超出信用证规定的 5% 范围。信用证规定每公吨单价 USD1, 540. 00，按 412 公吨计算，其总金额即 USD634, 480. 00，是信用证允许的，所以说其不符点是不成立的。你认为轻工业品进出口公司的理由是否充分？其能否顺利收取货款？最后应如何处理为妥？

六、阅读理解

（一）阅读理解一

HUIZHOU TEA IMPORT & EXPORT CORPORATION

6 NANTAN EAST ROAD, HUIZHOU, GUANGDONG, CHINA

INVOICE

TO MESSRS.:
YAKAHUCHI CO., LTD.
NO.689 NADA－KU, KOBE,
JAPAN

INVOICE NO.: SHE01/7203
DATE: MAY 27, 2002
L/C NO.: COM 8722732
CONTRACT NO.: HZT(02)003

TRANSPORT DETAILS:
FROM SHENZHEN TO KOBE VIA HONGKONG
BY VESSEL

TERMS OF PAYMENT:
BY SIGHT L/C

MARKS & NOS.	DESCRIPTION	QUANTITY	UNIT PRICE (USD)	AMOUNT (USD)
R. AND D. RIO HAINA R. 10.990 D.	AS PER S/C NO.:HZT(02)003 APPLICANT'S REF NO. 3－1190			
	BLACK TEA	6,000KGS	1.22/KG	USD7,320.00
		TOTAL: 6,000KGS	CIF KOBE	USD7,320.00

WE CERTIFY THAT THE ABOVE GOODS ARE OF CHINESE ORIGIN.
FOB VALUE: USD6,620.00
FREIGHT CHARGES:USD600.00
INSURANCE PREMIUM:USD100.00

根据上面单据找出下列内容：

（1）出口商名称：

（2）发票抬头人：

（3）发票号码：

（4）发票日期：

（5）合同号码：

（6）付款方式：

（7）装运港：

（8）目的港：

（9）转运港：

（10）运输方式：

（11）货物描述：

（12）价格术语：

（13）商品单价：

（14）总值：

（15）唛头：

（16）运费：

（17）保险费：

（18）证明文句：

（二）阅读理解二

Issuer GAWEN COMPANY LIMITED, AUSTRALIA	**COMMERCIAL INVOICE**		
To JIANGXI JIANGHAI GARMENTS IMPORT AND EXPORT CO. ,LTD. NO. 25 CHANGDAI ROAD, NANCHANG CITY, JIANGXI, CHINA	No. GA289	Date 20/05/2004	
Transport details FROM: SYDNEY, AUSTRALIA W/T: TO: FUZHOU, CHINA VESSEL: Northern WIND	S/C No. J0254	L/C No. ZJJ04LC0300135	
	Terms of payment D/P At Sight		

Marks and Numbers	Number and kind of packages; Description of goods	Quantity	Unit price	Amount
	LEATHER GARMENTS H. S. CODE:62011210			
GAWEN	ART 1212/100	200 PCS	USD52.20	USD10,440.00
SYDNEY	ART 1212/32	500 PCS	USD54.20	USD27,100.00
NO. 1 - 160	ART 1213/00	400 PCS	USD56.40	USD22,560.00
	ART 1214/00	350 PCS	USD58.20	USD20,370.00
	ART 1215/00	500 PCS	USD62.00	USD31,000.00
	ART 1216/00	400 PCS	USD65.00	USD26,000.00
		TOTAL: 2,350 PCS	CFR FUZHOU	USD137,470.00

TOTAL: US DOLLARS ONE HUNDRED THIRTY SEVEN THOUSAND FOUR HUNDRED AND SEVENTY ONLY.

WE CERTIFY THAT THE GOODS ARE IN ACCORDANCE WITH PURCHASE ORDER NUMBER 8803.

根据上面单据找出下列内容：

（1）出票人名称：

（2）发票抬头人：

（3）发票号码：

（4）发票日期：

（5）合同号码：

（6）信用证号码：

（7）付款方式：

（8）装运港：

（9）目的港：

（10）转运港：

（11）运输方式：

（12）运输工具名称：

（13）货物名称：

（14）商品编码：

（15）价格术语：

（16）数量：

（17）总值：

（18）唛头：

（19）原产国：

（20）证明文句：

七、单据填制

（一）单据填制一

根据有关信用证条款和参考资料缮制发票。

A. 信用证有关条款。

Issuing bank：THE SAKURA BANK，LIMITED
56，NANIWA－CHO，CHUO－KU，KOBE，JAPAN

20 /documentary credit number：KUW25847

31c /date of issue：　May 15，2004

31d /date and place of expiry：June 30，2004 beneficiaries' country

50 /applicant：　MOMO CO.，LTD.
NO. 215 NADA－KU，KOBE，JAPAN

59 /beneficiary：HUNAN TEA IMPORT & EXPORT CORPORATION
WUYI ROAD，CHANGSHA，HUNAN，CHINA

32 /currency code amount：　USD26，640.00

39a /percent credit amt tolerance：　05 / 05

41d /available with... by...：　Any bank in China by negotiation

45a /descript. of goods and/or services：

As per S/C No. HNT（04）021

Applicant's Ref No. 3－1190

12，000 kgs Pu'er tea at USD2.22 per kg. CIF Kobe

Packed：in 50 kgs per carton

46a /documents required：

+commercial invoice in one original plus 6 copies，showing that the goods exported are of Chinese Origin，all of which must be manually signed.

47a/ additional conditions：

+all documents required under this credit must mention this L/C number and the issuing bank name.

B. 参考资料。

2004年6月12日装"FENGQING V. 25"从广州出运。

唛头自行设计。

发票号码：HT－04－28931

湖 南 茶 叶 进 出 口 公 司
HUNAN TEA IMPORT & EXPORT CORPORATION
WUYI ROAD, CHANGSHA, HUNAN, CHINA
商业发票
COMMERCIAL INVOICE ORIGINAL

Messrs.:

INVOICE NO. :
INVOICE DATE :
L/C NO. :
L/C DATE :
S/C NO. :

Exporter:

Transport details:

Terms of payment:

Marks & Numbers	Description of Goods	Quantity	Unit Price	Amount

（二）单据填制二

根据有关信用证条款和参考资料缮制发票。

A．信用证有关条款。

We hereby establish our Irrevocable Documentary Credit No. MNL030850 dated AUG. 25, 2003 by order and for account of MRISSINA GARMENTS INC (8/F EXECUTIVE BLDG. CENTER GIL PUYAT COR MAKATI AVE. MAKATI CITY PHILIPPINES) in favor of CHINA TEXTILES IMPORT AND EXPORT CORP. (8 DONG' AN ROAD, BEIJING, CHINA) for the amount of USD179,700.00 available by your manually signed Drafts drawn on us at sight for full invoice value. Covering the following goods:

CIF MANILA, DISCOUNT OF 5% DEDUCTED

54, 000 YARDS 100PCT COTTON DARK NAVY DENIM, 12 OZ. CTW0945 USD2.75 PER YARD

12, 000 YARDS 100PCT COTTON INDIGO BLACK DENIM, 11 OZ. CTW0939 USD2.60 PER YARD

AS PER PROFORMA INVOICE NOS. PI－187/2003 DATED 08AUG. 2003

ACCOMPANIED BY THE FOLLOWING DOCUMENTS:

+SINGED COMMERCIAL INVOICE IN QUADRUPLICATE INDICATING L/C NUMBER AND TOTAL NUMBER OF PACKAGES.

B．参考资料。

INVOICE NO. MM024

INVOICE DATE: SEP. 10, 2003

SHIPPING MARKS:

M. G. I
MANILA
NO. 1－795

TOTAL PACKAGES: DARK NAVY DENIM 466 ROLLS
INDIGO BLACK DENIM 329 ROLLS
TOTAL 795 ROLLS

SHIPPED PER S. S. "MAYOR" V. 36 FROM DALIAN TO MANILA ON SEP. 8, 2003

中 国 纺 织 品 进 出 口 公 司
CHINA TEXTILES IMPORT & EXPORT CORP.
8 DONG'AN ROAD, BEIJING, CHINA
商业发票
COMMERCIAL INVOICE ORIGINAL

Messrs. :

INVOICE NO. :
INVOICE DATE :
L/C NO. :
L/C DATE :

Exporter:

Transport details:

Terms of payment:

Marks & Numbers	Description of Goods	Quantity	Unit Price	Amount

（三）单据填制三

根据有关信用证条款和参考资料缮制发票。

A. 信用证有关条款。

Type of Documentary Credit：IRREVOCABLE

Letter of Credit Number：LC84E0081/99

Date of Issue：990916

Date and Place of Expiry：991015 CHINA

Applicant Bank：FIRST SEOUL CITY BANK，LTD.

Applicant：SANGYONG CORPORATION
CPO BOX 110
SEOUL，KOREA

Beneficiary：DALIAN WEIDA TRADING CO.，LTD.

Currency Code Amount：about USD12，400，less 5% commission and 5% allowance（dis.）

Available with... by...：ANY BANK BY NEGOTIATION

Drafts at...：45 DAYS AFTER SIGHT

Drawee：US

Partial Shipments：NOT ALLOWED

Transshipment：NOT ALLOWED

Shipping on Board/Dispatch/Packing in Charge at/ from：DALIAN PORT，P. R. CHINA

Transportation to：INCHON KOREA

Latest Date of Shipment：991013

Description of Goods or Services：

PORCELAIN POT AS PER SALES CONTRACT NO. TH99/1689 DATED 13 JUN. 1999
6-1/2"DAI×6-1/2"H PORCELAIN FLOWER WHITE POT 4，000PCS
W/PINK/PURPLE FLOWER PATTERN
EACH/BUBBLE WRAPPED
4PCS/3-LAYER STRONG INNER
16PCS/5-LAYER STRONG CARTON
AT USD3.10 PER PC. CIF INCHON KOREA

Documents Required：

1. BENEFICIARY'S MANUALLY SIGNED ORIGINAL COMMERCIAL INVOICES IN DUPLICATE CERTIFYING MERCHANDISE OF CHINESE ORIGIN AND SHOWING HAMERNISED CODE 6913.9000.

B. 其他资料自拟。

大连威达贸易有限公司
DALIAN WEIDA TRADING CO. , LTD.
8 DONG'AN ROAD, BEIJING, CHINA
商业发票
COMMERCIAL INVOICE　　ORIGINAL

Messrs. :

INVOICE NO. :
INVOICE DATE :
L/C NO. :
L/C DATE :
S/C NO. :

Exporter:

Transport details:

Terms of payment:

Marks & Numbers	Description of Goods	Quantity	Unit Price	Amount

八、单据改错

（一）单据改错一

广东省华联贸易有限公司与加拿大的 EEN 公司成交了一笔出口交易，EEN 公司按期开来信用证，华联贸易有限公司备货出运后收妥提单，立即制作好全套单证并准备交单议付，请根据以下信用证提供的内容审核并修改其中的商业发票。

DOC. CREDIT NUMBER:	044/307587
APPLICANT:	EEN CO., VANCOUVER, CANADA
BENEFICIARY:	GUANGDONG HUALIAN TRADING CORPORATION 60 HUHAI ROAD, GUANGZHOU, CHINA
AMOUNT CURRENCY:	USD5,256.00
AVAILABLE WITH/BY:	FREELY NEGOTIABLE AT ANY BANK BY NEGOTIATION
LOADING IN CHARGE:	CHINA
FOR TRANSPORT TO:	VANCOUVER VIA HONGKONG
LATEST DATE OF SHIPMENT:	020131
DESCRIPTION OF GOODS:	2,920YDS OF 100PCT COTTON DENIM - 8 OZ - ROPE DYED INDIGO (CT - 121) DOUBLE P/SHRUNK RESIDUAL AHRINKAGE NOT MORE THAN 3 - 4PCT 82 × 50/14S × 14S - WIDTH: 58/59' AT USD1.80/YD AS PER PURCHASE ORDER NO. FAB10 - 20030087/01 - 02, CIF VANCOUVER
DOCUMENTS REQUIRED:	+ SIGNED COMMERCIAL INVOICE IN TRIPLICATE.

GUANGDONG HUALIAN TRADING CORPORATION

60 HUHAI ROAD, GUANGZHOU, CHINA

INVOICE

TO MESSRS. : EEN CO. ,
VANCOUVER, CANADA

INVOICE NO. : SHE01/7203
DATE: JAN. 28, 2002
L/C NO. : 044/387587
P. O. No. : FAB10 - 20030087/01 - 02

SHIPPED FROM GUANGZHOU TO VANCOUVER

MARKS & NOS.	DESCRIPTION	QUANTITY	UNIT PRICE	AMOUNT
GOLDTRON GARMENTS SDN BHD PO NO. FAB10 - 20030087/01 - 02 COLOR : INDIGO R/NO. : 1 - 4, 6 - 36				
		2, 928 YARDS	USD1. 80/YARD	USD5, 256. 00

100PCT COTTON DENIM - 8 OZ - ROPE DYED INDIGO (CT - 121)
DOUBLE P/SHRUNK RESIDUAL AHRINKAGE NOT MORE THAN
3 - 4PCT 82 × 50/14S × 14S - WIDTH: 58/59'
AS PER PURCHASE ORDER NO. FAB10 - 20030087/01 - 02

TOTAL: US DOLLARS FIVE THOUSAND TWO HUNDRED FITY SIX ONLY.

（二）单据改错二

天津体育用品进出口公司向日本的 Tokyo Keyboard Distributer 出口一批足球，该公司在货物出运后立即着手制单结汇，请根据以下提供的信用证内容审核并修改该公司制作的商业发票。

Name of Issuing Bank　：The Mitsui Bank Ltd., Tokyo, 15 Marunouche 3 – Chome
Place and date of issue　：3 March, 1999, Tokyo, Japan
To：Tianjin Sporting Goods Imp. & Exp. Corp.
68 Yentai Street, Tianjin, China

This Credit is advised through Bank of China, 50 Yentai Street, Tianjin, China.

Dear Sirs,

By order and for account of Tokyo Keyboard Distributer, 12 – 14 Monmachi 3 – Chome, Tokyo, Japan. We hereby issue an Irrevocable Documentary Credit No. 901026 for USD5,600.00 (say US dollars five thousand six hundred only) to expire on 30 June, 1999 in China available with any bank in China by negotiation against beneficiary's draft(s) at sight drawn on us and the documents detailed herein, marked with "×";

[×] Commercial Invoice in triplicate visaed by the chamber of commerce certifying goods origin.

[×] Full set 2/2 originals clean on board marine Bills of Lading made out to order and blank endorsed marked freight prepaid notifying Tokyo Keyboard Distributer, 12 – 14 Monmachi 3 – Chome, Tokyo, Japan.

[×] Packing List in triplicate.

[×] Certificate of Origin in China.

[×] Insurance Policy or Certificate covering All Risks and War Risk for 110% of the invoice value stipulating claim, if any, to be payable in currency of the draft.

[×] Certificate of Weight in triplicate.

[×] Certificate of Analysis in triplicate Evidencing shipment of 1,600PCS GBW32P Football USD3.5/PC CIF Tokyo AS PER S/C NO. TSG0215.

Shipping Marks：TTK/TOKYO/NO. 1 – 520

Shipment from Tianjin port to Tokyo not later than 16 June, 1999.

Partial shipment：allowed

Transshipment：not allowed

Documents to be presented within 15 days after the date of the transport documents but within the validity of the credit.

We hereby engage with drawers and /or bona fide holders that drafts drawn and negotiated in conformity with the terms of Credit will be fully honored on presentation.

Instructions to the advising bank：

Please advise the Credit to the beneficiary：

The number and the date of the Credit must be quoted on all documents required.

Please acknowledge receipt.

Reimbursement：The negotiating bank is authorized to claim reimbursement on The Mitsui Bank Ltd., New York by telex. All drafts and documents must be sent to us by airmail.

Yours faithfully,
The Mitsui Bank Ltd., Tokyo
Signature(s)

Tianjin Sporting Goods Imp. & Exp. Corp.

68 **Yentai Street, Tianjin, China**

TO MESSRS.: Tokyo Keyboard Distributer, 12 – 14 Monmachi 3 – Chome, Tokyo, Japan	INVOICE NO.: TS99012 INVOICE DATE: JUNE 12, 1999 L/C NO.: 901026 S/C NO.: TSG0205

TRANSPORT DETAILS:

From Tianjin port to Tokyo by Vessel

MARKS & NOS.	DESCRIPTION	QUANTITY	UNIT PRICE	AMOUNT
TK TOKYO NO. 1 – 520	GBW32P Football	1,600PCS	USD3.5/PC	USD5,600.00

TOTAL: US DOLLARS FIVE THOUSAND SIX HUNDRED ONLY.

受益人签章

第二节　汇　票

一、中英文术语、短语互译

（一）中译英

（1）商业汇票________________

（2）银行汇票________________

（3）即期汇票________________

（4）远期汇票________________

（5）提示________________

（6）承兑________________

（7）背书________________

（8）拒付________________

（9）付款________________

（10）跟单汇票________________

（二）英译中

（1）Drawer ________________

（2）Drawee ________________

（3）Payee ________________

（4）Protect ________________

（5）Without Recourse ________________

（6）Drawn on ________________

（7）Drawn under ________________

（8）Pay ××× Company Only ________________

（9）Payment at 60 Days after Sight ________________

（10）Available by Your Drafts on Us at Sight ________________

二、单项选择题

1. 一张汇票的收款人抬头注明："PAY TO THE ORDER OF ××× CO."即表示(　　)。

A. 该汇票只能由×××公司收取货款

B. 该汇票不能转让

C. 该汇票可以转让，但只能转让一次

D. 该汇票可以转让，而且可一直转让下去

2. 信用证上关于汇票的条款规定：AVAILABLE BY YOUR DRAFT AT 30 DAYS SIGHT DRAWN ON APPLICANT，那么汇票应填写为（　　）。

A. 付款期限为 AT 30 DAYS SIGHT，付款人为开证申请人的名称

B. 付款期限为 AT 30 DAYS SIGHT，付款人为开证行的名称

C. 付款期限为 AT ××× SIGHT，付款人为开证行的名称

D. 付款期限为 AT 30 DAYS SIGHT，付款人为“APPLICANT”

3. 如信用证未作规定，则汇票的付款人是（　　）。

A. 开证申请人　　B. 受益人

C. 开证行　　D. 议付行

4. 汇票的号码一般填写（　　）。

A. 汇票号码　　B. 商业发票号码

C. 提单号码　　D. 银行指定号码

5. 汇票的抬头人是汇票的（　　）。

A. 出票人　　B. 受票人

C. 付款人　　D. 受款人

6. 商业汇票是指汇票的（　　）为商业企业的汇票。

A. 受票人　　B. 受款人

C. 付款人　　D. 出票人

7. 托收汇票一般应在出票条款栏内加注（　　）。

A. COLLECTING　　B. FOR COLLECTION

C. COLLECTION　　D. ON COLLECTION

8. 当信用证规定“DRAWN ON US”，那么汇票应该（　　）。

A. 在付款人栏目处填写“US”

B. 在受款人栏目处填写“US”

C. 在付款人栏目处填写“开证行名称”

D. 在付款人栏目处填写“开证申请人名称”

9. 汇票的抬头做成指示样式，说明（　　）。

A. 汇票不能通过背书转让　　B. 汇票无须通过背书即可转让

C. 仅能由银行转让　　D. 须经过背书方能转让

10. 信用证规定：DRAFTS AT 90 DAYS SIGHT DRAWN ON SAKULA BANK LTD. USANCE DRAFTS DRAWN UNDER THIS L/C ARE TO BE NEGOTIATED AT SIGHT BASIS. DISCOUNT CHARGES AND ACCEPTANCE COMMISSION ARE FOR ACCOUNT OF ACCOUNTEE，汇票的付款期限和付款人应分别填写为（　　）。

A. AT 90 DAYS SIGHT 和 SAKULA BANK LTD.

B. AT 90 DAYS SIGHT 和开证申请人名称

C. AT 90 DAYS SIGHT AND NEGOTIABLE AT SIGHT DAYS 和 SAKULA BANK LTD.

D. AT ××× SIGHT 和开证申请人名称

三、多项选择题

1. 以下情况属于拒付的是（　　）。

A. 付款人破产

B. 付款人虽不拒绝付款，但承诺延缓一个月付款

C. 付款人拒绝付款

D. 付款人虽不拒绝付款，但承诺到期付款，并办理了承兑手续

2. 汇票的抬头限定“PAY TO ABC CO. ONLY”，表明（　　）。

A. 限付给 ABC CO.　　B. 凭 ABC CO. 公司指示

C. 可以转让　　D. 不能转让

3. 如果信用证没有规定出票依据，那么一般要填写的内容有（　　）。

A. 开证行名称　　B. 开证申请人名称

C. 信用证号码　　D. 开证日期

4. 汇票小写金额为 58,673.56 港元，那么汇票大写正确的是（　　）。

A. HONGKONG DOLLARS FIFTY EIGHT THOUSAND SIX HUNDRED AND SEVENTY THREE CENTS FIFTY SIX ONLY

B. HONGKONG DOLLARS FIFTY EIGHT THOUSAND SIX HUNDRED AND SEVENTY THREE 56/100 ONLY

C. HONGKONG DOLLARS FIFTY EIGHT THOUSAND SIX HUNDRED AND SEVENTY THREE POINT FIFTY SIX ONLY

D. HONGKONG DOLLARS FIFTY EIGHT THOUSAND SIX HUNDRED AND SEVENTY THREE 56% ONLY

5. 当来证规定：“INVOICE MUST SHOW CIF VALUE INCLUDING 5% COMMISSION AT THE TIME OF NEGOTIATION, 5% COMMISSION MUST BE DEDUCTED FROM DRAWINGS UNDER THIS CREDIT.”那么汇票金额应该（　　）。

A. 小于发票金额　　B. 大于发票金额

C. 是不含佣的 CIF 价　　D. 是含佣的 CIF 价

四、判断题

1. 汇票是出票人承诺在见票时或在未来某一规定的或可以确定的时间，对持票人或其指定人支付一定金额的书面文件。（　　）

2. 承兑是指持票人将汇票提交付款人要求承兑的行为。（　　）

3. A 公司因资金吃紧，把手头上的一张 6 个月期汇票经背书后转让给 B 公司，B 公司后来又转让给 C 公司，C 公司于汇票到期之日到银行收款，被告之汇票原付款人已破产，无力支付款项，C 公司转向 B 公司要求其付款，B 公司认为自己只是中间者，而要求 C 公司直接向 A 公司索款。B 公司的做法合理。（　　）

4. 商业汇票和银行汇票的主要区别在于前者的付款人是商业企业，后者的付款人是银行。（　　）

5. 出口人开具的汇票，如开证行付款后向开证人提示遭拒付时，开证行有权行使追索权。（　　）

6. L/C 条款规定：THIS L/C IS AVAILABLE WITH US BY PAYMENT AT 30 DAYS AFTER RECEIPT OF FULL SET OF DOCUMENTS AT OUR COUNTER，那么制单时应在汇票付款期限栏目填上：30 DAYS AFTER RECEIPT OF FULL SET OF DOCUMENTS AT OUR

COUNTER。(　　)

7. 一般汇票有两张正本，根据票据法规定，两张正本汇票具有同等效力，都可以同时收取款项。(　　)

8. 汇票出票人应该是信用证指定的受益人。(　　)

9. 假远期信用证项下汇票，其利息由卖方负担。(　　)

10. 远期汇票只有经过承兑才能转让。(　　)

五、案例分析

1. 2004 年 TW 进出口公司向 PU 有限公司出口一批大麻籽。对方开来信用证有关条款规定："... Credit available by the beneficiary's draft(s) at sight, pay to The Standard Bank, Ltd. only..."（……由受益人开具的即期汇票，只限付给标准银行……）TW 进出口公司在装运后，于 9 月 13 日将信用证所要求的单据向议付行交单议付。9 月 29 日开证行却提出如下单证不符：我信用证规定："... The beneficiary's draft (s) at sight, pay to The Standard Bank, Ltd. only..."（只限付给标准银行），你方提交的汇票收款人却只表示："pay to The Standard Bank, Ltd."（付给标准银行），漏"only"，违背了信用证规定。TW 进出口公司对开证行所提的不符点，经研究认为对方是无理挑剔，于 10 月 4 日作出如下反驳意见："汇票收款人名称有三种惯例填法，即记名式抬头、指示式抬头和来人式抬头。记名式抬头即直接指定某某人为收款人。你信用证所规定的和我提交的汇票均属于记名式标准银行，有无'only'，其作用没有很大的差别，均以标准银行为该汇票的收款人。我们认为我汇票的收款人缮制方法已符合你信用证要求，应认为单证一致。"你认为哪方有理呢？

2．2001 年 3 月 1 日，广州甲公司以广州乙公司为收款人，签发商业汇票一张，汇票金额为 50 万元人民币，汇票到期日为 2002 年 7 月 31 日。乙公司在接到该商业汇票后将该汇票背书转让给江门丙公司。江门丙公司在接到该商业汇票后将该汇票背书转让给佛山丁公司，同年 8 月 1 日，佛山丁公司持该商业汇票向银行提示付款。银行在接到该商业汇票后经查实，确认广州甲公司在银行的存款不足以支付票据款而将商业汇票退回给佛山丁公司。之后，佛山丁公司依法向其前手江门丙公司进行票据追索，江门丙公司在支付款项后又向其前手广州乙公司追偿，但广州乙公司拒绝偿付票据款项。

为此，江门丙公司向人民法院提起诉讼，诉称：被告广州乙公司背书转让给原告（丙公司）商业承兑汇票，被告广州乙公司系汇票出票人和付款人。在丙公司将汇票背书转让给后手后，当最后持票人在汇票到期日提示付款时，因广州甲公司银行存款不足被退票。要求判令广州乙公司支付票据款项及利息，并由广州甲公司承担连带清偿责任。广州乙公司辩称广州甲公司系商业汇票的出票人，应当由广州甲公司独立承担汇票款项的偿付责任。广州甲公司未答辩。请讨论该案例谁将会胜诉。

六、阅读理解

（一）阅读理解一

BILL OF EXCHANGE

NO. SHE01/7203　　　　DATE JUNE 5, 2002

EXCHANGE FOR USD7, 320. 00

AT ××× DAYS AFTER SIGHT OF THIS FIRST OF EXCHANGE (SECOND OF EXCHANGE BEING UNPAID)

PAY TO THE ORDER OF CONSTRUCTION BANK OF CHINA

THE SUM OF US DOLLARS SEVEN THOUSAND THREE HUNDRED AND TWENTY ONLY.

DRAWN UNDER L/C NO. COM 8722732　　DATED MAY 15, 2002

ISSUED BY THE SAKURA BANK, LIMITED

TO THE SAKURA BANK, LIMITED

56 NANIWA - CHO, CHUO - KU, KOBE,

JAPAN

HUIZHOU TEA IMPORT & EXPORT CORPORATION

根据上面汇票，找出以下所列内容：

（1）开证行名称：

（2）信用证号码：

（3）开证日期：

（4）出票人：

（5）付款人：

（6）受款人：

（7）付款期限：

（8）汇票大写金额：

（9）议付时间：

（10）汇票号码：

（二）阅读理解二

F11

凭 Drawn under NATIONAL COMMERCIAL BANK, THE JEDDAH (HEAD OFFICE)

信用证 L/C 第 No. 613M9732808 号

日期 dated Oct.02,1997 年 月 日

1

按 息 付款 Payable with interest @ ……… % per annum

号码 No. ……… 汇票金额 Exchange for USD37,800.00 中国，广州 Guangzhou, China 19 年 月 日

见票 At PAYABLE AFTER 60 DAYS FROM THE DATE OF RECEIPT OF ORIGINAL DOCTS BY NCB JEDDAH LC DEPT. sight of this FIRST of Exchange (Second of exchange being unpaid) 日后（本汇票之副本未付）付

pay to the order of BANK OF CHINA ,GUANG DONG ,BRANCH 或其指定人

金额 the sum of US DOLLARS THIRTY SEVEN THOUSAND EIGHT HUNDRED ONLY.

此致 To NATIONAL COMMERCIAL BANK, THE JEDDAH (JEDDAH, MAIN BRANCH)

广东省纺织品进出口针织品有限公司
GUANGDONG TEXTILES IMPORT & EXPORT KNITWEARS COMPANY LIMITED

林树宗

根据上面汇票，找出以下所列内容：

（1）开证行名称：

（2）信用证号码：

（3）开证日期：

（4）出票人：

（5）付款人：

（6）受款人：

（7）付款期限：

（8）汇票大写金额：

七、单据改错

（一）单据改错一

广东省华达食品有限公司按期收到香港 ABC 公司的信用证，请根据以下信用证内容审核并修改汇票。

FROM：KWANGTUNG PROVINCIAL BANK, HK
TO：BANK OF CHINA，GUANGZHOU BRANCH
HONG KONG NOV. 13，1994
IRREVOCABLE DOCUMENTARY CREDIT NO. ：002 – 10358
ADVISING BANK：　BANK OF CHINA，GUANGZHOU BRANCH
BENEFICIARY：　GUANGDONG HUADA FOOD CO.，LTD.
58 BEIJING ROAD，GUANGZHOU，CHINA
APPLICANT：　HONGKONG ABC CO.
3/F GUANGTEX BUILDING TAIKOKTSUI KOWLOON，HONGKONG
AMOUNT：　USD14，200. 00
EXPIRY DATE：　JAN. 15，1995
DEAR SIRS,
WE HEREBY ISSUE AN IRREVOCABLE DOCUMENT CREDIT IN YOUR FAVOUR WHICH IS AVAILABLE BY NEGOTIATION OF YOUR DRAFTS AT SIGHT DRAWN ON APPLICANT，FOR 100% INVOICE VALUE MARKED AS DRAWN UNDER THIS CREDIT ACCOMPANIED BY THE FOLLOWING DOCUMENTS：
SPECIAL CONDITIONS：ALL DOCUMENTS MENTIONING THIS CREDIT NUMBER. DOCUMENTS TO BE PRESENTED WITHIN 15 DAYS AFTER DATE OF ISSUANCE OF TRANSPORT DOCUMENTS BUT WITHIN VALIDITY OF CREDIT.
...

BILL OF EXCHANGE

NO. 002 – 10358　　　　DATE JAN. 10，1995

EXCHANGE FOR USD14，200. 00
AT 15 DAYS AFTER SIGHT OF THIS FIRST OF EXCHANGE（SECOND OF EXCHANGE BEING UNPAID）
PAY TO THE ORDER OF KWANGTUNG PROVINCIAL BANK, HK
THE SUM OF US DOLLARS FOURTEEN THOUSAND TWO HUNDRED.
DRAWN UNDER THIS CREDIT
TO KWANGTUNG PROVINCIAL BANK, HK

HONGKONG ABC CO.
（签名）

（二）单据改错二

广东省五矿进出口公司收到沙特阿拉伯的 MIGHWLLI STEEL PRODUCTS CO. 的信用证后，如期交货，请按其开来的信用证内容审核并修改该公司制单员制作的一份汇票。

TO：BANK OF CHINA，GUANGDONG

FM：ARAB NATIONAL BANK

P. O. BOX 18745 JEDDAH SAUDI ARABIA

DEAR SIRS，

KINDLY ADVISE BENEFICIARY'S M/S GUANGDONG METALS AND MINERALS I/E CORP. 5 TIANHE ROAD，GUANGZHOU，CHINA

OF OUR OPENING WITH YOU AN IRREVOCABLE DOCUMENTARY CREDIT DATED 10 MARCH，2002 IN THEIR FAVOUR ON BEHALF OF M/S MIGHWLLI STEEL PRODUCTS CO. P. O. BOX 18741 JEDDAH SAUDI ARABIA FOR AMOUNT ABOUT USD75，683.00 VALID IN CHINA UNTIL 20 MAY 2002，AVAILABLE WITH YOU BY PAYMENT AGAINST PRESENTATION OF BENEFICIARYS' DRAFT(S) AT 30 DAYS AFTER B/L DATE DRAWN ON OURSELVES AND MARKED "DRAWN UNDER ARAB NATIONAL BANK CREDIT NO. 254LK254".

5% COMMISSION MUST BE DEDUCTED FROM DRAWINGS UNDER THIS CREDIT.

F14

1

凭
Drawn under ARAB NATIONAL BANK

信用证 第 号
L/C *No.*

日期 年 月 日
dated 10 MARCH, 2002

按 息 付 款
Payable with interest @ ______ *%per annum*

号码 汇票金额 中国 广州 年 月 日
No. ______ **Exchange** *for* USD75, 683.00 *Guangzhou,China* ______ 20 ______

见票 日 后（本汇票之副本未付）付
At 30 DAYS *sight of this* **FIRST** *of Exchange (second of exchange bein paid)*

pay to the order of BANK OF CHINA, GUANGDONG 或其指定人

金 额
the sum of US DOLLARS SEVENTY FIVE THOUSAND SIX HUNDRED AND EIGHTY THREE

此致
To: MIGHWLLI STEEL PRODUCTS CO.
P.O.BOX 18741 JEDDAH
SAUDI ARABIA

GUANGDONG METALS AND MINERALS I/E CORP.
（签名）

八、单据填制

（一）单据填制一

根据以下内容，填写一份汇票。

INVOICE NO.：TU231

ISSUING BANK：KUWAIT REAL ESTATE BANK

L/C NO.：SP00256　　DATED MARCH 21，2002

INVOICE AMOUNT：USD9,785.00

BENEFICIARY：BEIJING NATIONAL NATIVE PRODUCT IMP. & EXP. CORPORATION

APPLICANT：HAMEED ALI AL TUHOO CO.，KUWAIT

NEGOTIATING BANK：THE INDUSTRIAL & COMMERCIAL BANK OF CHINA

DATE OF NEGOTIATION：APRIL 18，2002

... AVAILABLE WITH YOUR DRAFT AT SIGHT DRAWN ON US FOR THE FULL INVOICE VALUE. ALL DRAFTS MUST BE MARKED "DRAWN UNDER KUWAIT REAL ESTATE BANK".

BILL OF EXCHANGE

NO. ____________________　　　　DATE ____________________

EXCHANGE FOR ______________________________

AT ________ SIGHT OF THIS FIRST OF EXCHANGE (SECOND OF EXCHANGE BEING UNPAID)

PAY TO THE ORDER OF ____

THE SUM OF ____

DRAWN UNDER ____

____

TO ______________________________

____

____

____

（二）单据填制二

根据以下内容，填写一份汇票。

WE HEREBY ISSUE OUR IRREVOCABLE DOCUMENTARY LETTER OF CREDIT NO. 45BC123 DATED JAN. 02, 2003 AVAILABLE WITH US BY PAYMENT AT 30 DAYS AFTER RECEIPT OF FULL SET OF DOCUMENTS AT OUR COUNTERS FOR ACCOUNT OF STG99, 012. 52.

INVOICE NO.: NL0321

ISSUING BANK: THE CHARTERED BANK LONDON, ENGLAND

BENEFICIARY: CHINA NATIONAL LIGHT INDUSTRIAL PRODUCTS IMP. & EXP. CORP.
GUANGDONG BRANCH, NO. 87 THE BUND, GUANGHZHOU, CHINA

APPLICANT: LONDON EXPORT CO., LTD.
P. O. BOX 56387 LONDON, ENGLAND

NEGOTIATING BANK: BANK OF CHINA

DATE OF NEGOTIATION: FEB. 23, 2003

F14

1

凭
Drawn under --

信用证　第　号
L/C　*No.* ------------------------

日期　年　月　日
dated ------------------------------------

按　息　付款
Payable with interest @ ---------------- *%per annum*

号码　汇票金额　中国　广州　年　月　日
No. ------------ **Exchange** *for* ______ *Guangzhou,China* ---------- 20 ----------

见票　日后（本汇票之副本未付）付
At ------------ *sight of this* **FIRST** *of Exchange (Second of exchange being unpaid)*

pay to the order of -- 或其指定人

金　额
the sum of ______

此致
To: ----------------------

（三）单据填制三

根据以下内容，制作一份托收项下汇票：

COVERING 3,000 DOZ OF GARMENTS AT JPY20.2 PER DOZ. UNDER CONTRACT NO.: 02PT744. THE BUYERS SHALL DULY ACCEPT THE DOCUMENTARY DRAFT DRAWN BY THE SELLERS AT 90 DAYS SIGHT UPON FIRST PRESENTATION AND MAKE PAYMENT ON ITS MATURITY. THE SHIPPING DOCUMENTS ARE TO BE DELIVERED AGAINST PAYMENT ONLY.

COLLECTING BANK: THE BANK OF TOKYO, LTD.
P. O. BOX 240, NAGOYA - NAKA, NAGOYA, 460 - 91 JAPAN

PRINCIPAL: SHANGHAI FENGHUA TEXTILES I/E CORP.
25 GUANGDONG ROAD, SHANGHAI, CHINA

PAYER: TOYOHANM AND CO., LTD.
58 NISHIKI 6 - CHOME, NAKAKU

INVOICE NO.: YU25868

DATE OF NEGOTIATION: APR. 14, 2002

BILL OF EXCHANGE

NO. ________________________ DATE ________________

EXCHANGE FOR ________________________

AT ________ SIGHT OF THIS FIRST OF EXCHANGE (SECOND OF EXCHANGE BEING UNPAID)

PAY TO THE ORDER OF ____

THE SUM OF ____

DRAWN UNDER ____

____

TO ________________________

____

____

____

第三节 海运提单

一、中英文术语、短语互译

（一）中译英

（1）全套清洁已装船提单________

（2）指示提单________

（3）多式联运提单________

（4）托运人________

（5）装运港________

（6）收货人________

（7）卸货港________

（8）交货地点________

（9）集装箱货运站________

（10）集装箱堆场________

（二）英译中

（1）Freight Prepaid ________

（2）Freight Collect ________

（3）THC ________

（4）ORC ________

（5）GP ________

（6）S. T. C. ________

（7）Consignor ________

（8）Shipper's Load and Count ________

（9）Made Out to Order ________

（10）Blank Endorsed ________

二、单项选择题

1. 海运提单的签发日期是指（　　）。

A. 货物实际装船完毕的日期　　B. 托运人填写托运单的日期

C. 货物开始装船的日期　　D. 托运人办理报关的日期

2. 下列提单中，只有经过背书才能转让的提单是（　　）。

A. 指示提单　　B. 不记名提单

C. 记名提单　　D. 清洁提单

3. 我国某公司与外商签订一份 CIF 出口合同，以 L/C 为支付方式。国外银行开来的信用证中规定："信用证有效期为 8 月 8 日，最迟装运期为 7 月 31 日。"我方加紧备货出运，于 7 月 21 日取得大副收据，并换回正本已装船清洁提单，我方应不迟于（　　）向银行提交单据。

A. 7月21日　　B. 7月31日

C. 8月8日　　D. 8月11日

4. 信用证的到期日为12月31日，最迟装运期为12月16日，最迟交单日期为运输单据出单后15天，出口人备妥货物安排出运的时间是12月10日，则出口人最迟应于（　　）向银行交单议付。

A. 12月16日　　B. 12月25日

C. 12月28日　　D. 12月31日

5. 按《UCP600》解释，若信用证条款中未明确规定是否“允许分批装运”、“允许转运”，则应视为（　　）。

A. 可允许分批装运，但不允许转运　　B. 可允许分批装运和转运

C. 可允许转运，但不允许分批装运　　D. 不允许分批装运和转运

6. 信用证条款：

DOCUMENTS REQUIRED：FULL SET OF CLEAN ON BOARD OCEAN B/L MADE OUT TO THE ORDER OF SHIPPER，MARKED FREIGHT PREPAID，NOTIFY APPLICANT.

假定：货物的承运人为 COSCO，船长为 MARK TOE，承运人的代理人为 ABC SHIPPING CO.，提单由承运人的代理签发，签发人为张三，如果提单表面未表明承运人的身份，则提单的签发应为（　　）。

A. ABC SHIPPING CO.
MARK TOE AS THE CARRIER

B. ABC SHIPPING CO.
张三 AS AGENT FOR THE CARRIER：COSCO

C. COSCO
张三 AS CARRIER

D. COSCO
MARK TOE AS MASTER

7. 信用证条款：

APPLICANT：ABC CO.

BENEFICIARY：GD TRADING CO.，LTD.

DOCUMENTS REQUIRED：FULL SET OF CLEAN ON BOARD BILL OF LADING CONSIGNED TO THE ORDER OF APPLICANT，MARKED FREIGHT PREPAID，NOTIFY APPLICANT.

信用证未对提单作任何其他规定，则提单的收货人应为（　　）。

A. TO THE ORDER OF APPLICANT

B. TO ORDER

C. TO THE ORDER OF ABC CO.

D. CONSIGNED TO THE ORDER OF APPLICANT

8. 信用证条款：

FROM：VOLKSBANK SCHORNDORF，GERMANY

TO：DG－BANK，HONGKONG/HONGKONG

APPLICANT：ABC CO.

BENEFICIARY：GD TRADING CO.，LTD.

DOCUMENTS REQUIRED：FULL SET OF CLEAN ON BOARD OCEAN BILL OF LADING MADE OUT TO OUR ORDER，MARKED FREIGHT PREPAID，NOTIFY APPLICANT.

信用证未对提单作任何其他规定，则提单的收货人应为（　　）。

A. TO OUR ORDER

B. TO ORDER OF VOLKSBANK SCHORNDORF，GERMANY

C. TO ORDER OF ABC CO.

D. TO ORDER OF GD TRADING CO.，LTD.

9. 信用证条款：

FROM：VOLKSBANK SCHORNDORF，GERMANY

TO：DG－BANK，HONGKONG/HONGKONG

APPLICANT：ABC CO.

BENEFICIARY：GD TRADING CO.，LTD.

PARTIAL SHIPMENTS：ALLOWED

TRANSSHIPMENT：ALLOWED

LOADING IN CHARGE：CHINA PORTS

FOR TRANSPORT TO：ROTTERDAM PORT BY SEAFREIGHT

LATEST DATE OF SHIPMENT：JANUARY 3，1998

DOCUMENTS REQUIRED：FULL SET OF CLEAN ON BOARD MARINE BILL OF LADING，MADE OUT TO ORDER OF WIM BOSMAN BV，P. O. BOX 54064，NL－3008 JB ROTTERDAM，NETHERLANDS.

信用证未对提单作任何其他规定，提单签发日期为 JANUARY 2，1998，实际装船日期为 JANUARY 3，1998，则收妥备运提单的装船批注应为（　　）。

A. JANUARY 2，1998

B. JANUARY 3，1998

C. ON BOARD DATE：JANUARY 2，1998

D. ON BOARD DATE：JANUARY 3，1998

10. 信用证条款：

DOCUMENTS REQUIRED：FULL SET OF CLEAN ON BOARD CHARTER PARTY BILL OF LADING MADE OUT TO ORDER，MARKED FREIGHT PAYABLE AS PER CHARTER PARTY.

假定：船东为 XYZ SHIPPING CO.，货运代理人 ABC SHIPPING CO. 作为船东的代理人签发租船提单，签发人为张三，如果租船提单表面未表明船东及货运代理人的名称和身份，则提单的签发应为（　　）。

A. ABC SHIPPING CO.
张三 AS THE CARRIER

B. ABC SHIPPING CO.
张三 AS AGENT FOR THE CARRIER：XYZ SHIPPING CO.

C. ABC SHIPPING CO.
张三 AS AGENT FOR THE OWNER：XYZ SHIPPING CO.

D. XYZ SHIPPING CO.
张三 AS THE OWNER

三、多项选择题

1. 下列应向提单持有人交付货物的提单有（　　）。

A. Blank B/L　　B. Open B/L

C. Straight B/L　　D. Bearer B/L

2. 海运提单的作用主要有（　　）。

A. Receipt for the Goods　　B. Documents of Title

C. Evidence of Contract of Carrier　　D. Commercial Bill

3. 已知货物承运人为 XYZ SHIPPING CO.，承运人提单签发人为张三，承运人的代理人为 ABC SHIPPING CO.，承运人的代理人提单签发人为李四，如果提单表面未表明承运人及代理人的名称和身份，则提单的签发应为（　　）。

A. ABC SHIPPING CO.
李四 AS THE CARRIER

B. ABC SHIPPING CO.
张三 AS AGENT FOR THE CARRIER：XYZ SHIPPING CO.

C. ABC SHIPPING CO.
李四 AS AGENT FOR THE CARRIER：XYZ SHIPPING CO.

D. XYZ SHIPPING CO.
张三 AS THE CARRIER

4. 信用证有关条款：

ISSUING BANK：XYZ BANK

APPLICANT：ABC CO.

BENEFICIARY：GD TRADING CO.，LTD.

DOCUMENTS REQUIRED：FULL SET OF CLEAN ON BOARD BILL OF LADING MADE OUT TO ORDER OR TO OUR ORDER，MARKED FREIGHT PREPAID NOTIFY APPLICANT.

信用证未对提单作任何其他规定，则提单的收货人应为（　　）。

A. TO ORDER

B. TO ORDER OF XYZ BANK

C. TO ORDER OF ABC CO.

D. TO ORDER OF GD TRADING CO.　，LTD.

5. 信用证有关提单条款：

DOCUMENTS REQUIRED：FULL SET OF CLEAN ON BOARD MARINE BILL OF LADING，MADE OUT TO ORDER OF WIM BOSMAN BV，P. O. BOX 54064，NL－3008 JB ROTTERDAM，NETHERLANDS.

信用证未对提单作任何其他规定，提单正本的签发份数（NO. OF ORIGINAL B(S)/L）应为（　　）。

A. 1 份　　B. 2 份

C. 3 份　　D. 选项 A 和 B 错误

6. 如果货物运输的装运港为 GUANGZHOU，目的港为 LONDON，转运港为 HONGKONG，且合同和信用证没有对提单中的转运港有特别要求，那么，海运提单对转运港的标示方式可采用（　　）。

A. 在装运港栏目填写 GUANGZHOU/HONGKONG

B. 在目的港栏目填写 LONDON W/T HONGKONG

C. 在目的港栏目填写 LONDON VIA HONGKONG

D. 在海运提单上注明 FROM GUANGZHOU TO LONDON VIA HONGKONG

7. 对集装箱运输，由托运人装箱的整箱货，只要海关已对集装箱封箱，承运人对箱的内容和数量不负责，因此，提单在填写装运数量时应加注（　　）。

A. SHIPPER'S LOAD AND COUNT

B. SAID TO CONTAIN

C. SHIPPER'S LOAD AND COUNT AND SEAL

D. SAID BY SHIPPER

8. 海运提单中运费缴付方式填写为"FREIGHT PREPAID"，如果信用证没有特别要求，那么此缴付方式一般适用于（　　）。

A. FOB　　B. CFR

C. CIP　　D. CIF

四、判断题

1. 海运提单只有签发日期而没有已装船日期，按惯例，提单的签发日期可视为装船日期。如果海运提单上批注有已装船日期，则该批注的日期不得早于海运提单的签发日期。（　）

2. 信用证的有关条款表明："FULL SET OF CLEAN ON BOARD BILL OF LADING MADE OUT TO OUR ORDER，MARKED FREIGHT PREPAID NOTIFY APPLICANT."则出具的正本提单托运人必须空白背书。（　　）

3. 来证对提单没有特殊要求，正本提单上有如下批注："FREIGHT CHARGES：USD2,700.00;ORC：USD500.00；DOCUMENTATION FEE：USD100.00"，银行将接受该提单。（　　）

4. 来证对提单没有特殊要求，有关提单的信用证条款如下："FULL SET OF CLEAN ON BOARD BILL OF LADING MADE OUT TO OUR ORDER，MARKED FREIGHT PREPAID NOTIFY APPLICANT."如果正本提单上没有特别标明开证人的名称和地址，则正本提单的被通知人应填写为"APPLICANT"。（　　）

5. TEU 是标准吨的缩语。（　　）

6. 对于托运人托运整箱货，海运提单上常批注有 CFS/CFS。（　　）

7. 海运提单上装运港栏目填写："INTENDED：DONGFANGHONG V. 001"，如果实际装运船只也是 DONGFANGHONG V. 001，则海运提单不必另行批注。（　　）

8. 国外开来信用证规定的装运期限为"after 12th May 2001"，则正本提单的装运日期应理解为在 2001 年 5 月 12 日或以后。（　　）

9. 正本海运提单上批注有："TOTAL FIVE HUNDRED CARTONS ONLY. BUT TEN BROKEN CARTONS."若来证对提单没有特别要求，银行将不接受该提单。（　　）

10. 在规定装运期条文时，如使用了"迅速"、"立即"、"尽速"或类似词句者，按《UCP600》规定，银行将不予置理。（　　）

五、案例分析

1. 某农产品进出口公司向国外某贸易公司出口一批花生仁，国外客户在合同规定的开证时间内开来一份不可撤销信用证，证中的装运条款规定："Shipment from Chinese Ports to Singapore in May，Partial shipment prohibited."农产品进出口公司按证中规定，于5月15日将200公吨花生仁在福州港装上"嘉陵"号轮，又由同轮在厦门港续装300公吨花生仁，5月20日农产品进出口公司同时取得了福州港和厦门港签发的两套提单。该农产品公司在信用证有效期内到银行交单议付，却遭到银行以单证不符为由拒付货款。问：银行的拒付是否有理？为什么？

2. 国外开来不可撤销信用证，证中规定最迟装运期为2000年12月31日，议付有效期为2001年1月15日。我方按证中规定的装运期完成装运，并取得签发日为2000年12月10日的提单，当我方备齐议付单据于2001年1月4日向银行议付交单时，银行以我方单据已过期为由拒付货款。问：银行的拒付是否有理？为什么？

六、阅读理解

(一) 阅读理解一

Shipper GUANGDONG TEXTILES IMP. AND WOOLEN KNITWEAR CO., LTD.
13/F.,GUANGDONG TEX. MANSION .NO.168
XIAOBEI RD,GUANGZHOU,CHINA

BL No. KRL030523

COMBINED TRANSPORT BILL OF LADING

KINGROAD LOGISTICS LTD.

Consignee

CONSIGNED TO CANADIAN IMPERIAL BANK OF COMMERCE,QUEEN AND SIMCOE, TORONTO,ONTARIO,CANADA

Notify

A B C CO.

RECEIVED in apparent good order and condition except as otherwise noted the total number of Containers or other packages or units enumerated below (*) for transportation from the place of receipt to the place of delivery subject to the terms hereof.
One of the original Bills of Lading must be surrendered duly endorsed in exchange for the Goods or Delivery Order.
On presentation of this document (duly endorsed) to the Carrier by or on behalf of the Holder, the rights and liabilities arising in accordance with the terms hereof shall (without prejudice to any rule of common law or statute rendering them binding on the Merchant) become binding in all respects between the Carrier and the Holder as though the contract evidenced hereby had been made between them. IN WITNESS whereof the number of original Bills of Lading stated have been signed, one of which being accomplished, the other(s) to be void.

(Terms of Bill of Lading continued on the back hereof)

Place of Receipt GUANGZHOU, CHINA

Ocean Vessel	Port of loading
REPULSE BAY V.48E21	GUANGZHOU,CHINA
Port of discharge	**Place of delivery**
VANCOUVER,CANADA	VANCOUVER,CANADA

Marks and numbers	Number and kind of packages	Description of goods	Gross weight	Measurement
P.O.# STYLE#: QUANTITY PRE-PACK MADE IN CHINA CARTON #.	30CTNS	LADIES 95 PERCENT COTTON, 5 PERCENT (SPANDEX) KNITTED TOP. GOODS HAVE BEEN LOADED ON BOARD VESSEL NAME : REPULSE BAY V.48E21 DATE: 2003/5/21 THE ESTIMIATED ARRIVAL DATE : 2003.6.20 THE L/C NO., P/O NO.06674 STYLE NO.05-168 SHIPPED QUANTITY OF EACH ORDER.: 1,260 PCS	285 KGS	1.85 CBM
	CFS-CFS	FREIGHT PREPAID & DDC COLLECT		

SAY: TOTAL THIRTY (30) CARTONS ONLY.

According to the declaration of the merchant

For delivery of goods please apply to:
THE FORWARDER AGENT IN CANADA:
WSA LINE INT'L (VANCOUVER) INC
#213-3889 HENNING DRIVE
BURNAY,BC V5C 5N5 CANADA
TEL: 804-2986448 FAX: 804-2928834
ATTN: MR. KEVIM MOK

Freight amount	Freight payable at GUANGZHOU	Place and date of issue GUANGZHOU MAY 15,2003
Cargo Insurance through the undersigned ☐ not covered ☐ Covered according to attached Policy	Number of Original BL's THREE	For and on behalf of KINGROAD LOGISTICS LTD. KINGROAD LOGISTICS LIMITED
Laden on board the vessel Date: MAY 15,2003 By: KINGROAD LOGISTICS LTD.	BO SHI JI 282 V.0227S	AS CARRIER Authorized Signature

根据上面单据回答下列问题：

（1）托运人：

（2）收货人：

（3）被通知人：

（4）提单号码：　（5）船名：

（6）装货港：　（7）目的港：

（8）唛头：　（9）件数和包装：

（10）总毛重：

（11）总尺码：

（12）货物名称：　（13）运费缴付方式：

（14）“DDC COLLECT”的中文意思为：

（15）正本提单件数：

（16）提单日期及签发地点：

（17）货物的装运日期：

（二）阅读理解二

根据下面单据回答问题：

（1）提单的承运人是哪个公司？

（2）按运输过程中是否转船分类，提单属于何种提单？

（3）按提单收货人抬头分类，提单属于何种提单？

（4）提单是承运人签发还是代理人签发？

（5）提单是否需要托运人背书？

（6）提单为何有两个船名？

（7）提单中批注有“SHIPPER'S LOAD & SEAL S. T. C.”，该批注是何意思？

（8）提单中批注有“CY/CY FCL”，该批注是何意思？

（9）提单中批注的特殊条款有“THIS IS TO CERTIFY THAT THE CARRYING VESSEL IS NOT OVER 15 YEARS OF AGE AT THE TIME OF LOADING. THE AGE IS 8 YEARS. L/C NO. IS 613R9846106”，该批注是何意思？

（10）提单是否有运输标志？如果有，是什么？

（11）提单标明的运费缴付方式是什么？

（12）提单标明承运船只在卸货港的代理人的名称、地址和电话号码，请找出来。

Carrier Hapag-Lloyd Container Linie GmbH, Hamburg

Bill of Lading

Multimodal Transport or Port to Port Shipment

Hapag-Lloyd

Shipper

WENZHOU E.T.D.Z. GENERAL ECONOMIC AND
TECHNICAL DEVELOPMENT CORP.
ROOM 906 BLOCK C. 30 LUCHENG ROAD WENZHOU CHINA
TEL 86-577-8236094　　FAX NO. 86-577-8236091

Carrier's Reference:	B/L-No.:	Page:
	KCT-9808181	

Export References: (PG831005)

Consignee or Order:

TO ORDER OF N. C. B JEDDAH

Forwarding Agent:

Notify Address (Carrier not responsible for failure to notify; see clause 20 (1) hereof):

AL-KHAIRAT CORP.
P.O.BOX 42369 JEDDAH 21541 SAUDI ARABIA
TEL 6515536　FAX NO.6520532

Consignee's Reference:

Place of Receipt:

Precarrying Vessel: SUI YUE NO.1　　**Voyage-No.:**

Ocean Vessel(s): KITANO V.50WE35　　**Voyage-No.:**

Port of Loading: GUANGZHOU　　**Port of Discharge:** JEDDAH

Port(s) of Transhipment: SHEKOU

Place of Delivery: JEDDAH

Container Nos., Seal Nos.; Marks and Nos.	Number and Kind of Packages, Description of Goods	Gross Weight:	Measurement:
	SHIPPER'S LOAD & COUNT & SEAL S.T.C.		
A.K.C - jeddah	310 CTNS　　STATIONERY GOODS	6,780KGS	29.048CBM
	FREIGHT PAYABLE AT DESTINATION		
1×20' CY/CY FCL HLCU2044684			
	THIS IS TO CERTIFY THAT THE CARRYING VESSEL IS NOT OVER 15 YEARS OF AGE AT THE TIME OF LOADING. THE AGE IS 8 YEARS. L/C NO. IS 613R9846106		

NAME ,ADDRESS AND TEL NO. OF THE CARRYING VESSELS' AGENT
AT THE PORT OF DISCHARGE:
HAJI ABDULLAH ALIREZA & CO., LTD.
P.O.BOX 7158, KIMG ABDUL AZIZ STREET,
JEDDAH 21462, PHONE(2)6472233,
TELEX 601037 REZASJ, FAX(2)6484644
CABLE ZAINAL - REZASHIP

ORIGINAL

Shipper's declared Value [see clause 7(1) and 7(2)]

Total No. of Containers received by the Carrier:	Packages received by the Carrier:
ONE (20') CONTAINER ONLY	

Movement:	Currency:
CY/CY	

Charge	Rate	Basis	Wt/Vol/Val	P/C	Amount

Total Freight Prepaid	Total Freight Collect	Total Freight

90116745

Above Particulars as declared by shipper. Without responsibility or warranty as to correctness by carrier [see clause 11(1) and (2)]

RECEIVED by the Carrier from the Shipper in apparent good order and condition (unless otherwise noted herein) the total number or quantity of Containers or other packages or units indicated in the box opposite entitled "Total No. of Containers/Packages received by the Carrier" for Carriage subject to all the terms and conditions hereof (INCLUDING THE TERMS AND CONDITIONS ON THE REVERSE HEREOF AND THE TERMS AND CONDITIONS OF THE CARRIER'S APPLICABLE TARIFF) from the Place of Receipt or the Port of Loading, whichever is applicable, to the Port of Discharge or the Place of Delivery, whichever is applicable. One original Bill of Lading, duly endorsed, must be surrendered by the Merchant to the Carrier in exchange for the Goods or a delivery order. In accepting this Bill of Lading the Merchant expressly accepts and agrees to all its terms and conditions whether printed, stamped or written, or otherwise incorporated, notwithstanding the non-signing of this Bill of Lading by the Merchant.

IN WITNESS WHEREOF the number of original Bills of Lading stated below all of this tenor and date has been signed, one of which being accomplished the others to stand void.

Place and date of issue: GUANGZHOU, AUG.24,1998

Freight payable at:	Number of original Bs/L:
	THREE

SHIPPED ON BOARD

For Hapag-Lloyd Container Linie GmbH, Hamburg (as Carrier)

AS AGENT FOR THE CARRIER: HAPAG-LLOYD

CHINA OCEAN SHIPPING AGENCY GUANGZHOU
AS AGENTS (8)

(Signature)

七、单据改错

（一）单据改错一

广东省荣华贸易有限公司与芬兰 ABC 公司成交一笔出口交易。ABC 公司按期开来信用证，荣华公司按期出运，并填制好海运提单，请根据下面信用证提供的内容审核海运提单编号①至⑧的内容，对单证不符的内容在单据上进行修改。

ISSUING BANK：	METITA BANK LTD. FIN－00020 METITA，FINLAND
Form of Doc. Credit：	IRREVOCABLE
Credit Number：	LRT9802457
Date of Issue：	020505
Expiry：	Date 020716 Place CHINA
Applicant：	ABC CORP. AKEKSANTERINK AUTO P. O. BOX 9，FINLAND
Beneficiary：	GUANGDONG RONGHUA TRADE CO.，LTD. 168 DEZHENG ROAD SOUTH，GUANGZHOU，CHINA
Amount：	Currency USD Amount 36，480.00（SAY US DOLLARS THIRTY SIX THOUSAND FOUR HUNDRED AND EIGHTY ONLY.）
Pos./Neg. Tol.（%）：	5/5
Available with/by：	ANY BANK IN ADVISING COUNTRY BY NEGOTIATION
Partial Shipments：	Not Allowed
Transshipment：	Allowed
Loading in Charge：	GUANGZHOU
For Transport to：	HELSINKI
Shipment Period：	AT THE LATEST JULY 16，2002
Descript. of Goods：	9，600PCS OF WOMEN'S SWEATERS UNIT PRICE：USD3.80/PC PACKING：12PCS/CTN TOTAL 800CTNS OTHER DETAILS AS PER S/C NO. 98SGQ468001 CFR HELSINKI
Documents Required：	FULL SET OF CLEAN ON BOARD MARINE BILLS OF LADING，MADE OUT TO ORDER OF METITA BANK LTD.，FINLAND，MARKED "FREIGHT PREPAID" AND NOTIFY APPLICANT（AS INDICATE ABOVE）
Additional Cond.：	1. T. T. REIMBURSEMENT IS PROHIBITED. 2. ALL DOCUMENTS MUST BE MARKED THE S/C NO. 3. SHIPPING MARKS：ABC/HELSINKI/ NO. 1－800.

BILL OF LADING

Shipper

GUANGDONG RONGHUA TRADE CO., LTD.
168 DEZHENG ROAD SOUTH, GUANGZHOU, CHINA
①

B/L No.　KFT2582588

Combined Transport BILL OF LADING

RECEIVED in apparent good order and condition except as otherwise noted the total number of containers or other packages or units enumerated below for transportation from the place of receipt to the place of delivery subject to the terms and conditions hereof. One of the Bills of Lading must be surrendered duly endorsed to the Carrier by or on behalf of the Holder of the Bill of Lading, the rights and liabilities arising in accordance with the terms and conditions hereof shall, without prejudice to any rule of common law or statute rendering them binding on the Merchant, become binding in all respects between the Carrier and the Holder of the Bill of Lading as though the contract evidenced hereby had been made between them.

IN WITNESS whereof the number of original Bills of Lading stated under have been signed. All of this tenor and date, one of which being accomplished, the other(s) to be void.

Consignee

ABC CORP. AKEKSANTERINK AUTO
P. O. BOX 9, FINLAND
②

Notify Address

METITA BANK LTD.,
FIN－00020 METITA, FINLAND
③

For delivery of goods please apply to:

Pre-carriage by	Place of Receipt	
DONGFANGHONG		
Ocean Vessel　Voy. No. SUISUN 103	Port of Loading GUANGZHOU	
Port of Discharge HELSINKI VIA HONGKONG	Place of Delivery	Final Destination for the Merchant's Reference only

Container, Seal No. & Marks & Nos.	No. of Package & Description of Goods	Gross Weight KGS	Measurement m^3
N/M ④	9,600PCS WOMEN'S SWEATERS ⑤ TOTAL: EIGHT HUNDRED CARTONS ONLY. ⑥ S/C NO.: LRT9802457 ⑦	13,600.00KGS FREIGHT COLLECT ⑧	25CBM

FREIGHT & CHARGES	Revenue Tons.	Rate　Per	Prepaid	Collect

Prepaid at	Payable at	Place and Date of Issue GUANGZHOU　MAY 20, 2002
Total Prepaid	No. of Original B(s)/L THREE(3)	Stamp & Signature ABC SHIPPING CO. 刘五 AS MASTER

LADEN ON BOARD THE VESSEL
Date

By..................................
(TERMS CONTINUED ON BACK HEREOF)

（二）单据改错二

广东省荣华贸易有限公司与芬兰ABC公司成交一笔出口交易。ABC公司按期开来信用证，荣华公司按期出运，并填制好海运提单，请根据下面信用证提供的内容审核海运提单编号①至⑧的内容，对单证不符的内容在单据上进行修改。

ISSUING BANK:	METITA BANK LTD. FIN－00020 METITA, FINLAND
Term of Doc. Credit:	IRREVOCABLE
Credit Number:	LRT9802457
Date of Issue:	020505
Expiry:	Date 020716 Place CHINA
Applicant:	ABC CORP. AKEKSANTERINK AUTO P. O. BOX 9, FINLAND
Beneficiary:	GUANGDONG RONGHUA TRADE CO., LTD. 168 DEZHENG ROAD SOUTH, GUANGZHOU, CHINA
Amount:	Currency USD Amount 36, 480. 00 (SAY US DOLLARS THIRTY SIX THOUSAND FOUR HUNDRED AND EIGHTY ONLY.)
Pos. / Neg. Tol. (%):	5/5
Available with/by:	ANY BANK IN ADVISING COUNTRY BY NEGOTIATION
Partial Shipments:	Not Allowed
Transshipment:	Allowed
Loading in Charge:	GUANGZHOU
For Transport to:	HELSINKI
Shipment Period:	AT THE LATEST JULY 16, 2002
Descript. of Goods:	9, 600PCS OF WOMEN'S SWEATERS UNIT PRICE: USD3. 80/PC PACKING: 12PCS/CTN OTHER DETAILS AS PER S/C NO. 98SGQ468001 CFR HELSINKI
Documents Required:	FULL SET OF CLEAN ON BOARD MARINE BILLS OF LADING, MADE OUT TO THE ORDER OF ISSUING BANK, MARKED "FREIGHT PREPAID" AND NOTIFY APPLICANT (AS INDICATE ABOVE)
Additional Cond.:	1. T. T. REIMBURSEMENT IS PROHIBITED. 2. ALL DOCUMENTS MUST BE MARKED THE S/C NO. AND THE L/C NO. 3. SHIPPING MARKS: ABC/HELSINKI/NO. I－UP.

BILL OF LADING

Shipper GUANGDONG RONGHUA TRADE CO. ,LTD. 168 DEZHENG ROAD SOUTH, GUANGZHOU,CHINA	B/L No. KEN－98－25401
Consignee TO THE ORDER OF ISSUING BANK ①	Combined Transport BILL OF LADING RECEIVED in apparent good order and condition except as otherwise noted the total number of containers or other packages or units enumerated below for transportation from the place of receipt to the place of delivery subject to the terms and conditions hereof. One of the Bills of Lading must be surrendered duly endorsed to the Carrier by or on behalf of the Holder of the Bill of Lading, the rights and liabilities arising in accordance with the terms and conditions hereof shall, without prejudice to any rule of common law or statute rendering them binding on the Merchant, become binding in all respects between the Carrier and the Holder of the Bill of Lading as though the contract evidenced hereby had been made between them. IN WITNESS whereof the number of original Bills of Lading stated under have been signed. All of this tenor and date, one of which being accomplished, the other(s) to be void.
Notify Address ABC CORP. AKEKSANTERINK AUTO P. O. BOX 9,FINLAND	For delivery of goods please apply to :

Pre-carriage by	Place of Receipt	
Ocean Vessel Voy. No. DONGFANGHONG/SUISUN 103 ②	Port of Loading HELSINKI VIA HONGKONG ③	
Port of Discharge GUANGZHOU ④	Place of Delivery	Final Destination for the Merchant's Reference only

Container, Seal No. & Marks & Nos.	No. of Package & Description of Goods	Gross Weight KGS	Measurement m^3
ABC/HELSINKI/NO.I－UP 1×20'DHSU3654872 SEAL NO. 123456 CY/CY FCL	SHIPPER'S LOAD & COUNT & SEAL S. T. C. 9,720PCS WOMEN'S SWEATERS ⑤ TOTAL:EIGHT HUNDRED AND TEN CARTONS ONLY. ⑥ SHIPPED ON BOARD DATE:MAY 22,2002 ⑦ L/C NO. :LRT9802457	13,600.00KGS	25CBM

FREIGHT & CHARGES	Revenue Tons.	Rate	Per	Prepaid	Collect
FREIGHT PREPAID					

Prepaid at	Payable at	Place and Date of Issue
GUANGZHOU		GUANGZHOU MAY 20,2002
Total Prepaid	No. of Original B(s)/L THREE(3)	Stamp & Signature XYZ SHIPPING CO. 刘五 ⑧ AS AGENT FOR THE CARRIER: ABC SHIPPING CO.

LADEN ON BOARD THE VESSEL
Date

By.................................
(TERMS CONTINUED ON BACK HEREOF)

八、单据填制

（一）单据填制一

根据给出的信用证条款和其他资料缮制提单。

A. 信用证条款。

Issuing Bank:	METITA BANK LTD. FIN－00020 METITA, FINLAND
Term of Doc. Credit:	IRREVOCABLE
Credit Number:	KHL02－22457
Date of Issue:	020505
Expiry:	Date 020716 Place CHINA
Applicant:	FFK CORP. AKEKSANTERINK AUTO P. O. BOX 9, FINLAND
Beneficiary:	GUANGDONG RONGHUA TRADE CO., LTD. 168 DEZHENG ROAD SOUTH, GUANGZHOU, CHINA
Amount:	Currency USD Amount 38, 400. 00
Pos. / Neg. Tol. (%):	5/5
Available with/by:	ANY BANK IN ADVISING COUNTRY BY NEGOTIATION
Partial Shipments:	Not Allowed
Transshipment:	Allowed
Loading in Charge:	GUANGZHOU
For Transport to:	HELSINKI
Shipment Period:	AT THE LATEST JULY 16, 2002
Description of Goods:	9, 600PCS OF WOMEN'S SWEATERS Unit Price: USD4. 00/PC, CFR HELSINKI Packing: 12PCS/CTN
Documents Required:	FULL SET OF CLEAN ON BOARD MARINE BILLS OF LADING, MADE OUT TO ORDER OF METITA BANK LTD., FINLAND, MARKED "FREIGHT PREPAID" AND NOTIFY APPLICANT

B. 其他资料。

提单号码：KTT0245678

货物总毛重：6, 500KGS

货物总尺码：25CBMS

船名：MAKIS V. 002

唛头：ABC/ HELSINKI/ NO. 1－800

集装箱号码：SIHU365487－2（20'）SEAL NO. 123456 CY/CY

提单签发日期：2002 年 7 月 10 日

提单签发地点：广州

承运人：ABC SHIPPING CO.

提单签发人：张三

货物由托运人负责装箱及计数。

BILL OF LADING

Shipper		B/L No.	
Consignee		Combined Transport BILL OF LADING RECEIVED in apparent good order and condition except as otherwise noted the total number of containers or other packages or units enumerated below for transportation from the place of receipt to the place of delivery subject to the terms and conditions hereof. One of the Bills of Lading must be surrendered duly endorsed to the Carrier by or on behalf of the Holder of the Bill of Lading, the rights and liabilities arising in accordance with the terms and conditions hereof shall, without prejudice to any rule of common law or statute rendering them binding on the Merchant, become binding in all respects between the Carrier and the Holder of the Bill of Lading as though the contract evidenced hereby had been made between them. IN WITNESS whereof the number of original Bills of Lading stated under have been signed. All of this tenor and date, one of which being accomplished, the other(s) to be void.	
Notify Address		For delivery of goods please apply to:	
Pre-carriage by	Place of Receipt		
Ocean Vessel Voy. No.	Port of Loading		
Port of Discharge	Place of Delivery	Final Destination for the Merchant's Reference only	
Container, Seal No. & Marks & Nos.	No. of Package & Description of Goods	Gross Weight KGS	Measurement m^3

FREIGHT & CHARGES	Revenue Tons.	Rate Per	Prepaid	Collect

Prepaid at	Payable at	Place and Date of Issue
Total Prepaid	No. of Original B(s)/L	Stamp & Signature

LADEN ON BOARD THE VESSEL
Date

By..................................

(TERMS CONTINUED ON BACK HEREOF)

（二）单据填制二

根据给出的信用证条款和其他资料缮制提单。

A. 信用证条款。

Issuing Bank:	METITA BANK LTD. FIN -00020 METITA, FINLAND
Term of Doc. Credit:	IRREVOCABLE
Credit Number:	KHL02 -22457
Date of Issue:	020505
Expiry:	Date 020716 Place CHINA
Applicant:	FFK CORP. AKEKSANTERINK AUTO P. O. BOX 9, FINLAND
Beneficiary:	GUANGDONG RONGHUA TRADE CO., LTD. 168 DEZHENG ROAD SOUTH, GUANGZHOU, CHINA
Amount:	Currency USD Amount 38,400.00
Pos. / Neg. Tol. (%):	5/5
Available with/by:	ANY BANK IN ADVISING COUNTRY BY NEGOTIATION
Partial Shipments:	Not Allowed
Transshipment:	Allowed
Loading in Charge:	GUANGZHOU
For Transport to:	HELSINKI
Shipment Period:	AT THE LATEST JULY 16, 2002
Description of Goods:	9,600PCS OF WOMEN'S SWEATERS UNIT PRICE: USD4.00/PC, OTHER DETAILS AS PER S/C NO. 98SGQ468001 PACKING: 12PCS/CTN CFR HELSINKI (INCOTERMS 2000)
Documents Required:	FULL SET OF CLEAN ON BOARD MARINE BILLS OF LADING, MADE OUT TO ORDER OF ISSUING BANK, MARKED FREIGHT PREPAID AND DDC COLLECT, SHOWING INSURANCE PREMIUM, SURCHARGE AND TRADE TERMS NOTIFY APPLICANT
Additional Cond.:	1. T. T. REIMBURSEMENT IS PROHIBITED. 2. ALL DOCUMENTS MUST BE MARKED THE S/C NO. AND L/C NO.

B. 其他资料。

提单号码：KTT0245678	货物总毛重：6,500KGS
货物总尺码：25CBMS	唛头：ABC/ HELSINKI/ NO. 1 -800
转运港：香港	船名：第一程 DONGFANG 第二程 MAKIS V. 002
集装箱号码：SIHU365487 -2（20'）	SEAL NO. 123456
保险费：USD100.00	附加费：USD300.00
提单签发地点：广州	提单签发日期：2002 年 7 月 10 日
承运人：ABC SHIPPING CO.	承运人代理人：XYZ SHIPPING CO.
提单签发人：李四	提单装船批注日期：2002 年 7 月 11 日

货物由托运人负责装箱、计数和封箱，整箱装，由集装箱堆场至集装箱堆场。

BILL OF LADING

Shipper		B/L No.		
Consignee		Combined Transport BILL OF LADING RECEIVED in apparent good order and condition except as otherwise noted the total number of containers or other packages or units enumerated below for transportation from the place of receipt to the place of delivery subject to the terms and conditions hereof. One of the Bills of Lading must be surrendered duly endorsed to the Carrier by or on behalf of the Holder of the Bill of Lading, the rights and liabilities arising in accordance with the terms and conditions hereof shall, without prejudice to any rule of common law or statute rendering them binding on the Merchant, become binding in all respects between the Carrier and the Holder of the Bill of Lading as though the contract evidenced hereby had been made between them. IN WITNESS whereof the number of original Bills of Lading stated under have been signed. All of this tenor and date, one of which being accomplished, the other (s) to be void.		
Notify Address		For delivery of goods please apply to:		
Pre-carriage by	Place of Receipt			
Ocean Vessel Voy. No.	Port of Loading			
Port of Discharge	Place of Delivery	Final Destination for the Merchant's Reference only		
Container, Seal No. & Marks & Nos.	No. of Package & Description of Goods	Gross Weight KGS	Measurement m^3	

FREIGHT & CHARGES	Revenue Tons.	Rate Per	Prepaid	Collect

Prepaid at	Payable at	Place and Date of Issue
Total Prepaid	No. of Original B(s) /L	Stamp & Signature

LADEN ON BOARD THE VESSEL
Date

By……………………………………

(TERMS CONTINUED ON BACK HEREOF)

第四节 保险单

一、中英文术语、短语互译

（一）中译英

（1）保险单______

（2）预约保险单______

（3）航空运输险______

（4）仓至仓条款______

（5）平安险______

（6）罢工险______

（7）单独海损______

（8）淡水雨淋险______

（9）中国人民保险公司海洋运输货物保险条款______

（10）保费______

（二）英译中

（1）Insurance Certificate ______

（2）Combined Insurance Certificate ______

（3）Covering All Risks and War Risks ______

（4）Amount Insured ______

（5）Institute Cargo Clauses ______

（6）Made out to Order ______

（7）Theft Pilferage & Non-delivery Risk ______

（8）Irrespective of Percentage ______

（9）General Average ______

（10）Insured ______

二、单项选择题

1. 以 CIF 术语达成的交易，如信用证没有特别规定，保险单的被保险人一栏应填写（　）。

A. 开证申请人的名称　　B. 受益人的名称

C. TO ORDER　　D. TO WHOM IT MAY CONCERN

2. 如信用证没有特别规定，按国际保险市场惯例，保险金额一般在发票金额的基础上（　）填写。

A. 加一成　　B. 加两成

C. 加三成　　D. 加四成

3. 如信用证规定"COVERING MARINE RISKS OF THE PEOPLE'S INSURANCE COMPANY OF CHINA DD 1/1/1982"，则出口公司（　　）。

A. 只能投保平安险　　B. 只能投保水渍险

C. 只能投保一切险　　D. 可投保平安险、水渍险及一切险中的任一种

4. 信用证中规定"COVERING RISKS AS PER 'INSTITUTE CARGO CLAUSES（A）', INCLUDING WAREHOUSE TO WAREHOUSE CLAUSE"，其中的"WAREHOUSE TO WAREHOUSE CLAUSE"是指（　　）责任起讫的条款。

A. 出口方负责的交货　　B. 承运人负责的运输

C. 进口方负责的收货　　D. 保险人负责的保险

5. 信用证中规定"ALL DOCUMENTS SHOULD INDICATE THE SHIPPING MARK"，出口公司在保单的"Marks & Nos."一栏应填写（　　）。

A. 实际唛头

B. AS PER INVOICE NO. ×××

C. AS PER B/L NO. ×××

D. 既可按实际唛头填写，也可按"AS PER INVOICE NO. ×××"填写

6. 假设提单的签发日期为"MARCH 24，2005"，那么以下保单的开航日期中，（　　）的填写是错误的。

A. MARCH 24，2005　　B. AS PER B/L

C. MARCH 30，2005　　D. MARCH 23，2005

7. 保险的赔付地点一般填写（　　）。

A. 起运港（地）　　B. 目的港（地）

C. 投保人所在地　　D. 保险公司所在地

8. 预约保险是指根据预约保险合同，投保人以（　　）替代投保单，保险公司负自动承保的责任。

A. 大副收据　　B. 买卖合同

C. 海运提单　　D. 国外寄来的装运通知

9. 我方按 CIF 条件出口一批陶瓷制品，由于信用证中没有规定具体的投保险别，我方在办理投保手续时，一般可按（　　）投保。

A. 一切险 + 碰损破碎险　　B. 平安险 + 水渍险

C. 平安险 + 碰损破碎险　　D. 一切险 + 水渍险

10. 某公司以 CIF 条件出口一批货物，在广州港装上船只"DONGFENG"号运往香港，在香港装上第二程船"NATA"号后运往旧金山，该公司在保单的载运输工具栏（Per conveyance S. S.）应填写为（　　）。

A. DONGFENG　　B. NATA

C. DONGFENG/NATA　　D. DONGFENG/NATA W/T HONGKONG

三、多项选择题

1. 根据伦敦保险协会制定的《协会货物条款》，以下险别能单独投保的有（　　）。

A. ICCA　　B. ICCB

C. 战争险　　D. 恶意损害险

2. 按照我国《海洋货物运输保险条款》的规定，以下险别属于特殊附加险的是（　　）。

A. 偷窃提货不着险　　B. 交货不到险

C. 甲板险　　D. 舱面险

3. 信用证中规定“MARINE INSURANCE POLICY OF CERTIFICATE IN DUPLICATE, COVERING FPA AS PER OCEAN MARINE CARGO CLAUSE OF THE PEOPLE'S COMPANY OF CHINA DATED 1/1/1981，INCLUDING T. P. N. D. LOSS AND DAMAGE CAUSED BY HEAT，SHIP'S SWEAT AND ODOUR，BREAKAGE OF PACKING”，按此规定，应投保的一般附加险有（　　）。

A. 偷窃提货不着险　　B. 受潮受热险

C. 串味险　　D. 破碎险

4. 按照我国《海洋货物运输保险条款》的规定，以下险别属于我国海洋运输货物保险中的基本险的是（　　）。

A. FPA　　B. ICCA

C. WPA　　D. WAR RISKS

5. 共同海损分摊时，涉及的受益方包括（　　）。

A. 船方　　B. 货方

C. 救助方　　D. 运费方

四、判断题

1. 保险单俗称“大保单”，保险凭证俗称“小保单”，由于保险凭证背面没有列入保险条款，因而它们不具有同等的法律效力。（　　）

2. 保险单的签发日期应该不迟于海运提单的签发日期。（　　）

3. 我某外贸公司以 CIF 条件出口，代客户投保一切险，对于从装运港运往目的港途中由于任何外来原因所造成的损失，客户均可向保险公司索赔。（　　）

4. 我某公司以 CFR 术语进口钢材一批，我方在收到国外发来的装船通知后，按事先签订的预约保险合同，将该通知交保险公司，保险公司的承保责任起讫应该为“仓至仓”。（　　）

5. 如信用证规定按 ICC 条款投保，根据中国人民保险公司的现行做法是不能接受的，应要求对方修改信用证。（　　）

6. 当信用证要求提交的保险单份数为“IN TWO COPIES”时，我方应提交两份副本。（　　）

7. 按照我国现行的《海洋货物运输保险条款》的规定，保险公司对于海运战争险的保险责任起讫不采用仓至仓条款，而是仅负责水上风险。（　　）

8. 某出口公司按 CIF 条件出口服装一批，我方按信用证要求投保水渍险，运输途中由于食用水管破裂，造成部分服装被浸泡，该损失保险公司将予以赔偿。（　　）

9. 按照我国《海洋货物运输保险条款》的规定，战争险与罢工险均能单独投保。(　　)

10. 保险公司按伦敦保险协会制定的《协会货物条款》中的ICCA、ICCB和ICCC三种险别承保的责任范围与按我国《海洋货物运输保险条款》中ALL RISKS、WPA和FPA承保的责任范围大致相同。(　　)

五、案例分析

1. 我某外贸公司以CFR条件出口货物一批，应买方要求，我方在装船前代为投保了一切险，保单的被保险人为买方。货物用驳船从广州乌冲码头运往盐田港装船时，由于触礁而全部灭失，卖方认为保险公司的保险责任范围为“仓至仓”，而该损失又在一切险的承保范围以内，因此持相关保险单向保险公司索赔。问保险公司对该损失应不应该赔偿？为什么？

2. 我某公司以CIF条件出口一批羊肉到中东某国，信用证规定投保平安险加战争险、罢工险。货到目的港后由于码头工人罢工而致无人卸货，一个星期后由于无法补充燃料，货轮上的冷冻设备停止运转，等到罢工结束，该批羊肉已变质，无法食用。问保险公司对于该损失是否赔偿？为什么？

六、阅读理解

(一) 阅读理解一

中保财产保险有限公司
The People's Insurance (Property) Company of China, Ltd.
PICC PROPERTY

№ 0071897

发票号码 97-257-501367
Invoice No.

No.of Original: One
保险单号次
Policy No. KC04 97011505104

海洋货物运输保险单
MARINE CARGO TRANSPORTATION INSURANCE POLICY

被保险人：
Insured: G M G HARDWARE & TOOLS IMP. & EXP. COMPANY LTD.

中保财产保险有限公司（以下简称本公司）根据被保险人的要求，及其所缴付约定的保险费，按照本保险单承保险别和背面所载条款与下列特别条款承保下述货物运输保险，特签发本保险单。

This policy of Insurance witnesses that The People's Insurance (Property) Company of China, Ltd.(hereinafter called "The Company"),at the request of the Insured and in consideration of the agreed premium paid by the Insured, undertakes to insure the undermentioned goods in transportation subject to the conditions of this Policy as per the Clauses printed overleaf and other special clauses attached hereon.

保险货物项目 Descriptions of Goods	包装 单位 数量 Packing Unit Quantity	保险金额 Amount Insured
HAND TOOLS	203 PACKAGES	USD7,391.84
TOTAL: 203 PACKAGES		

承保险别
Conditions

Covering All Risks as per Ocean Marine Cargo Clauses (1/1/1981) (Warehouse to Warehouse Clause is included) of The People's Insurance Company of China.

货物标记
Marks of Goods

GIATRAKIS

COPY

总保险金额：
Total Amount Insured: US Dollar SEVEN THOUSAND THREE HUNDRED & NINETY-ONE CENTS EIGHTY-FOUR ONLY.

保费
Premium as arranged

载运输工具
Per conveyance S.S. NING GLORY V.98/207W

开航日期
Slg. on or abt. DEC.10, 1997

起运港
From GUANGZHOU

目的港
To PIRAEUS

所保货物，如发生本保险单项下可能引起索赔的损失或损坏，应立即通知本公司下述代理人查勘。如有索赔，应向本公司提交保险单正本（本保险单共有　份正本）及有关文件。如一份正本已用于索赔，其余正本则自动失效。

In the event of loss or damage which may result in a claim under this Policy, immediate notice must be given to the Company's Agent as mentioned hereunder. Claims, if any, one of the Original Policy which has been issued in　Original (s) together with the relevant documents shall be surrendered to the Company, If one of the Original Policy has been accomplished, the others to be void.

Macrymichalos Brothers S.A.
2, Gounari Street, Piraeus.

中保财产保险有限公司
THE PEOPLE'S INSURANCE (PROPERTY) COMPANY OF CHINA,LTD.

THE PEOPLE'S INSURANCE (PROPERTY) CO. OF CHINA, LTD.
GUANGDONG PROVINCIAL BRANCH
INTERNATIONAL DEPT

赔款偿付地点
Claim payable at PIRAEUS

日期
Date DEC.10, 1997

在
at GUANGZHOU

地址：
Address: 2 Guangwei Road, Guangzhou,China
Fax:83324566 Tlx:440462 PICC CN

UNDERWRITING SIGNATORY (220)

如果该交易以 CIF 条件达成，请根据上面单据回答下列问题：

（1）该笔交易是进口贸易还是出口贸易？

（2）受益人到银行办理议付前，是否需要对该保单进行背书转让？

（3）保险金额为 USD7,391.84，该金额是否就是发票金额？

（二）阅读理解二

如果该交易以 CIF 条件达成，请根据下面单据回答下列问题：

（1）保险货物的名称是什么？

（2）该保单投保什么险别？采用什么保险条款？

（3）保险货物在运输过程中是否发生了转运？

PICC 中国人民保险公司
The People's Insurance Company of China

总公司设于北京　　一九四九年创立
Head Office: BEIJING　　Established In 1949

No. 0010951

发票号码
Invoice No. 2000057WBS-5

海洋货物运输保险单
MARINE CARGO INSURANCE POLICY

保险单号次
Policy No. KC04 000110081000

被保险人：
Insured: GUANGDONG TEXTILES IE WOOLEN KNITWEARS CO. LTD. HELD TO ORDER OF (THE) A B C CO.

中国人民保险公司(以下简称本公司)根据被保险人的要求，及其所缴付约定的保险费，按照本保险单承保险别和背面所载条款与下列特别条款承保下述货物运输保险，特签发本保险单。
This policy of Insurance witnesses that The People's Insurance Company of China (hereinafter called "The Company"), at the request of the Insured and in consideration of the agreed premium paid by the insured, undertakes to insure the undermentioned goods in transportation subject to the conditions of this Policy as per the Clauses printed overleaf and other special clauses attached hereon.

保险货物项目　标记　数量及包装
Description, Marks, Numbers & Quantity of Goods:

承保条件
Conditions:

PRATEX-TOR
P.O.#
STYLE#
COLOUR
QUANTITY
SIZE RATIO
LABEL
PREPACKS RATIO/

COVERING ALL RISKS AS PER OCEAN MARINE CARGO CLAUSES(1/1/1981) (WAREHOUSE TO WAREHOUSE CLAUSE IS INCLUDED) OF THE PEOPLE'S INSURANCE COMPANY OF CHINA

MEN'S / WOMEN'S SWEATERS

2,297PCS (192CTNS)

COPY

Including Year 2000 Problem Exclusion Clause.

总保险金额
Total Amount Insured: US DOLLARS TWENTY-TWO THOUSAND EIGHT HUNDRED AND SEVENTY TWO ONLY. (USD22,872)

保费
Premium as arranged

装载运输工具
Per conveyance S.S APL JAPAN V.043-2

开航日期
Sig. on or abt July 30,2000

自 from (YANTIAN), GUANGDONG, CHINA 至 TORONTO, CANADA

所保货物，如发生本保险单项下可能引起索赔的损失或损坏，应立即通知本公司下述代理人查勘。如有索赔，应向本公司提交保险单正本(本保险单共有 2 份正本)及有关文件。如一份正本已用于索赔，其余正本则自动失效。
In the event of loss or damage which may result in a claim under this Policy, immediate notice must be given to the Company's Agent as mentioned hereunder. Claims, if any, one of the Original Policy which has been issued in TWO Original(s) together with the relevant documents shall be surrendered to the Company, If one of the Original Policy has been accomplished, the others to be void.

... NAME AND ADDRESS:
BOYD PHILLIPS & CO., LTD.
145 WELLINGTON ST.W., SUITE 310
TORONTO, ONT. CANADA M5J 1HB
TEL.:416-9719744 FAX.416-5917673
TELEX.06-218844"ADJUSTOR CABLE:"ADJUSTERS"

中国人民保险公司广东省分公司
THE PEOPLE'S INSURANCE CO. OF CHINA
GUANGDONG PROVINCIAL BRANCH

THE PEOPLE'S INSURANCE CO. OF CHINA
GUANGDONG PROVINCIAL BRANCH
INTERNATIONAL DEPT.
丘小山
AUTHORIZED SIGNATORY

赔款偿付地点
Claim payable at TORONTO, CANADA

日期　　广州
Date: July 29,2000　　Guangzhou

地址：中国广州广卫路2号
Address: 2, Guangwei Road, Guangzhou China
Tlx: 44462 PICCG CN　Fax: 0086 20 83324566

七、单据改错

（一）单据改错一

请根据以下材料修改一份保险单。

THE SAKURA BANK, LTD.
INT'L OPERATIONS CENTER
P. O. BOX 166, TOKYO, JAPAN

CREDIT NO.: 645 - 3000511
DATE OF ISSUE: OCTOBER 23, 1997　　　　EXPIRY DATE: DECEMBER 15, 1997

APPLICANT: SHITAYA KINSOKU CO., LTD. 6 - 11 7 - CHONE UENO TAITO - KU TOKYO, JAPAN	BENEFICIARY: GUANGDONG MACHINERY IMP. & EXP. CORP. (GROUP) 720 DONGFENG ROAD EAST GUANGZHOU, CHINA
ADVISING BANK: BANK OF CHINA, GUANGDONG BRANCH GUANGZHOU	AMOUNT: USD15,880.00 US DOLLARS FIFTEEN THOUSAND EIGHT HUNDRED AND EIGHTY ONLY.
PARTIAL SHIPMENTS ARE NOT ALLOWED TRANSSHIPMENT IS ALLOWED FROM: CHINESE PORTS TO: YOKOHAMA, JAPAN NOT LATER THAN NOVEMBER 30, 1997	CREDIT AVAILABLE WITH ANY BANK BY NEGOTIATION AGAINST PRESENTATION OF DOCUMENTS DETAILED HEREIN AND BENEFICIARY'S DRAFT(S) AT SIGHT DRAWN ON THE SAKURA BANK LTD., TOKYO FOR FULL INVOICE VALUE

LIST OF DOCUMENTS TO BE PRESENTED:
1) SIGNED COMMERCIAL INVOICES IN 2 COPIES.
2) FULL SET OF CLEAN ON BOARD OCEAN BILLS OF LADING MADE OUT TO ORDER OF SHIPPER AND BLANK ENDORSED, MARKED "FREIGHT PREPAID" AND NOTIFY APPLICANT.
3) INSURANCE POLICY OR CERTIFICATE IN DUPLICATE, ENDORSED IN BLANK FOR 110% OF THE CIF INVOICE VALUE COVERING OCEAN MARINE CARGO CLAUSES (ALL RISKS) AND OCEAN MARINE CARGO WAR RISK CLAUSES OF THE PEOPLE'S INSURANCE CO. OF CHINA OF 1981. CLAIMS PAYABLE IN JAPAN IN CURRENCY OF DRAFT(S).
4) PACKING LIST IN 2 COPIES.
5) G. S. P. CERTIFICATE OF ORIGIN FORM A IN 2 COPIES.

COVERING SHIPMENT:
"RABBIT" BRAND SHOVEL WITH METAL HANDLE
S501MH 210 DOZ @ USD38.00/DOZ
S503MH 200 DOZ @ USD39.50/DOZ
AS PER S/C NO. A97JP19900247　　CIF YOKOHAMA

OTHER MATERIALS:
INV. NO.: 97GD003511　　INV. DATE: NOV. 2, 1997
B/L DATE: NOV. 25, 1997　　POLICY NO.: AA3546897
NAME OF STEAMER: NEDLLOYD HONSHU V. 3165　　PACKING: 1DOZ/CTN
SHIPPING MARK: SK/YOKOHAMA/NOS. 1 - 410

PICC PROPERTY

中保财产保险有限公司
The People's Insurance (Property) Company of China, Ltd.

发票号码
Invoice No. 97GD003511

保险单号次
Policy No.

海 洋 货 物 运 输 保 险 单
MARINE CARGO TRANSPORTATION INSURANCE POLICY

被保险人：
Insured： GUANGDONG MACHINERY IMP. & EXP. CORP.（GPOUP）

中保财产保险有限公司（以下简称本公司）根据被保险人的要求，及其所缴付约定的保险费，按照本保险单承担险别和背面所载条款与下列特别条款承保下列货物运输保险，特签发本保险单。

This policy of Insurance witnesses that the People's Insurance (Property) Company of China, Ltd. (hereinafter called "the Company"), at the request of the Insured and in consideration of the agreed premium paid by the Insured, undertakes to insure the undermentioned goods in transportation subject to the conditions of this Policy as per the Clauses printed overleaf and other special clauses attached hereon.

保险货物项目 Descriptions of Goods	包装 单位 数量 Packing Unit Quantity	保险金额 Amount Insured
"RABBIT" BRAND SHOVEL WITH METAL HANDLE TOTAL：410CTNS	410CTNS	USD17,468.00

承保险别
Conditions

COVERING OCEAN MARINE CARGO CLAUSES (ALL RISKS) AND OCEAN MARINE CARGO WAR RISK CLAUSES OF THE PEOPLE'S INSURANCE CO. OF CHINA OF 1981

货物标记
Marks of Goods

SK
TOKYO
NOS. 1－410

总保险金额：
Total Amount Insured： US DOLLARS SEVENTEEN THOUSAND FOUR HUNDRED AND SIXTY EIGHT ONLY.

保费
Premium as arranged

载运输工具
Per conveyance S. S. HEDLLOYD HONSHU V. 3165

开航日期
Slg. on or abt NOV. 25, 1997

起运港
From GUANGZHOU

目的港
to YOKOHAMA

所保货物，如发生本保险单项下可能引起索赔的损失或损坏，应立即通知本公司下述代理人查勘。如有索赔，应向本公司提交保险单正本（本保险单共有　份正本）及有关文件。如一份正本已用于索赔，其余正本则自动失效。

In the event of loss or damage which may result in a claim under this Policy, immediate notice must be given to the Company's Agent as mentioned hereunder. Claims, if any, one of the Original Policy which has been issued in ONE Original(s) together with the relevant documents shall be surrendered to the Company. If one of the Original Policy has been accomplished, the others to be void.

中保财产保险有限公司
THE PEOPLE'S INSURANCE (PROPERTY) COMPANY OF CHINA, LTD.

赔款偿付地点
Claim payable at TOKYO

日期
Date NOV. 24, 1997

在
at GUANGZHOU

地址：
Address：

（二）单据改错二

请根据以下材料修改一份保险单。

A. 信用证条款。

APPLICANT	: HALSSEN & LYON GMBH PICKHUBEN 9, 20457 HAMBURG
BENEFICIARY	: CHINA TUHSU GUANGDONG TEA IMP. & EXP. CORP. 26 – 30 FLOOR, GUANGDONG FOREIGN ECONOMICS & TRADE BUILDING 351 TIANHE ROAD, GUANGZHOU, CHINA
AMOUNT	: DEM31, 428.00 (DEUTSCHE MARK THIRTY ONE THOUSAND FOUR HUNDRED AND TWENTY EIGHT ONLY.)
PARTIAL SHIPMENTS	: NOT PERMITTED
TRANSSHIPMENT	: PERMITTED
LOADING IN CHARGE	: GUANGZHOU/HUANGPU, CHINA
FOR TRANSPORT TO	: HAMBURG
DESCRIPT. OF GOODS	: 4439 CHINA BLACK TEA ABT. 8,000 KGS @ DEM4.05/KG CIFC3% HAMBURG (1 × 20' FCL/200 PAPERSACKS) PACKED IN PAPERSACKS, PALLETIZED AND CONTAINERIZED AS PER THE SALES CONFIRMATION NO. BT7095 THE PRICE IS TO BE UNDERSTOOD PER KILO NET SHIPPED WEIGHT CIF HAMBURG LESS 3 PERCENT COMMISSION, INCLUDING PACKING
DOCUMENTS REQUIRED	: MARINE INSURANCE POLICY/CERTIFICATE, COVERING ALL RISKS AND WAR RISKS, ISSUED FOR 110 PERCENT OF THE CIF INVOICE VALUE

B. 其他资料。

INVOICE NO. : TA7149

INV. DATE: AUGUST 11, 1997

B/L NO. : GSG97 – 723

B/L DATE: AUGUST 23, 1997

PACKING: 200 PAPERSACKS

SHIPPING MARKS: H&L/HAMBURG/6580

POLICY NO. : 1997A512

NAME OF STEAMER: PUDONG SENATOR WN743

中保财产保险有限公司

The People's Insurance (Property) Company of China, Ltd.

PICC PROPERTY

发票号码　　　　　　　　　　　　　　　　　　　保险单号次

Invoice No.　　　　　　　　　　　　　　　　　Policy No. 1997A512

海 洋 货 物 运 输 保 险 单

MARINE CARGO TRANSPORTATION INSURANCE POLICY

被保险人：

Insured: CHINA TUSHU GUANGDONG TEA IMPORT & EXPORT CORP. (被保险人背书转让)

中保财产保险有限公司(以下简称本公司)根据被保险人的要求,及其所缴付约定的保险费,按照本保险单承担险别和背面所载条款与下列特别条款承保下列货物运输保险,特签发本保险单。

This policy of Insurance witnesses that the People's Insurance (Property) Company of China, Ltd. (hereinafter called "the Company"), at the request of the Insured and in consideration of the agreed premium paid by the Insured, undertakes to insure the undermentioned goods in transportation subject to the conditions of this Policy as per the Clauses printed overleaf and other special clauses attached hereon.

保险货物项目 Descriptions of Goods	包装　单位　数量 Packing　Unit　Quantity	保险金额 Amount Insured
4439 CHINA BLACK TEA TOTAL:200 PAPERSACKS	200 PAPERSACKS	DEM34,571.00

承 保 险 别　　　　　　　　　　　　　　　　　　　货 物 标 记

Conditions　　　　　　　　　　　　　　　　　　　Marks of Goods

COVERING ALL RISKS AND WAR RISKS AS PER OCEAN MARINE CARGO CLAUSES(1/1/1981)(WAREHOUSE TO WAREHOUSE CLAUSE IS INCLUDED)

H&L
HAMBURG
65805

总保险金额：

Total Amount Insured: DEUTSCHE MARK THIRTY ONE THOUSAND FOUR HUNDRED AND TWENTY EIGHT ONLY.

保费　　　　　　　　载运输工具　　　　　　　　　　　开航日期

Premium as arranged　Per conveyance S. S. PUDONG SENATOR WN743　Slg. on or abt. SEPT. 23,1997

起运港　　　　　　　　　　　　目的港

From GUANGZHOU　　to　　HAMBURG

所保货物,如发生本保险单项下可能引起索赔的损失或损坏,应立即通知本公司下述代理人查勘。如有索赔,应向本公司提交保险单正本(本保险单共有　　份正本)及有关文件。如一份正本已用于索赔,其余正本则自动失效。

In the event of loss or damage which may result in a claim under this Policy, immediate notice must be given to the Company's Agent as mentioned hereunder. Claims, if any, one of the Original Policy which has been issued in ONE Original(s) together with the relevant documents shall be surrendered to the Company. If one of the Original Policy has been accomplished, the others to be void.

中保财产保险有限公司

THE PEOPLE'S INSURANCE(PROPERTY) COMPANY OF CHINA,LTD.

赔款偿付地点

Claim payable at　HAMBURG

日期　　　　　　　　　　在

Date SEPT. 22,1997　at　GUANGZHOU

地址：

Address:

八、单据填制

（一）单据填制一

请根据以下材料填制一份保险单。

A. 信用证条款。

Applicant	*50	:	ZELLERS INC., ATTN. IMPORT DEPT. 401 BAY STREET, 10/FL. TORONTO ON MJH. 2Y4, CANADA
Beneficiary	*59	:	G. M. G. HARDWEAR & TOOLS IMP. & EXP. COMPANY LTD. 726 DONGFENG ROAD EAST, GUANGZHOU, CHINA
Loading in Charge	44 A	:	GUANGZHOU, CHINA
For Transport to...	44 B	:	VANCOUVER, CANADA
Descript. of Goods	45 A	:	HANDLE TOOLS

ITEM NO.	QUANTITY	UNTI PRICE
A 0214	2,000 DOZ	USD 10.50
A 0012	1,000 DOZ	USD 11.50
M 0102	500 DOZ	USD 28.00

AS PER SALES CONFIRMATION NO. 02GP520471
DD 03 JAN. 02
CIF VANCOUVER CANADA

Documents Required　46 A :

+MARINE INSURANCE POLICY OR CERTIFICATE IN DUPLICATE, ENDORSED IN BLANK, FOR FULL INVOICE VALUE PLUS 10 PERCENT, STATING CLAIM PAYABLE IN CANADA COVERING INSTITUTE CARGO CLAUSES(A) AND WAR RISKS.

B. 其他资料。

发票号码：KW-030419
发票日期：2002年4月10日
发票金额：USD46,500.00
提单日期：2002年4月19日
船名：CHAOHE /ZIM CANADA V. 44E（在香港转运）
唛头：ZELLERS CANADA/VANCOUVER
保险单号码：KC03-85362
货物装箱情况：10DOZ/PACKAGE　350 PACKAGES

PICC PROPERTY

中保财产保险有限公司

The People's Insurance (Property) Company of China, Ltd.

发票号码　　　　保险单号次

Invoice No.　　　　Policy No.

海　洋　货　物　运　输　保　险　单

MARINE CARGO TRANSPORTATION INSURANCE POLICY

被保险人：

Insured: ______________________________

中保财产保险有限公司（以下简称本公司）根据被保险人的要求，及其所缴付约定的保险费，按照本保险单承担险别和背面所载条款与下列特别条款承保下列货物运输保险，特签发本保险单。

This policy of Insurance witnesses that the People's Insurance (Property) Company of China, Ltd. (hereinafter called "the Company"), at the request of the Insured and in consideration of the agreed premium paid by the Insured, undertakes to insure the undermentioned goods in transportation subject to the conditions of this Policy as per the Clauses printed overleaf and other special clauses attached hereon.

保险货物项目 Descriptions of Goods	包装　单位　数量 Packing　Unit　Quantity	保险金额 Amount Insured

承保险别　　　　货物标记

Conditions　　　　Marks of Goods

总保险金额：

Total Amount Insured: ______________________________

保费　　　　载运输工具　　　　开航日期

Premium　as arranged　　Per conveyance S. S. __________　　Slg. on or abt __________

起运港　　　　目的港

From __________　　to __________

所保货物，如发生本保险单项下可能引起索赔的损失或损坏，应立即通知本公司下述代理人查勘。如有索赔，应向本公司提交保险单正本（本保险单共有　　份正本）及有关文件。如一份正本已用于索赔，其余正本则自动失效。

In the event of loss or damage which may result in a claim under this Policy, immediate notice must be given to the Company's Agent as mentioned hereunder. Claims, if any, one of the Original Policy which has been issued in　　　Original(s) together with the relevant documents shall be surrendered to the Company. If one of the Original Policy has been accomplished, the others to be void.

中保财产保险有限公司

THE PEOPLE'S INSURANCE (PROPERTY) COMPANY OF CHINA, LTD.

赔款偿付地点

Claim payable at ______________________________

日期　　　　在

Date __________　　at __________

地址：

Address:

（二）单据填制二

请根据以下材料填制一份保险单。

A. 信用证条款。

Applicant	*50	: INTERCONTOR, ZENTRALEINKAUF UND HANDELS SIGMUND STR. 220 90431 NUERNBERG
Beneficiary	*59	: GUANGDONG TEXTILES IMP. & EXP. COTTON MANUFACTURED GOODS COMPANY LTD. 14/F., GUANGDONG TEXTILES MANSION NO. 168 XIAOBEI ROAD, GUANGZHOU
Loading in Charge	44 A	: GUANGZHOU
For Transport to...	44 B	: HAMBURG
Descript. of Goods	45 A	: GUITAR ITEM NO.　QUANTITY　UNTI PRICE 948　1,700 PCS　USD 7.42 AS PER SALES CONFIRMATION NO. 2002MCGS02007 DD 8.3.2002 TOTAL AMOUNT USD12,614.00 CIF HAMBURG
Documents Required	46 A	:

MARINE INSURANCE POLICY OR CERTIFICATE IN DUPLICATE, ENDORSED IN BLANK, FOR FULL INVOICE VALUE PLUS 10 PERCENT, STATING CLAIM PAYABLE IN HAMBURG COVERING INSTITUTE CARGO CLAUSES (A) AND WAR RISKS, MARKED PREMIUM PAID.

B. 其他资料。

发票号码：020603GTB
发票日期：2002 年 6 月 20 日
发票金额：USD12,614.00
提单日期：2002 年 6 月 25 日
保险单号码：KC53696265
唛头：KCHCSB /HAMBURG
船名：NANTU V. 832
货物装箱情况：10PCS/CTN

中保财产保险有限公司

The People's Insurance (Property) Company of China, Ltd.

PICC PROPERTY

发票号码　　保险单号次

Invoice No.　　Policy No.

海　洋　货　物　运　输　保　险　单

MARINE CARGO TRANSPORTATION INSURANCE POLICY

被保险人：

Insured: ....

中保财产保险有限公司（以下简称本公司）根据被保险人的要求，及其所缴付约定的保险费，按照本保险单承担险别和背面所载条款与下列特别条款承保下列货物运输保险，特签发本保险单。

This policy of Insurance witnesses that the People's Insurance (Property) Company of China, Ltd. (hereinafter called "the Company"), at the request of the Insured and in consideration of the agreed premium paid by the Insured, undertakes to insure the undermentioned goods in transportation subject to the conditions of this Policy as per the Clauses printed overleaf and other special clauses attached hereon.

保险货物项目 Descriptions of Goods	包装　单位　数量 Packing　Unit　Quantity	保险金额 Amount Insured

承保险别　　货物标记

Conditions　　Marks of Goods

总保险金额：

Total Amount Insured: ....

保费　　载运输工具　　开航日期

Premium ....　Per conveyance S. S. ....　Slg. on or abt ....

起运港　　目的港

From ....　to ....

所保货物，如发生本保险单项下可能引起索赔的损失或损坏，应立即通知本公司下述代理人查勘。如有索赔，应向本公司提交保险单正本（本保险单共有　　份正本）及有关文件。如一份正本已用于索赔，其余正本则自动失效。

In the event of loss or damage which may result in a claim under this Policy, immediate notice must be given to the Company's Agent as mentioned hereunder. Claims, if any, one of the Original Policy which has been issued in　　　Original(s) together with the relevant documents shall be surrendered to the Company. If one of the Original Policy has been accomplished, the others to be void.

中保财产保险有限公司

THE PEOPLE'S INSURANCE (PROPERTY) COMPANY OF CHINA, LTD.

赔款偿付地点

Claim payable at ....

日期　　在

Date ....　at ....

地址：

Address:

第五节　原产地证明书

一、中英文术语、短语互译

（一）中译英

（1）目的地国家（地区）________

（2）发票号码和日期________

（3）签证机构________

（4）工业联合会________

（5）货物的原产地在中国________

（6）回签________

（7）成分________

（8）代表处________

（9）影印本________

（10）与以色列没有任何直接或间接关系________

（二）英译中

（1）Certificate of Origin ________

（2）GSP ________

（3）Origin Criterion ________

（4）Chamber of Commerce ________

（5）Competent Authorities ________

（6）For Official Use ________

（7）Means of Transport and Route ________

（8）H. S. Code ________

（9）Number and Kind of Packages ________

（10）Declaration by the Exporter ________

二、单项选择题

1. 根据我国的规定，企业最迟于货物报关出运前（　　）向签证机构申请办理原产地证。

A. 7 天　　　　B. 3 天

C. 10 天　　　　D. 5 天

2. 在我国，签发普惠制原产地证 FORM A 的机构是（　　）。

A. 海关总署及各省市海关

B. 中国质检总局及各省市出入境检验检疫局

C. 商务部及各省市经贸厅

D. 各省市对外贸易促进委员会

3. 普惠制原产地证明书 FORM A 原产地标准栏目，如果出口商品完全是出口国自产的，不含有进口成分的商品，出口到所有给惠国，填写（　　）。

A. “P”　　B. “W”

C. “Y”　　D. “F”

4. 信用证条款：GSP Certificate of Origin，Form A，certifying goods of origin in China，issued by competent authorities，根据该条款，FORM A 的签发机构为（　　）。

A. 对外贸易促进委员会]　　B. 出入境检验检疫局

C. 公证处　　D. 海关

5. 信用证条款：Certificate of Origin in two fold indicating that goods are of Chinese origin issued by Chamber of Commerce，根据该条款，原产地证的签发机构为（　　）。

A. 商会　　B. 出入境检验检疫局

C. 公证处　　D. 海关

6. 普惠制是（　　）对来自发展中国家的出口产品给予的一种关税优惠制度。

A. 发达国家　　B. 发展中国家

C. 美国　　D. 欧盟

7. 下列不属于普惠制原则的是（　　）。

A. 普遍原则　　B. 非互惠原则

C. 严格符合原则　　D. 非歧视原则

8. 下列不属于普惠制原产地规则的是（　　）。

A. 原产地标准　　B. 直接运输规则

C. 书面证明　　D. 单边优惠规则

三、多项选择题

1. 出口企业在办理原产地证时，必须提交的单证有（　　）。

A.《中华人民共和国出口货物原产地证书/加工装配证明申请书》

B.《中华人民共和国出口货物原产地证书》一式四份

C. 出口货物商业发票

D. 签证机构认为必要的其他证明文件

2. 在我国，签发原产地证的机构包括（　　）。

A. 海关总署及各省市海关　　B. 各省市出入境检验检疫局

C. 商务部及各省市经贸厅　　D. 各省市对外贸易促进委员会

3. 下列国家中，给予我国普惠制待遇的是（　　）。

A. 保加利亚　　B. 美国

C. 新西兰　　D. 加拿大

4. 普惠制原产地证明书 FORM A 原产地标准栏目，如果出口商品完全是出口国自产的，不含有进口成分的商品，出口到澳大利亚、新西兰，该栏目可填写（　　）。

A. “P”　　B. “W”

C. “Y”　　D. 留空

5. 普惠制原产地证明书 FORM A 的申报日期，可以（　　）。

A. 早于发票日期　B. 不得早于发票日期
C. 与发票日期同日　D. 与提单日期同日

四、判断题

1. 普惠制原产地证明书 FORM A 一般使用英文填制，应进口商的要求，也可使用法文，除此之外，证书不得使用其他语种。(　　)

2. 普惠制原产地证明书 FORM A 的收货人应填写最终收货人的名称。如果信用证未明确最终收货人，可以填写商业发票的抬头人，也可填写中间商的名称。(　　)

3. 含有进口成分的产品，出口到加拿大，普惠制原产地证明书 FORM A 的原产地标准栏目填“W”。(　　)

4. 根据日本政府的规定，普惠制原产地证明书 FORM A 的有效期为自进口之日起 4 个月内。(　　)

5. 普惠制的原则有非普遍原则、非互惠原则和非歧视原则。(　　)

6. 非互惠原则是指非对等的，发达国家应单方面给予发展中国家优惠关税待遇，而不要求发展中国家给予同等待遇。(　　)

7. 非歧视原则是指应对所有的发展中国家都给予优惠待遇，不应区别对待，不应有例外。(　　)

五、阅读理解

（一）阅读理解一

ORIGINAL

1. Exporter	Certificate No.
GUANGDONG TEXTILES IMPORT AND EXPORT KNITWEARS COMPANY LTD.15/F GUANGDONG TEXTILES MANSION 168 XIAOBEI ROAD, GUANGZHOU 510045, CHINA TEL 83856391 FAX NO.83866713	971697422 CERTIFICATE OF ORIGIN OF THE PEOPLE' S REPUBLIC OF CHINA
2. Consignee M/S ALAMOUDI SPORT CENTER P.O.BOX 40616 JEDDAH 21511 K.S.A. TEL 6447453 FAX NO.6447433	
3. Means of transport and route FROM GUANGZHOU CHINA TO JEDDAH BY VESSEL	5. For certifying authority use only
4. Country / region of destination JEDDAH	

6. Marks and numbers	7. Number and kind of packages;description of goods	8. H.S.Code	9. Quantity	10. Number and date of invoices
ALAMOUDI SPORT CENTER JEDDAH	ONE HUNDRED AND FIFTY (150) CARTONS OF BOY'S SPORT SUIT THE NAME OF THE MANUFACTURERS:SAME AS EXPORTER GOODS EXPORTED ARE WHOLLY OF DOMESTIC ORIGIN. ****************************	6112	600 DOZ	97.229KES OCT. 28 1997

11. Declaration by the exporter	12. Certification
The undersigned hereby declares that the above details and statements are correct, that all the goods were produced in China and that they comply with the Rules of Origin of the People's Republic of China. 广东省纺织品进出口针织品有限公司 GUANGDONG TEXTILES IMPORT & EXPORT KNITWEARS COMPANY LIMITED 林樹宗 GUANGZHOU NOV. 01,1997	It is hereby certified that the declaration by the exporter is correct. GUANGZHOU NOV. 01,1997
Place and date. signature and stamp of authorized signatory	Place and date, signature and stamp of certifying authority

请根据上面的原产地证明书回答问题：

（1）出口商：

（2）收货人：

（3）运输方式和路线：

（4）目的地国家（地区）：

（5）运输标志：

（6）商品名称：

（7）包装数量：

（8）商品编码：

（9）发票号码：

（10）发票日期：

（11）申请日期：

（12）签发日期：

（13）签证机构：

（二）阅读理解二

请根据下面的 FORM A 回答问题：

（1）出口商：

（2）收货人：

（3）运输方式和路线：

（4）FORM A 号码：

（5）运输标志：

（6）商品名称：

（7）包装数量：

（8）原产地标准：

（9）发票号码：

（10）发票日期：

（11）申请日期：

（12）签发日期：

（13）签证机构：

ORIGINAL

1. Goods consigned from (Exporter's business name, address, country) GUANGDONG TEXTILES IMP. AND EXP. COTTON MANUFACTURED GOODS COMPANY LTD. 14/F,GUANGDONG TEXTILES MANSION NO.168 XIAOBEI ROAD, GUANGZHOU CHINA	Reference No. GZ8/80293/0120 GENERALIZED SYSTEM OF PREFERENCES CERTIFICATE OF ORIGIN (Combined declaration and certificate) FORM A Issued in THE PEOPLE'S REPUBLIC OF CHINA (country) See Notes overleaf
2. Goods consigned to (Consignee's name, address, country) BRUSSELS LACES AND GIFTS SERV.SA RUE DE LUSAMBO,21/23 1190 BRUXELLES,BELGIUM	
3. Means of transport and route (as far as known) ON/AFTER APR.24,"1998 FROM GUANGZHOU GUANGDONG CHINA TO ANTWERP BELGIUM VIA HONGKONG BY SEA	4. For official use THIS IS TO CERTIFY THAT THE GOODS STATED IN THIS CERTIFICATE HAD NOT BEEN SUBJECTED TO ANY PROCESSING DURING THEIR STAY/TRANSHIPMENT IN HONG KONG. SIGNATURE: DATE: 14 MAY 1998 CHINA INSPECTION COMPANY LIMITED 中国检验有限公司

5. Item number	6. Marks and numbers of packages	7. Number and kind of packages; description of goods	8. Origin criterion (see Notes overleaf)	9. Gross weight or other quantity	10. Number and date of invoices
1.	BLGS VIA ANTWERP P.O.NO.970366 ART.NR.... BEACH TOWELS C.C. SIZE:75X150 CM QTY.:24 PCS	ONE HUNDRED AND SIXTY-FOUR (164) CARTONS OF COTTON PRINTED VELVET TOWELS(WOVEN) **************************	"P"	3,936 PCS	98.422CBS APR.21, 1998

11. Certification	12. Declaration by the exporter
It is hereby certified, on the basis of control carried out, that the declaration by the exporter is correct. GUANGZHOU APR.23,1998 Place and date, signature and stamp of certifying authority	The undersigned hereby declares that the above details and statements are correct; that all the goods were produced in CHINA (country) and that they comply with the origin requirements specified for those goods in the Generalized System of Preferences for goods exported to BELGIUM (importing country) GUANGZHOU APR.22,1998 Place and date, signature of authorized signatory

六、单据改错

广东省东风进出口公司（GUANGDONG DONGFENG IMPORT AND EXPORT CORP. 122 DONGFENG ROAD EAST，GUANGZHOU）与 SANYEI HONG KONG 14/F.，KAISER ESTATE 1，MANYUE STREET，HUNG HOM，SYDNEY，AUSTRALIA 达成一笔交易，内容主要有：2 400 件不锈钢铲头（STAINLESS STEEL SPADE HEAD），每 12 件扎成 1 捆，2002 年 12 月 1 日出运，该公司填制好如下“FORM A”，请审核并修改。

ORIGINAL

<table>
<tr><td colspan="3">1. Goods consigned from (Exporter's business name, address, country)
GUANGDONG DONGFENG IMPORT AND EXPORT CORP.
122 DONGFENG ROAD EAST, GUANGZHOU</td><td colspan="3" rowspan="2">Reference No.
GZ9/12078/6311
GENERALIZED SYSTEM OF PREFERENCES
CERTIFICATE OF ORIGIN
(Combined declaration and certificate)
FORM A
issued in THE PEOPLE'S REPUBLIC OF CHINA
(country)
See Notes overleaf</td></tr>
<tr><td colspan="3">2. Goods consigned to (Consignee's name, address, country)
SANYEI HONG KONG
14/F., KAISER ESTATE 1, MANYUE STREET,
HUNG HOM, SYDNEY</td></tr>
<tr><td colspan="3">3. Means of transport and route (as far as known)
ON/AFTER NOV. 11, 2002
FROM GUANGZHOU TO SYDNEY</td><td colspan="3">4. For official use</td></tr>
<tr><td>5. Item number</td><td>6. Marks and numbers of packages</td><td>7. Number and kind of packages; description of goods</td><td>8. Origin criterion (see Notes overleaf)</td><td>9. Gross weight or other quantity</td><td>10. Number and date of invoices</td></tr>
<tr><td>1</td><td>KMART
SYDNEY
NO. 1 – 200</td><td>TWO THOUDAND FOUR HUNDRED (2,400) PCS OF STAINLESS STEEL SPADE HEAD
* *</td><td>“P”</td><td>2,400PCS</td><td>YSM199901
NOV. 11, 2002</td></tr>
<tr><td colspan="3">11. Certification
It is hereby certified, on the basis of control carried out, that the declaration by the exporter is correct.

GUANGZHOU NOV. 20, 2002
Place and date, signature and stamp of certifying authority</td><td colspan="3">12. Declaration by the exporter
The undersigned hereby declares that the above details and statements are correct; that all the goods were produced in
GUANGZHOU
(country)
and that they comply with the origin requirements specified for those goods in the Generalized System of Preferences for goods exported to
SYDNEY
(importing country)

GUANGZHOU NOV. 21，2002
Place and date, signature of authorized signatory</td></tr>
</table>

七、单据填制

（一）单据填制一

广东省纺织品进出口针织品有限公司向希腊某商出口一批塑胶玩具，该出口公司产地证申报员张强拟于 2003 年 10 月 7 日向广州检验检疫局申报，公司电话：78787878。请你根据下面的商业发票帮张强填制“一般原产地证明书”。

广东省纺织品进出口针织品有限公司

GUANGDONG TEXTILES IMP. & EXP. KNITWEARS COMPANY LIMITED.

15/F, GUANGDONG TEXTILES MANSION 168 XIAOBEI ROAD, GUANGZHOU, CHINA

商业发票

COMMERCIAL INVOICE

Messrs.:
JOHNSON
KREONTOS 30 STR.
GREECE

INVOICE NO. : YSM1999B
INVOICE DATE : OCT. 05, 2003
L/C NO. : KDTT524250
L/C DATE : AUG. 20, 2003
S/C NO. : GD－98TX2509

Exporter:
GUANGDONG TEXTILES IMP. & EXP.
KNITWEARS COMPANY LIMTIED.
15/F, GUANGDONG TEXTILES MANSION
168 XIAOBEI ROAD, GUANGZHOU, CHINA

Transport details:
FROM GUANGZHOU TO PIRAIEV'S GREECE
BY VESSEL SAILING DATE: OCT. 15, 2003

Terms of Payment:
BY L/C

MARKS AND NUMBERS	DESCRIP. OF GOODS	QUANTITY	UNIT PRICE	AMOUNT
JOHNSON	H. S. NO. : 9503. 90			
97KCS05111	PLASTIC TOYS	10, 000PCS	USD0. 60/PC	USD6, 000. 00
NO. 1－500				
MADE IN CHINA				

FOB GUANGZHOU　USD6, 000. 00

TOTAL QUANTITY: 10, 000PCS　PACKING: 500CARTONS
TOTAL: US DOLLARS SIX THOUSAND ONLY.

广东省纺织品进出口针织品有限公司
GUANGDONG TEXTILES IMP. & EXP.
KNITWEARS COMPANY LIMITED
（签章）

ORIGINAL

1. Exporter	Certificate No. CERTIFICATE OF ORIGIN OF THE PEOPLE'S REPUBLIC OF CHINA
2. Consignee	
3. Means of transport and route	5. For certifying authority use only
4. Country/region of destination	

6. Marks and numbers of packages	7. Number and kind of packages; Description of goods	8. H. S. Code	9. Quantity	10. Number and date of invoices

11. Declaration by the exporter The undersigned hereby declares that the above details and statements are correct, that all the goods were produced in China and that they comply with the Rules of Origin of the People's Republic of China. Place and date, signature and stamp of certifying authority	12. Certification It is hereby certified that the declaration by the exporter is correct. Place and date, signature of authorized signatory

（二）单据填制二

广东省轻工家电有限公司出口一批产品到比利时，该产品完全为我国江西浪花毛织厂自产，不含任何进口成分，请你根据下面的商业发票帮该公司产地证申报员张强（2005年3月18日申报，预定出口装运日期为3月22日）填制“普惠制产地证明书FORM A”。

广东省轻工家电有限公司

GUANGDONG LIGHT ELECTRICAL APPLIANCES COMPANY LIMITED

52 DEZHENG ROAD SOUTH, GUANGZHOU, CHINA

商业发票

COMMERCIAL INVOICE

MESSRS.:

BRUSSELSLACES AND GIFTS SERV. SA
RUE DE LUSAMBO. 21/23
1190 BRUXELLES, BE

INVOICE NO. : GD05753
INVOICE DATE : FEB. 28, 2005
L/C NO. : 21036414276424
S/C NO. : D/269/97

EXPORTER:

GUANGDONG LIGHT ELECTRICAL
APPLIANCES COMPANY LIMITED

TRANSPORT DETAILS:

FROM GUANGZHOU TO ANTWERP BELGIUM
W/T HONG KONG BY VESSEL

TERMS OF PAYMENT:

BY L/C

MARKS & NUMBERS	DESCRIP. OF GOODS	QUANTITY	UNIT PRICE	AMOUNT
AL SHAMALI ANTWERP	COTTON PRINTED VELVET TOWELS H. S. CODE: 6302. 5900	3,936PCS	@ USD3. 64/PC	USD14,327. 04
			CIF ANTWERP	USD14,327. 04

TOTAL QUANTITY: 3,936PCS　PACKING: 160CTNS

TOTAL: US DOLLARS FOURTEEN THOUSAND AND THREE HUNDRED TWENTY-SEVEN POINT FOUR ONLY.

GUANGDONG LIGHT ELECTRICAL
APPLIANCES COMPANY LIMITED
（签章）

ORIGINAL

1. Goods consigned from (Exporter's business name, address, country)	Reference No. GENERALIZED SYSTEM OF PREFERENCES CERTIFICATE OF ORIGIN (Combined declaration and certificate) FORM A issued in THE PEOPLE'S REPUBLIC OF CHINA (country) See Notes overleaf
2. Goods consigned to (Consignee's name, address, country)	
3. Means of transport and route (as far as known)	4. For official use

5. Item number	6. Marks and numbers of packages	7. Number and kind of packages; description of goods	8. Origin criterion (see Notes overleaf)	9. Gross weight or other quantity	10. Number and date of invoices

11. Certification It is hereby certified, on the basis of control carried out, that the declaration by the exporter is correct. --- Place and date, signature and stamp of certifying authority	12. Declaration by the exporter The undersigned hereby declares that the above details and statements are correct; that all the goods were produced in --- (country) and that they comply with the origin requirements specified for those goods in the Generalized System of Preferences for goods exported to --- (importing country) --- Place and date, signature of authorized signatory

第六节 装箱单

一、中英文术语、短语互译

（一）中译英

（1）装箱单/重量单/尺码单________

（2）集装包和集装袋________

（3）托盘________

（4）散装________

（5）习惯包装________

（6）麻袋装________

（7）每袋一打________

（二）英译中

（1）Bundle ________

（2）Roll ________

（3）Drum ________

（4）Teu ________

（5）Sea-Worthy Packing ________

（6）Packed in Wooden Case ________

（7）Each Carton Contains 2 Sets ________

二、单项选择题

1. 对于价值较低的农产品，买卖双方往往采用（　　）计算其重量。

A. 法定重量　　B. 理论重量

C. 净重　　D. 以毛作净

2. 买卖双方以 CIF 条件达成 10 万吨散装小麦的交易合同，卖方如不希望在交货时因数量产生纠纷，最好在合同中订立（　　）。

A. 品质机动幅度　　B. 仓至仓条款

C. 溢短装条款　　D. 禁止转运条款

3. 某贸易公司向英国客商出口平纹印花纯棉坯布，信用证中规定“数量约为 100 000 码”，根据《UCP600》的规定，卖方可以理解为交货数量有不超过（　　）的增减幅度。

A. 3%　　B. 5%

C. 10%　　D. 15%

4. 信用证中规定“PACKING LIST IN FIVE COPIES”，则受益人提交的装箱单的份数为（　　）。

A. 5 份副本　　B. 1 份正本 4 份副本

C. 不需提交正本　　D. 5 份正本及 5 份副本

5. 某公司出口货物，从黄埔港发运，运往汉堡，在香港转船，在装箱单“TRANSPORT DETAILS”一栏填写错误的是（　　）。

A. FROM HUANGPU TO HAMBURG W/T HONGKONG

B. FROM HUANGPU TO HAMBURG VIA HONGKONG

C. FROM HUANGPU TO HONGKONG AND THENCE TO HAMBURG

D. FROM HUANGPU TO HAMBURG WITH TRANSSHIPMENT AT HONGKONG

三、多项选择题

1. 印刷在运输包装上的唛头，其作用是在运输过程中使有关人员易于辨认货物，便于核对单证，按习惯做法，唛头由（　　）提供。

A. 卖方　　B. 买方

C. 船方　　D. 货代公司

2. 根据在流通过程中所起作用不同，商品包装可分为（　　）。

A. 运输包装　　B. 装卸包装

C. 储存包装　　D. 销售包装

3. 买卖双方在合同中对交货数量规定了溢短装条款，溢短装的选择权可以在合同中规定由（　　）行使。

A. 买方　　B. 卖方

C. 拖车公司　　D. 船公司

4. 当合同中规定采用净重计算商品重量时，对于如何计算包装的重量，国际上通常采用以下几种做法（　　）。

A. 按实际皮重计算　　B. 按约定皮重计算

C. 按平均皮重计算　　D. 按习惯皮重计算

5. 运输包装分为单件运输包装和集合运输包装，以下哪些包装属于集合运输包装（　　）。

A. 托盘　　B. 箱

C. 集装箱　　D. 包

四、判断题

1. 装箱单的主要作用是补充商业发票内容的不足，便于买方掌握商品的包装、数量及供进口国海关检查和核对货物。（　　）

2. 某工厂出口货物一批，合同中规定使用纸箱包装，为了更好地保护商品，卖方在交货时没有经过买方的同意就采用了木箱包装，这种替客户着想的做法是对的。（　　）

3. 信用证中规定包装采用“SEAWORTHY PACKING”，受益人在出口时根据货物情况采用了纸箱作为运输包装，在制作装箱单时，包装材料一栏应填制为“SEAWORTHY PACKING”。（　　）

4. 国际贸易中的习惯做法是将包装包括在货价以内，不另计收。（　　）

5. 受益人在制作相关单据时，必须将运输包装上的标志都注明在单据上。（　　）

五、案例分析

1．某公司出口羊肉罐头到科威特，合同规定使用木箱装，每箱 24 听。卖方按合同规定的数量交付了货物，但其中部分包装使用的是 12 听的小箱。货到目的港后，买方以包装与合同不符为由拒绝收取货物，卖方却坚持要买方收取全部货物，其称：根据我方在科威特市场的销售人员及客户的反映，不论是使用每箱 24 听的包装还是使用每箱 12 听的包装，并不影响羊肉罐头的市场销售价格。请问买方有无权利拒收货物？为什么？

2．我某外贸公司从日本进口鱼粉 5 000 公吨，合同条款如下：价格为 CIF 广州每公吨 100 美元，单层新麻袋包装，每袋 50 千克，以即期信用证方式付款。货到广州港后，我方发现货物扣除麻袋重量后不足 5 000 公吨，于是要求卖方将短量部分的货款退还。问我方要求是否合理？为什么？

六、单据改错

(一) 单据改错一

请根据以下材料修改装箱单。

A. 信用证条款。

Date of Issue	: 971020
Form of Doc. Credit	: IRREVOCABLE
Doc. Credit Number	: M20K2710NS00032
Expiry	: Date 971115 Place IN BENEFICIARY'S COUNTRY
Applicant	: SE BANG TRADING CO., LTD. 148 NAMCHEON - 2 DONG, SUYOUNG - KU PUSAN, KOREA
Beneficiary	: GUANGZHOU ARTS & CRAFTS IMP. & EXP. CORP. 628 GUANGZHOU DADAO ZHONG ROAD, GUANGZHOU, CHINA
Partial Shipments	: ALLOWED
Transshipment	: ALLOWED
Loading in Charge	: GUANGZHOU, CHINA
For Transport to...	: PUSAN, KOREA
Latest Date of Ship.	: 971105
Descript. of Goods	: CHINA ORIGIN CIF PUSAN ARTIFICIAL FLOWERS AB - 06001　　5,184DOZ @ USD2.50/DOZ AB - 07049　　2,880DOZ @ USD2.50/DOZ AS PER S/C NO. 97A/KF002A DATE OCT. 15, 1997, ISSUED BY GUANGZHOU ARTS & CRAFTS IMP. & EXP. CORP.
Documents Required	: PACKING LIST IN TRIPLICATE
Additional Cond.	: ALL DOCUMENTS MUST INDICATE THIS CREDIT NUMBER THE DETAILS SUCH AS ART NO. , COLOR, Q'TY SHOULD BE MARKED ON THE EACH INNER BOX AND CARTON EXACTLY

B. 其他资料。

INV. NO. : 97KF335　　INV. DATE: OCT. 28, 1997

B/L NO. : DSA97 - 1102　　SHIPPING MARKS: SE BANG/PUSAN

PACKING: AB - 06001 36DOZ/CTN　G. W. : 23KGS/CTN　N. W. : 18KGS/CTN

AB - 07049 36DOZ/CTN　G. W. : 19KGS/CTN　N. W. : 13KGS/CTN

NAME OF STEAMER: SUI 301/NORASIA V. 49 - 3　W/T HONGKONG

CONTAINER NO. MSCU 4097615 (40')

MEASUREMENT: (40 × 50 × 80) CM/CTN

广州工艺品进出口公司

GUANGZHOU ARTS & CRAFTS IMP. & EXP. CORP.

628 GUANGZHOU DADAO ZHONG ROAD, GUANGZHOU, CHINA

装 箱 单

PACKING LIST

ORIGINAL

Exporter:
GUANGZHOU ARTS & CRAFTS IMP. & EXP. CORP.
628 GUANGZHOU DADAO ZHONG ROAD,
GUANGZHOU, CHINA

DATE: OCT. 28, 1997
INVOICE NO.: 97KF335
B/L NO.: OCT. 31, 1997
S/C NO.: 97A/KF002A
L/C NO.: M20K2710NS00032

TRANSPORT DETAILS:
FROM GUANGZHOU TO PUSAN
BY VESSEL

标记 Marks & numbers	货名 Description of goods	件数 Quantity	净重 N. W.	毛重 G. W.	尺码 Measurement
SE BANG	ARTIFICIAL FLOWERS				
PUSAN	ART NO.: AB-06	36DOZ/CTN	@18.00KGS	@23.00KGS	@(40×50×80)CM
	5,184DOZ	144CTNS	2,592.00KGS	3,312.00KGS	23.04CBMS
	ART NO.: AB-07049	36DOZ/CTN	@13.00KGS	@19.00KGS	@(40×50×80)CM
	2,880DOZ	80 CTNS	1,040.00KGS	1,520.00KGS	12.80CBMS
		224CTNS	3,632.00KGS	4,832.00KGS	35.84CBMS

TOTAL QUANTITY: 224CTNS
TOTAL: TWO HUNDRED AND TWENTY-FOUR CARTONS ONLY.

GUANGZHOU ARTS & CRAFTS IMP. & EXP. CORP.
628 GUANGZHOU DADAO ZHONG ROAD, GUANGZHOU, CHINA

（二）单据改错二

请根据以下材料修改装箱单。

A. 信用证条款。

NANYANG COMMERCIAL BANK LTD. , HONGKONG

HONGKONG 1ST MARCH, 1997

TO: BANK OF CHINA, GUANGZHOU, CHINA
DOCUMENTARY CREDIT NO. 97 - 34985

FOR THE ACCOUNT OF ABC TRADING CO. , LTD. , 312 SOUTHBRIDGE STREET, HONGKONG

DEAR SIRS,

WE OPEN AN IRREVOCABLE DOCUMENTARY CREDIT IN FAVOUR OF GUANGDONG FOREIGN TRADE IMP. AND EXP. CORP. , 267 TIANHE ROAD, GUANGZHOU, CHINA. FOR A SUM NOT EXCEEDING HKD980,000.00 (SAY HONGKONG DOLLARS NINE HUNDRED AND EIGHTY THOUSAND ONLY.) AVAILABLE BY THE BENEFICIARY'S DRAFT (S) AT SIGHT DRAWN ON US, BEARING THE CLAUSE: "DRAWN UNDER NANYANG CMMERCIAL BANK LTD. , HONGKONG IRREVOCABLE DOCUMENTARY CREDIT NO. 97 - 34985 DATED 1ST MARCH, 1997." ACCOMPANIED BY THE FOLLOWING DOCUMENTS:

...

(4) PACKING LIST IN TRIPLICATE.

(5) CERTIFICATE OF ORIGIN ISSUED BY GUANGZHOU IMPORT AND EXPORT COMM ODITY INSPECTION BUREAU OF THE PEOPLE'S REPUBLIC OF CHINA IN TRIPLICATE. EVIDENCING SHIPMENT OF THE FOLLOWING MERCHANDISE:

AIR CONDITIONER (HUALING BRAND), 500 SETS KF - 23GW AND 500 SETS KF - 25GW, PACKING: IN CARTON BOX, 50 KILOS NET EACH CARTON, 1SET/CTN, @HKD1,000/SET, CIFC2% DUBAI, OTHER TERMS AND CONDITIONS AS PER S/C NO. AB44001, FROM GUANGZHOU TO DUBAI VIA HONGKONG. PARTIAL SHIPMENT PERMITIED. TRANSSHIPMENT PROHIBITED. LATEST DATE FOR SHIPMENT: 30TH APRIL, 1997. EXPIRY DATE: 15TH MAY, 1997. IN PLACE OF BENEFICIARY FOR NEGOTIATION.

WE HEREBY ENGAGE WITH THE DRAWERS, ENDORSERS AND BONAFIDE HOLDERS OF DRAFT(S) DRAWN UNDER AND COMPLIANCE WITH THE TERMS OF THIS CREDIT THAT SUCH DRAFT(S) SHALL BE DULY HONOURED ON DUE PRESENTATION.

BENEFICIARY'S DECLARATION ON THE INVOICE THAT THE PRODUCTION COMPANY IS A STATE-OWNED ENTERPRISE AND IS NO RELATION WITH ISRAEL WHATSOEVER.

SHIPPING MARKS: ABC/DUBAI/NOS1 - 1000

THIS CREDIT IS SUBJECT TO "UNIFORM CUSTOMS AND PRACTICE FOR DOCUMENTARY CREDITS" (1993 REVISION) INTERNATIONAL CHAMBER OF COMMERCE PUBLICATION NO. 500.

YOURS FAITHFULLY,
NANYANG COMMERCIAL BANK LTD. , HONGKONG

B. 其他资料。

发票号码	GDF-97-22341	发票日期	APR. 15, 1997	船　名	MECUE/DONGFENG M0123
毛　重	55 KGS/CTN	提单号码	SWHK-970156	尺　码	(50×80×100) CM/CTN

广东对外贸易进出口公司

GUANGDONG FOREIGN TRADE IMP. AND EXP. CORP.
267 TIANHE ROAD, GUANGZHOU, CHINA

装 箱 单
PACKING LIST

ORIGINAL

Exporter:
GUANGDONG FOREIGN TRADE IMP. AND EXP. CORP.
267 TIANHE ROAD,
GUANGZHOU, CHINA

DATE: APR. 15, 1997
INVOICE NO.: GDF-97-2234
B/L NO.: SWHK-970156
S/C NO.: AB44001
L/C NO.: 97-34985

TRANSPORT DETAILS:
FROM GUANGZHOU TO DUBAI VIA
HONGKONG BY VESSEL

标记 Marks & numbers	货名 Description of goods	件数 Quantity	净重 N. W.	毛重 G. W.	尺码 Measurement
ABC	AIR CONDITIONER (HUALING BRAND)				
DUBAI	ART NO.: KF-23GW	1SET/CTN	@50.00KGS	@55.00KGS	@ (50×80×100) CM
NOS.1-100	500SETS	500CTNS	2,500.00KGS	2,750.00KGS	200CBMS
	ART NO.: KF-25GW	1SET/CTN	@50.00KGS	@55.00KGS	@(50×80×100)CM
	500SETS	500CTNS	2,500.00KGS	2,750.00KGS	200CBMS
		1,000CTNS	5,000.00KGS	5,500.00KGS	400CBMS

TOTAL QUANTITY: 1,000SETS
TOTAL: ONE THOUSAND PIECES ONLY.

GUANGDONG FOREIGN TRADE IMP. AND EXP. CORP.
267 TIANHE ROAD, GUANGZHOU, CHINA

七、单据填制

（一）单据填制一

请根据以下材料填制一份装箱单。

A. 信用证条款。

WE HEREBY ESTABLISH OUR IRREVOCABLE DOCUMENTARY CREDIT（DC NO.：FK28093）FOR AMOUNT OF USD8,335.00 US DOLLARS EIGHT THOUSAND THREE HUNDRED THIRTY FIVE ONLY.
CFR KARACHI

AVAILABLE BY BENEFICIARY'S MANUALLY SIGNED DRAFTS DRAWN ON US IN DUPLICATE ACCOUNT OPENERS AT SIGHT FOR FULL INVOICE VALUE OF SHIPMENT PURPORTING TO BE：
（H. S. CODE NO. 8539.2900）FILAMENT LAMPS
TW－3050（1.5M）　3,000 PCS　AT USD0.65 PER PC
TW－3018（3YD）　3,800 PCS　AT USD0.65 PER PC
TW－8031（2YD）　3,000 PCS　AT USD0.98 PER PC
TW－6013（2YD）　500 PCS　AT USD0.65 PER PC

AS PER BENEFICIARY'S FAX PROFORMA INVOICE NO. 97SGQ469011 DTD 26/4/97

ACCOMPANIED BY THE FOLLOWING DOCUMENTS：
+PACKING LIST IN DUPLICATE
...
PARTIAL SHIPMENT PROHIBITED
TRANSSHIPMENT ALLOWED
SHIPMENT FROM P. R. OF CHINA TO KARACHI BY VESSEL

ALL DOCUMENTS TO EVIDENCE SHIPMENT AS INDICATED ABOVE
B/L MUST BE DATED NOT BEFORE THE DATE OF THIS CREDIT
AND NOT LATER THAN 30/6/97.

B. 其他资料。

发票号码：97SGP7528
发票日期：1997 年 6 月 20 日
提单号码：CANE124004
装运港：黄埔港
船名：HANJIN V. 008W
尺码：(40×40×50)CM/CTN
净重：10.00KGS/CTN
毛重：12.00KGS/CTN
货物装箱情况：100PCS/CTN

广东轻工家电有限公司

GUANGDONG LIGHT ELECTRICAL APPLIANCES CO., LTD.

52 DEZHENG ROAD SOUTH, GUANGZHOU, CHINA

装 箱 单

PACKING LIST

ORIGINAL

Exporter:

DATE :

INVOICE NO. :

B/L NO. :

S/C NO. :

L/C NO. :

TRANSPORT DETAILS:

标记 Marks & numbers	件数 Quantity	货名 Description of goods	净重 N. W.	毛重 G. W.	尺码 Measurement

（二）单据填制二

请根据以下材料填制一份装箱单。

A. 信用证条款。

DOC. Credit Number	*20		: KRT2899302
Date of Issue	31	C	: 970912
Expiry	*31	D	: Date 971205 place CHINA
Applicant	*50		: CURRENT FUNDS LIMITED ROOM 1110 CHINACHEM GOLDEN PLAZA NO. 77 MODY ROAD, TSIM SHA TSUI EAST, KOWLOON, HONG KONG
Beneficiary	*59		: GUANGDONG TEXTILES IMPORT AND EXPORT KNITWEARS COMPANY LIMITED. 15/F, GUANGDONG TEXTÍLES MANSION, 168 XIAOBEI ROAD, GUANGZHOU, CHINA
Amount	*32	B	: CURRENCY USD AMOUNT 30, 384. 00
Available with / by	*41	D	: CREDIT ISSUING OFFICE BY PAYMENT
Partial Shipments	43	P	: FORBIDDEN
Transshipment	43	T	: PROHIBITED
Loading in Charge	44	A	: GUANGDONG, CHINA
For Transport to...	44	B	: SANTOS, BRAZIL
Latest Date of Ship.	44	C	: 971115
Descript. of Goods	45	A	:

DESCRIPTION: CHILDREN'S 65 PERCENT COTTON 35 PERCENT POLYESTER
KNITTED JOGGING SUIT

QUANTITY: 720 DOZEN SETS

UNIT PRICE: USD42. 2 PER DOZEN SET

FOB GUANGDONG, CHINA

ALL OTHER DETAILS AS PER CONFIRMATION NO. DY－039

SHIPMENT TO BE EFFECTED BY 1×20 CONTAINER (FCL)

Documents Required 45 A :

PACKING LIST IN TRIPLICATE SHOWING DETAILS OF PACKING.

BREAKDOWN OF QUANTITY, GROSS WEIGHT, NET WEIGHT AND MEASUREMENT OF EACH CARTON.

B. 其他资料。

发票号码：9703SP023

发票日期：1997 年 11 月 2 日

提单号码：SA75214

货物装箱情况：30DOZ/BALE

船名：FANDU V. 336

装运港：广州港

净重：180. 00KGS/BALE

毛重：195. 00KGS/BALE

尺码：(100×100×120)CM/BALE

广东纺织品进出口针织品有限公司

GUANGDONG TEXTILES IMPORT & EXPORT KNITWEARS COMPANY LIMITED.

15/F，GUANGDONG TEXTILES MANSION，168 XIAOBEI ROAD，GUANGZHOU，CHINA

装 箱 单
PACKING LIST

ORIGINAL

Exporter：

DATE：

INVOICE NO.：

B/L NO.：

S/C NO.：

L/C NO.：

TRANSPORT DETAILS：

标记 Marks & numbers	件数 Quantity	货名 Description of goods	净重 Net weight	毛重 Gross weight	尺码 Measurement

第三章
其他结汇单据

第一节　商检证书

一、中英文术语、短语互译

（一）中译英

（1）商品检验________________

（2）品质检验证书________________

（3）重量/体积检验证书________________

（4）数量检验证书________________

（5）开证人的代表________________

（二）英译中

（1）Inspection Certificate of Sanitary or Health ________________

（2）Inspection Certificate of Disinfection ________________

（3）Inspection Certificate of Fumigation ________________

（4）Inspection Certificate of Hold ________________

（5）China Commodity Inspection Bureau ________________

二、单项选择题

1. 根据《联合国国际货物销售合同公约》的规定，买方向卖方提出索赔的最后期限是(　　)。

A. 货物在装运港经检验机构检验并签发检验证书之日起两年内

B. 货物到达目的港经检验机构检验并签发检验证书之日起两年内

C. 买方在实际收到货物之日起两年内

D. 货物到达目的港（地）进入买方仓库之日起两年内

2. 根据出入境检验检疫局的规定，出境货物最迟应于报关或装运前(　　)天报验。

A. 3 天　　B. 7 天

C. 10 天　　D. 15 天

3. 以下哪一项不是国家质量监督检验检疫总局的主要职责(　　)。

A. 主管全国质量、计量　　B. 出入境商品检疫

C. 出入境卫生检疫　　D. 流通领域商品质量监督管理

4. 有关商品检验的时间和地点比较公平合理，能够兼顾买卖双方的利益的规定是(　　)。

A. 离岸质量、重量（或数量）为准　　B. 到岸质量、重量（或数量）为准

C. 出口国检验、目的国复验　　D. 提交第三国检验机构进行检验

5. 对于规格复杂、精密程度高，需要在一定操作条件下用精密仪器或设备检验的货物一般在(　　)进行检验。

A. 生产设备的工厂　　B. 设备在装运港装船前

C. 进口国卸货地　　D. 最终用户所在地

三、多项选择题

1. 根据我国《商检法》，地方检验检疫机构在进出口商品检验方面的基本任务是(　　)。

A. 实施法定检验　　B. 办理鉴定业务

C. 实施监督管理　　D. 发放检验证书

2. 在合同中规定买方有检验权的情况下，商检条款中应进一步明确以下问题(　　)。

A. 复验地点　　B. 复验时间

C. 复验机构　　D. 复验方法

3. 在合同中商品检验时间和地点的规定的基本做法有(　　)。

A. 在出口国检验　　B. 将货物运到双方同意的第三国检验

C. 在进口国检验　　D. 出口国检验，进口国复验

4. 在国际贸易中，检验证书所起的作用有(　　)。

A. 公证证明的作用

B. 买卖双方交接货物、结算货款和进行索赔和理赔的依据

C. 通关的有效凭证

D. 以信用证支付时，通常是银行议付货款的依据

5. 根据国家质量监督检验检疫总局的规定，出境货物报验时须提交的有关单据是(　　)。

A. 外贸合同（确认书）　　B. 信用证

C. 提单　　D. 发票

四、判断题

1. 根据《进出口商品检验法》的规定，列入“种类表”的进出口商品，必须经过商检机构的检验。(　　)

2. 根据《联合国国际货物销售合同公约》的规定，若买方没有利用合理的机会检验货物，就是放弃了选择权，从而丧失了声称货物不符合合同的权利。(　　)

3. 在合同中规定为“离岸品质，离岸重量”时，买方在货物到达目的港或目的地

后，可自行委托检验机构对货物进行复验，并有权在规定的时间内凭复验证书向卖方提出异议和索赔。(　　)

4．“出口国检验，进口国复验”是国际货物买卖中最常见的一种规定检验时间和地点的方法。(　　)

5．根据《中华人民共和国进出口商品检验法》的规定，对出口食品的卫生检验不属于我国法定检验的范围。

6．凡属法定检验范围的商品，在办理进出口清关手续时，必须向海关提供检验检疫机构签发的检验证书，海关方予以验放。(　　)

7．已在所在地检验检疫机构办理报验登记备案的单位，可以自行办理报验或代理他人报验。(　　)

8．经商检机构检验合格发给检验证单的出口商品，应当在商检机构规定的期限内报关出口；超过期限的，可向商检机构申请延长检验证单的期限。(　　)

9．《中华人民共和国进出口商品检验法》规定，必须经商检机构检验的进出口商品以外的进出口商品，根据国家规定全部免予检验。(　　)

10．实行“到岸品质、重量”检验条件时，买方无须分清卖方、船公司或保险公司的责任，而有权根据货物到达目的港时的检验结果，直接向卖方提出索赔。(　　)

五、案例分析

1．我某出口企业以 CIF 旧金山向美国 A 公司出口了 400 套家具，该公司又将货物转手出售给了加拿大 B 公司。货物抵达旧金山后，A 公司发现家具质量存在问题，但仍将货物转运至加拿大。B 公司收到家具后，在合同规定的索赔期限内凭加拿大商检机构签发的检验证书，向我出口企业提出索赔。问我方企业是否需要进行赔偿？为什么？

2．我方公司以 FOB 条件向法国某经销商出口 5 000 打男式衬衣，合同规定：“货物在黄埔港装运前由中国出入境检验检疫局进行检验，交货品质以该机构出具的检验证书为准。”我方在货物装运后制作了整套结汇单据，其中的品质检验证书声明我方所交货物符合合同规定。我方在办理完结汇手续后，收到了法国经销商的传真，声称我方所交衬衣的质量与合同严重不符，要求我方赔偿，法方还提交了该国检验机构出具的检验证明。问我方公司是否要进行赔偿？为什么？

六、阅读理解

根据下面的单据，找出下列内容：

（1）货物名称及 H. S. 编码：

（2）货物总值：

（3）包装种类及数量：

（4）运输工具名称号码：

（5）贸易方式：

（6）货物存放地点：

（7）合同号：

（8）用途：

（9）发货日期：

（10）输往国家（地区）：

（11）起运地：

（12）到达口岸：

（13）标记及号码：

（14）领取单证日期：

（15）需要证单名称：

（16）检验检疫费：

中华人民共和国出入境检验检疫
出境货物报检单

2-1035

报检单位(加盖公章)：广东市华实业发展有限公司　　*编　号 442200205000589E

报检单位登记号：4401004824　联系人：吴会芳　电话：82170725　报检日期：2005 年 05 月 20 日

发货人	(中文)	广东市华实业发展有限公司
	(外文)	***
收货人	(中文)	***
	(外文)	***

货物名称(中/外文)	H.S. 编码	产地	数/重量	货物总值	包装种类及数量
木雕	44201090.90 P/Q	广东省	4,000件 4,000千克	20,000 港币	200纸箱
木家具	94036099.00 P/Q	广东省	60件 2,500千克	12,000 港币	60捆装
木家具	94016900.00 P/Q	广东省	80件 2,000千克	12,000 港币	80纸箱
竹雕	44201010.90 P.Q	广东省	100件 500千克	4,000 港币	50纸箱
				USD 60,000.-	

运输工具名称号码	船舶	贸易方式	一般贸易	货物存放地点	永业码头
合同号	DH050322	信用证号	***	用途	其他
发货日期	2005-06-20	输往国家(地区)	中国台湾	许可证/审批号	***
起运地	天河永业码头口岸	到达口岸	中国台湾省	生产单位注册号	***
集装箱规格、数量及号码	***				

合同、信用证订立的检验检疫条款或特殊要求	标记及号码	随附单据(划"✓"或补填)	
***	N/M	□合同 □信用证 □发票 □换证凭单 □装箱单 □厂检单	□包装性能结果单 □许可/审批文件 □ □ □ □

需要证单名称(划"✓"或补填)				*检验检疫费	
□品质证书	_正_副	□植物检疫证书	_正_副	总金额(人民币元)	66.-
□重量证书	_正_副	□熏蒸/消毒证书	_正_副	计费人	李平
□数量证书	_正_副	□出境货物换证凭单	1 正 2 副	收费人	陈欣
□兽医卫生证书	_正_副	□出境货物通关单			
□健康证书	_正_副	□			
□卫生证书	_正_副	□			
□动物卫生证书	_正_副	□			

报检人郑重声明：	领取证单	
1.本人被授权报检。 2.上列填写内容正确属实，货物无伪造或冒用他人的厂名、标志、认证标志，并承担货物质量责任。 签名：吴会芳	日期	05.6.20
	签名	唐毅

注：有"*"号栏由出入境检验检疫机关填写

◆国家出入境检验检疫局制
[1-2(2004)-1]

七、单据改错

请根据以下资料修改一份出境货物报检单。

广东纺织品进出口针织品有限公司

GUANGDONG TEXTILES IMPORT & EXPORT KNITWEARS COMPANY LIMITED

15/F, GUANGDONG TEXTILES MANSION, 168 XIAOBEI ROAD, GUANGZHOU CHINA

COMMERCIAL INVOICE

ORIGINAL

Messrs.:
CURRENT FUNDS LIMITED
ROOM 1110 CHINACHEM GOLDEN PLAZA
NO. 77 MODY ROAD, TSIM SHA TSUI EAST
KOWLOON, HONGKONG

INVOICE NO. : 9703S9023
INVOICE DATE: NOV. 2, 1997
L/C NO. : WFH515950F
L/C DATE : AUG. 26, 1997
S/C NO. : DY－039

Transport details:
FROM GUANGZHOU TO SANTOS W/T HONGKONG
BY VESSEL

Terms of payment:
BY L/C

Marks & numbers	Description of goods	Quantity	Unit price	Amount
N/M	MEN'S 100 PCT COTTON WOVEN UNDER PANTS	7, 200 DOZ	USD 4. 2/DOZ	USD 30, 240. 00
			CIF SANTOS	USD 30, 240. 00

TOTAL QUANTITY: 7, 200 DOZ　　PACKING: 240CTNS
TOTAL WEIGHT: N. W.: 720 KGS　　G. W.: 800 KGS
TOTAL: US DOLLARS THIRTY THOUSAND TWO HUNDRED AND FORTY ONLY.
SHIPPED PER: XINDA/FANDU V. 336
SHIPPED ON BOARD: NOV. 10, 1997

GUANGDONG TEXTILES IMPORT & EXPORT
KNITWEARS COMPANY LIMITED

有关资料

商品编码：6207. 1100　　用途：其他

货物存放地点：大朗仓库　　产地：广州

报检人：何涛　　报检日期：1997 年 11 月 3 日

报验时提交的随附单据：合同、信用证、发票、装箱单

需要的证单：品质证书 1 正 1 副

中华人民共和国出入境检验检疫
出境货物报检单

报检单位（加盖公章）： *编 号

报检单位登记号： 联系人：何涛 电话： 报检日期：1997 年 11 月 3 日

发货人	（中文）广东纺织品进出口针织品有限公司				
	（外文）GUANGDONG TEXTILES IMPORT & EXPORT KNITWEARS COMPANY LIMITED				
收货人	（中文）				
	（外文）CURRENT FUNDS LTMTTED				
货物名称（中/外文）	H. S. 编码	产地	数/重量	货物总值	包装种类及数量
男式内裤 MEN'S 100 PCT COTTON WOVEN UNDER PANTS		广东省广州市	7，200 件	30，240 美元	240 纸箱

运输工具名称号码	XINDA/FANDU V. 336	贸易方式	来料加工	货物存放地点	大朗仓库
合同号	DY－093	信用证号	WFH5159590F	用途	其他
发货日期	1997 年 11 月 10 日	输往国家（地区）	巴西	许可证/审批号	/
起运地	广州	到达口岸	圣保罗	生产单位注册号	/
集装箱规格、数量及号码	/				

合同、信用证订立的检验检疫条款或特殊要求	标 记 及 号 码	随附单据（划“√”或补填）	
/	N/M	☑合同 ☑信用证 ☑发票 ☐换证凭单 ☑装箱单 ☐厂检单	☐包装性能结果单 ☐许可/审批文件 ☐ ☐ ☐ ☐

需要证单名称（划“√”或补填）				*检验检疫费	
☑品质证书	1 正 1 副	☐植物检疫证书	__正__副	总金额（人民币元）	
☐重量证书	__正__副	☐熏蒸/消毒证书	__正__副		
☐数量证书	__正__副	☐出境货物换证凭单	__正__副		
☐兽医卫生证书	__正__副	☐		计费人	
☐健康证书	__正__副	☐			
☐卫生证书	__正__副	☐			
☐动物卫生证书	__正__副	☐		收费人	

报检人郑重声明：	领 取 证 单	
1. 本人被授权报检。 2. 上列填写内容正确属实，货物无伪造或冒用他人的厂名、标志、认证标志，并承担货物质量责任。	日期	
签名：何涛	签名	

注：有“*”号栏由出入境检验检疫机关填写

八、单据填制

（一）单据填制一

请根据以下材料填制一份出境货物报检单。

四川长虹电器股份有限公司

SICHUAN CHANGHONG ELECTRIC CO., LTD.

35, EAST MIANXING ROAD, HIGH-TECH PARK, MIANYANG, CHINA

COMMERCIAL INVOICE

Messrs.:
YOUTA TRADING COMPANY LTD.
52 JULAN SULTAN
ROOM 1510 KOONA PLAZA
SINGAPORE

INVOICE NO. : TB - M85062
INVOICE DATE : JULY 25, 2003
S/C NO. : SM9806263
L/C NO. : HU65926

Transport details:
FROM SHENZHEN TO SINGAPORE BY VESSEL
PER S. S.: TAO LA V. 441

Terms of payment:
BY L/C

Marks & numbers	Description of goods	Quantity	Unit price	Amount
			CIF SINGAPORE	
YOUTA SINGAPORE NOS. 1 - 500	"CHANGHONG" BRAND COLOUR TELEVISION SET MODEL RT560 WITH REMOTE CONTROL, PACKED IN EXPORT CARTONS OF ONE SET EACH	500SETS	USD160.00 PER SET	USD 80,000.00

四川长虹电器股份有限公司
SICHUAN CHANGHONG ELECTRIC CO., LTD.

有关资料：

商品编码：8528.1291　　　　CONTAINER NO.: 1 * 40'COSU829234 - 2

发货日期：AUG. 10, 2003　　　　货物存放地点：中山南头

用途：其他　　　　产地：四川省绵阳市

报检人：李明　　　　报检日期：2003 年 7 月 27 日

报验时提交的随附单据：合同、信用证、发票、装箱单

需要的证单：品质证书（1 正 2 副）日出境货物换证凭单（1 正 1 副）

中华人民共和国出入境检验检疫
出境货物报检单

报检单位（加盖公章）：　　　　　　　　　　　　　　　　＊编　号＿＿＿＿＿＿

报检单位登记号：　　　　联系人：　　　　电话：　　　　报检日期：　　年　　月　　日

发货人	（中文）	
	（外文）	
收货人	（中文）	
	（外文）	

货物名称（中/外文）	H.S. 编码	产地	数/重量	货物总值	包装种类及数量

运输工具名称号码		贸易方式		货物存放地点	
合同号		信用证号		用途	
发货日期		输往国家（地区）		许可证/审批号	
起运地		到达口岸		生产单位注册号	
集装箱规格、数量及号码					

合同、信用证订立的检验检疫条款或特殊要求	标记及号码	随附单据（划“√”或补填）	
		□合同	□包装性能结果单
		□信用证	□许可/审批文件
		□发票	□
		□换证凭单	□
		□装箱单	□
		□厂检单	□

需要证单名称（划“√”或补填）				＊检验检疫费	
□品质证书	＿正＿副	□植物检疫证书	＿正＿副	总金额（人民币元）	
□重量证书	＿正＿副	□熏蒸/消毒证书	＿正＿副		
□数量证书	＿正＿副	□出境货物换证凭单	＿正＿副		
□兽医卫生证书	＿正＿副	□		计费人	
□健康证书	＿正＿副	□			
□卫生证书	＿正＿副	□		收费人	
□动物卫生证书	＿正＿副	□			

报检人郑重声明：	领取证单	
1. 本人被授权报检。	日期	
2. 上列填写内容正确属实，货物无伪造或冒用他人的厂名、标志、认证标志，并承担货物质量责任。		
签名：＿＿＿＿＿＿	签名	

注：有“＊”号栏由出入境检验检疫机关填写

（二）单据填制二

请根据以下材料填制一份出境货物报检单。

厦门富乐贸易发展公司

FULE TRADE DEVELOPMENT CO. LTD.

INVOICE

L/C NO.: KC－65284　　INVOICE NO.: FL69536874

S/C NO.: TL652C063　　DATE: MARCH 15, 2002

MESSRS.: L. Y. CONSULTANT CO., LTD.

ADDRESS: 21 OTEMON CHUO—KU FUKUODA, JAPAN

PER S. S.: HONG YAN V. 5021　DATE OF DEPARTURE: APR. 25, 2002

FROM XIAMEN　TO MOJI

MARK	PACKAGE	DESCRIPTION	QUANTITY	UNIT PRICE	AMOUNT
N/M	15,000CTNS	FRESH WINTER BAMBOO SHOOTS	15,000KGS	USD1.60/KG	USD24,000.00
				CFR MOJI	

有关资料：

集装箱号码：CCLU 850114－5（20'）　CCLU850500－6（20'）

商品编码：0709.9010

货物存放地点：石狮

用途：食用

报检人：王雅丽

报检日期：2002 年 4 月 15 日

产地：福建省厦门特区

报验时提交的随附单据：信用证、合同、发票、装箱单

需要的证单：品质证书 1 正 1 副、卫生检验证书 1 正 1 副、出境货物换证凭单 1 正 2 副

中华人民共和国出入境检验检疫
出境货物报检单

报检单位（加盖公章）：　　　　　　　　　　　　　　　　＊编　号________

报检单位登记号：　　　　联系人：　　　　电话：　　　　报检日期：　　年　　月　　日

发货人	（中文）	
	（外文）	
收货人	（中文）	
	（外文）	

货物名称（中/外文）	H. S. 编码	产地	数/重量	货物总值	包装种类及数量

运输工具名称号码		贸易方式		货物存放地点	
合同号		信用证号		用途	
发货日期		输往国家(地区)		许可证/审批号	
起运地		到达口岸		生产单位注册号	
集装箱规格、数量及号码					

合同、信用证订立的检验检疫条款或特殊要求	标记及号码	随附单据（划“√”或补填）	
		□合同 □信用证 □发票 □换证凭单 □装箱单 □厂检单	□包装性能结果单 □许可/审批文件 □ □ □ □

需要证单名称（划“√”或补填）				＊检验检疫费	
□品质证书	__正__副	□植物检疫证书	__正__副	总金额（人民币元）	
□重量证书	__正__副	□熏蒸/消毒证书	__正__副		
□数量证书	__正__副	□出境货物换证凭单	__正__副		
□兽医卫生证书	__正__副	□		计费人	
□健康证书	__正__副	□			
□卫生证书	__正__副	□		收费人	
□动物卫生证书	__正__副	□			

报检人郑重声明：	领取证单	
1. 本人被授权报检。 2. 上列填写内容正确属实，货物无伪造或冒用他人的厂名、标志、认证标志，并承担货物质量责任。 签名：________	日期	
	签名	

注：有“＊”号栏由出入境检验检疫机关填写

第二节　受益人证明书

一、单据填制

(一) 单据填制一

请根据以下材料在下面方框中制作一份受益人证明书。

A. 信用证条款。

BENEFICIARY：SHANGHAI MACHINERY IMP. & EXP. CORPORATION

L/C NO.：HU65926

DOCUMENTS REQUIRED：

* BENEFICIARY'S CERTIFICATE CERTIFYING THAT COMMERCIAL INVOICE, PACKING LIST AND ORIGINAL EXPORT LICENCE HAVE BEEN DESPATCHED BY COURIER DIRECTLY TO YOUTA TRADING COMPANY.

B. 其他资料。

INVOICE NO.：TB－M85062

DATE OF ISSUING THE BENEFICIARY'S CERTIFICATE：AUG. 3, 2003

（二）单据填制二

请根据以下材料在下面方框中制作一份受益人证明书。

A. 信用证条款。

BENEFICIARY：FULE TRADE DEVELOPMENT CO.，LTD.

L/C NO.：KC－65284

DOCUMENTS REQUIRED：

* BENEFICIARY'S CERTIFICATE CERTIFYING THAT FIVE COPIES OF YOUR SAMPLE BOOK HAVE BEEN SENT BY REGISTERED AIRMAIL TO L. Y. CONSULTANT CO.，LTD.，21 OTEMON CHUO-KU FUKUODA，JAPAN.

B. 其他资料。

INVOICE NO.：FL69536874

DATE OF ISSUING THE BENEFICIARY'S CERTIFICATE：MARCH 30，2002

（三）单据填制三

请根据以下材料在下面方框中制作一份受益人证明书。

A. 信用证条款。

BENEFICIARY：GUANGDONG TEXTILES I/E（GROUP）GARMENTS CO.

L/C NO.：P－67971

DOCUMENTS REQUIRED：

* BENEFICIARY'S CERTIFICATE STATING THAT ALL THE SHIPPED GOODS ARE STRICTLY IN COMPLIANCE WITH THE TERMS OF THE RELATIVE SALES CONTRACT（NO. 98GTB0602）.

B. 其他资料。

INVOICE NO.：980602GTB

DATE OF ISSUING THE BENEFICIARY'S CERTIFICATE：SEP. 25，1998

二、单据改错

（一）单据改错一

请根据以下材料修改一份受益人证明书。

A. 信用证条款。

ISSUE OF A DOCUMENTARY CREDIT

APPLICANT：HALSSEN & LYON GMBH，GERMANY

BENEFICIARY：CHINA TUHSU GUANGDONG TEA IMP. & EXP. CORP.

L/C NO.：6005729745H3

DOCUMENTS REQUIRED：

* BENEFICIARY'S CERTIFICATE CERTIFYING THAT ONE COPY OF COMMERCIAL INVOICE，N/N B/L HAVE BEEN FAXED TO APPLICANT TO FAX NO. 78 – 025 – 605 WHITHIN 3 DAYS AFTER SHIPMENT.

B. 其他资料。

INVOICE NO.：TA7149

DATE OF ISSUING THE BENEFICIARY'S CERTIFICATE：AUGUST 28，1997

BENEFICIARY'S CERTIFICATE

DATE：AUG. 28，1997

INVOICE NO.：TAT149　　L/C NO.：6005729745H3

WE HEREBY CERTIFY THAT ONE COPY OF COMMERCIAL INVOICE NO. B/L HAVE BEEN FAXED TO APPLICANT TO FAX NO. 78 – 025 – 605 WHITHIN 3 DAYS AFTER SHIPMENT.

中国土畜产广东茶叶进出口公司

CHINA TUHSU GUANGDONG TEA IMP. & EXP. CORP.

（SIGNATURE）

（二）单据改错二

请根据以下材料修改一份受益人证明书。

A. 信用证条款。

ISSUE OF A DOCUMENTARY CREDIT

APPLICANT：DU PONT SINGAPORE FIBRES PTE LTD.

BENEFICIARY：SHANGHAI HUAYUAN TRADE ENTERPRISE LTD.

L/C NO.：XCBS07258

DOCUMENTS REQUIRED：

* BENEFICIARY'S CERTIFICATE CERTIFYING THAT ALL THE GOODS ARE PACKED IN STRONG SEAWORTHY CARTONS AND EACH CASE CLEARLY INDICATES THE SHIPPING MARKS AND NOS.：DU PONT/NO. 1 - 420/SINGAPORE.

B. 其他资料。

INVOICE NO.：IG20303465

DATE OF ISSUING THE BENEFICIARY'S CERTIFICATE：JULY 18，2001

BENEFICIARY'S CERTIFICATE

JULY 8，2001

INVOICE NO.：IG20303465　　　L/C NO.：XCBS07258

TO WHOM IT MAY CONCERN：

WE HEREBY CERTIFY THAT ALL THE GOODS ARE PACKED IN CARTONS AND EACH CASE CLEARLY INDICATES THE SHIPPING MARKS AND NOS.：DU PONT/NO. 1 - 420/SINGAPORE.

上海华源贸易有限公司

SHANGHAI HUAYUAN TRADE ENTERPRISE LTD.

（SIGNATURE）

第三节 航空运单

一、中英文术语、短语互译

1. Airway Bill ______
2. Airline Code Number ______
3. Declared Value for Customs ______
4. Airport of Destination ______
5. Chargeable Weight ______
6. Accounting Information ______
7. IATA ______
8. NCV ______
9. NVD ______
10. CHGS Code ______
11. AS ______
12. PPD ______
13. FC ______
14. COLL ______
15. IN ______
16. GT ______
17. RCP ______
18. NIL ______

二、单项选择题

1. 航空运单正本按国际惯例为(　　)。

A. 一式两份　　B. 一式三份

C. 一份　　D. 一式六份

2. 中国民航的代号为(　　)。

A. 999　　B. 131

C. 160　　D. 988

3. 香港机场代号为(　　)。

A. HGH　　B. HRB

C. HKG　　D. HAK

4. 广州机场的代号为(　　)。

A. SHA　　B. PEK

C. SZX　　D. CAN

5. 大阪机场的代号为(　　)。

A. TYO　B. OSA
C. OKA　D. NGO

6. 曼谷机场的代号为(　　)。
A. SIN　B. PEN
C. MNL　D. BKK

7. 巴黎机场的代号为(　　)。
A. LON　B. PAR
C. HAM　D. FRA

8. 旧金山的机场代号为(　　)。
A. SFO　B. NYK
C. WAS　D. LAX

9. 在航空运输中，当托运的货物中含有危险货物时，应分别填写，并把危险货物填列在(　　)。
A. 第一项　B. 第二项
C. 任意项　D. 最后一项

10. 在航空运单中的“Executed on date”栏目表示的日期，一般应是(　　)。
A. 航空公司接受托运货物的日期
B. 签发航空运单的日期
C. 信用证规定的最后装运日期
D. 实际起飞的日期

三、多项选择题

1. 航空运单可分为(　　)。
A. 出票航空公司标志的航空货运单　B. 指示航空运单
C. 无承运人任何标志的中性货运单　D. 记名航空运单

2. 航空运单的作用包括(　　)。
A. 航空运单是航空运输承运人与托运人之间的运输合同
B. 航空运单是航空公司或其代理人收运货物的证明文件
C. 航空运单是承运人核收运费的依据
D. 航空运单是承运人处理货物运输过程情况的依据

3. 下列机场代号中，属于我国机场的是(　　)。
A. LAS　B. TSN
C. SEL　D. XMN

4. 下列表述正确的是(　　)。
A. 航空运单不是物权凭证　B. 航空运单是物权凭证
C. 航空运单不可转让　D. 航空运单经背书后可以转让

5. 航空运单的托运人名称和地址栏目，一般填写(　　)。
A. 托运人的名称和地址　B. 托运人的国家（或国家两字代号）
C. 托运人的传真、电传号码　D. 托运人的电话号码

四、判断题

1．航空运单不是物权凭证，不能通过背书转移货物的所有权，但只有航空运单的持有人才能对货物要求所有权。(　　)

2．航空运单正本按国际惯例为一式三份，每份都印有背面条款。交单议付时必须提交全部三份正本航空运单。(　　)

3．与海运提单相同，航空运单只是运输契约的证明，它本身不是运输契约。(　　)

4．一张航空运单可用于一个托运人在同一时间、同一地点托运货物，运往不同目的站的不同收货人。(　　)

5．航空运单的货物运价细目，当一票货物中含有两种或两种以上不同运价类别计费的货物时应分别填写，每填写一项另起一行，如果含有危险品，则该危险货物应列在第一项。(　　)

五、阅读理解

988-2191 7184 DYN-8800845

Shipper's Name and Address:
GUANGDONG TEXTILES I/E WOOLEN KNITWEARS CO.,LTD.13/F GUANGDONG TEXTILES MANSION 168,XIAOBEI ROAD,GUANGZHOU CHINA

Shipper's Account Number:

Not negotiable
Air Waybill*
issued by
DYNASTY INTERNATIONAL, INC.

Consignee's Name and Address:
TO Q.T.SERVICES GROUP,INC.

Consignee's Account Number:

Copies 1, 2 and 3 of this Air Waybill are originals and have the same validity.

It is agreed that the goods described herein are accepted in apparent good order and condition (except as noted) for carriage SUBJECT TO THE CONDITIONS OF CONTRACT ON THE REVERSE HEREOF. ALL GOODS MAY BE CARRIED BY ANY OTHER MEANS INCLUDING ROAD OR ANY OTHER CARRIER UNLESS SPECIFIC CONTRARY INSTRUCTIONS ARE GIVEN HEREON BY THE SHIPPER, AND SHIPPER AGREES THAT THE SHIPMENT MAY BE CARRIED VIAINTERMEDIATE STOPPING PLACES WHICH THE CARRIER DEEMS APPROPRIATE. THE SHIPPER'S ATTENTION IS DRAWN TO THE NOTICE CONCERNING CARRIER'S LIMITATION OF LIABILITY. Shipper may increase such limitation of liability by declaring a higher value for carriage and paying a suppiemental charge if required.

Issuing Carrier's Agent Name and City:
DYNASTY INTERNATIONAL, INC.

Accounting Information:
ALSO NOTIFY:
DYNASTY CHB,INC.
365 CHELSEA ST., EAST BOSTON, MA
02128,PHONE 617.569.5969

Agent's IATA Code: | Account No.:

Airport of Departure (Addr. of first Carrier) and Requested Routing:
SHANGHAI,CHINA

to	By First Carrier / Routing and Destination	to	by	to	by	Currency	Chgs. Code	WT/VAL PPD	WT/VAL COLL	OTHER PPD	OTHER COLL	Declared Value for Carriage	Declared Value for Customs
						USD		PP		PP		N.V.D	AS PER INV

Airport of Destination	Flight/Date (For Carrier Use Only)	Flight/Date	Amount of Insurance
BOSTON,MA	OZ364/2OCT		

INSURANCE – If carrier offers insurance and such insurance is requested in accordance with conditions on reverse hereof indicate amount to be insured in figures in box marked Amount of Insurance.

Handling Information including marks, numbers and mehtods of packaging:
THIS SHPT CONTAINS NO SOLID WOOD PACKING MATERIALS.
A/S/D

SCI

No. of Pieces RCP	Gross Weight	kg/lb	Rate Class / Commodity Item No.	Chargeable Weight	Rate / Charge	Total	Nature and Quantity of Goods (Incl. Dimensions or Volume)
103 CTNS	691.00	K	FREIGHT PREPAID	1,371.00			WOMEN'S APPAREL (WOMEN'S 100% CASHMERE KNITTED SWEATERS) PO#703307,703308,703309 STYLE#44-3375M,44-3375P,44-3375W VOL:8.226CBM (60.5×40×33)CM×103

SHIPPING MARKS:
TO:QT SERVICES GROUP,INC
A J.JILL COMPANY
ATTN: RECEIVING DEPT
100 BIRCH POND DRIVE
TILTON, NH03276
TEL: 603-279-7051
FROM: DZ TRADING LTD
110 EAST 9TH STREET, SUITE A1103
LOS ANGELES, CA90079
TEL: 213-532-8000
MADE IN P.R.CHINA

Prepaid	Weight Charge	Collect
AS ARRANGED		
	Valuation Charge	
	Tax	
	Total other CHarges Due Agent	
AS ARRANGED		
	Total other CHarges Due Carrier	
Total prepaid		Total collect
AS ARRANGED		
Currency Conversion Rates		cc Charges in Dest. Currency
For Carriers Use only at Destination	Charges at Destination	Total Collect Charges

Other Charges:

Shipper certifies that the particulars on the face hereof are correct and that insofar as any part of the consignment contains dangerous goods such part is properly described by name and is in proper condition for carriage by air according to the applicable Dangerous Goods Regulations.

Signature of Shipper or His Agent

Executed on 2,OCT 2004 (Date) at SHANGHAI (Place) Signature of Issuing Carrier or its Agent

DYN-8800845

3.ORIGINAL (FOR SHIPPER)

（一）阅读理解一

根据以上单据找出有关内容：

（1）收货人：

（2）代理人的名称和地址：

（3）财务说明：

（4）始发站：

（5）到达站：

（6）航班：

（7）货币：

（8）供运输用声明价值：

（9）供海关用声明价值：

（10）处理情况：

（11）货物件数：

（12）计费重量：

（13）运费缴付方式：

（14）货物品名和数量：

（15）货物体积：

（16）航空运单填开日期：

（17）航空运单填开地点：

（二）阅读理解二

根据以下单据找出有关内容：

（1）托运人的名称及地址：

（2）收货人：

（3）航班日期：

（4）财务说明：

（5）始发站：

（6）到达站：

（7）航班：

（8）货币：

（9）供运输用声明价值：

（10）供海关用声明价值：

（11）货物件数：

（12）计费重量：

（13）运费缴付方式：

（14）货物品名和数量：

（15）货物体积：

（16）航空运单填开日期：

（17）航空运单填开地点：

（18）所附文件：

House Air Waybill Number: IFS-31661

160 HKG 36877175 FILE NO : AE05-02-0016

Shipper's Name and Address	Shipper's Account Number	Not negotiable Air Waybill (Air Consignment note) Issued by
STEP ELEGANT LTD. RM201,2/F,WAI CHING COMM BLDG, 77 WAI CHING ST,KLN,HONG KONG 27812910 DEREK CHENG		IFS 運航國際空運有限公司 IFS INTERNATIONAL AIR CARGO LIMITED Copies 1, 2 and 3 of this Air Waybill are originals and have the same validity.

Consignee's Name and Address	Consignee's Account Number	
TO ORDER OF BNP PARIBAS (CANADA)		It is agreed that the goods described herein are accepted in apparent good order and condition (except as noted) for carriage SUBJECT TO THE CONDITIONS OF CONTRACT ON THE REVERSE HEREOF. THE SHIPPER'S ATTENTION IS DRAWN TO THE NOTICE CONCERNING CARRIERS' LIMITATION OF LIABILITY. Shipper may increase such limitation of liability by declaring a higher value for carriage and paying a supplemental charge if required. FREIGHT PREPAID NOTIFY COSACO INC 9600 RUE MEILLEUR,MONTREAL, QC H2N 2E3 CONTACT PERSON:KAREN CRAWLEY TEL:(514)3824860 FAX:(514)3878086

Airport of Departure (Addr. of First Carrier) and Requested Routing: HONG KONG

to	By First Carrier	Routing and Destination	Air Waybill Number	Currency	CHGS Code	WT/VAL PPD	WT/VAL COLL	Other PPD	Other COLL	Declared Value for Carriage	Declared Value for Customs
YUL	CX			HKD		P		P		N.V.D.	AS PER INV

Airport of Destination	Flight/Date	For Carrier Use only	Flight/Date	Amount of Insurance	
MONTREAL	CX828		05 FEB.2005	NIL	INSURANCE - If Carrier offers insurance and such insurance is requested in accordance with conditions on reverse hereof, indicate amount to be insured in figures in box marked amount of insurance.

Handling Information

THIS SHIPMENT,INCLUDING ITS CONTAINERS,DOES NOT CONTAIN ANY NON-MANUFACTURED WOODEN PACKING MATERIAL,DUNNAGE,BRACING MATERIAL,PALLETS, CRATING OR OTHER NON-MANUFACTURED WOODEN PACKING MATERIAL.

No. of Pieces RCP	Gross Weight	kg/lb	Rate Class / Commodity Item No.	Chargeable Weight	Rate / Charge	Total	Nature and Quantity of Goods (incl. Dimensions or Volume)
22	189.0	K		189.0	PREPAID AS ARRANGED		LADIES' 95% COTTON 5% SPANDEX KNITTED SWEATER PO. C9588 STYLE NO.52309D5S/LD QTY:800PCS [D34×60×31CM×14] [D54×31×31CM×8] VOL. = 1300512.0CM BY VOL. 186.0K

MARKS:
OUR MARK
OUR P/O NO.
CONCECUTIVE
PACKAGE NUMBER
STYLE NO.
COLOR
SIZE
QTY
MADE IN CHINA
WEIGHT
MEASURMENT

INVOICE,PACKING LIST,ORIGINAL CHINA
C/O#040551659 ATT'D
E/L : E501221500005

Prepaid	Weight Charge	Collect	Other Charges
AS ARRANGED		PREPAID	
	Valuation Charge		
	Tax		
	Total other Charges Due Agent		Shipper certifies that the particulars on the face hereof are correct and that insofar as any part of the consignment contains restricted articles, such part is properly described by name and is in proper condition for carriage by air according to the applicable Dangerous Goods Regulations.
	Total other Charges Due Carrier		IFS INTERNATIONAL AIR CARGO LIMITED Signature of Shipper or his Agent
Total Prepaid		Total Collect	
Currency Conversion Rates		CC Charges in Dest. Currency	03 FEB.2005 HONG.KONG Executed on (Date) at (Place) Signature of Issuing Carrier or its Agent

(Stamp: IFS INTERNATIONAL AIR CARGO LIMITED 運航國際空運有限公司)

ORIGINAL 1 (FOR SHIPPER)

House Air Waybill Number: IFS-31661

六、单据填制

（一）单据填制一

根据给出的资料填制单据。

A. 信用证条款。

Applicant	*50	: YYY TRADING CO., LTD. 220 SIGMUND STR. 80035 NOLA (ITALY)
Beneficiary	*59	: GUANGDONG ABC IMPORT & EXPORT COMPANY LTD. NO. 188 XIAOGANG ROAD, GUANGZHOU
Loading in Charge	44 A	: FROM ANY CHINESE AIRPORT
For Transport to ...	44 B	: MILAN, ITALY
Descript. of Goods	45 A	:

1,700 PCS OF LADIES' 55% RAMIE 36% WOOL 9% NYLON KNITTED SWEATER
CFR MILAN AIRPORT
AS PER SALES CONFIRMATION NO. 2002MCGS02007 DD 8.3.2002
TOTAL AMOUNT USD12,614.00

Documents Required 46 A :

CLEAN AIR WAYBILL FOR GOODS AIR FREIGHTED TO YYY TRADING CO., LTD. 220 SIGMUND STR. 80035 NOLA (ITALY) MARKED FREIGHT PREPAID AND EVIDENCING THAT ORIGINAL INVOICE AND PACKING LIST ACCOMPANY THE GOODS, NOTIFY APPLICANT

B. 其他资料。

航空运单填开日期：2005 年 5 月 25 日
航空运单填开地点：广州
始发站：广州
货物装箱情况：1,700PCS/40CTNS
航班号及日期：CA1234/26, MAY, 2005
总毛重：400KGS
唛头：YYY/MILAN/NOS1 - 40
计费重量：420KGS
计费货币：美元
航空运单号码：03030030509
空运单注明没有声明价值和没有商业价值
尺码：(30 × 40 × 20)CM

999　　　　　　　　　　　　　　　　　　　　　　　　　999—

Shipper's Name and Address

Shipper's Account Number

NOT NEGOTIABLE 中国民航 CAAC

AIR WAYBILL AIR CONSIGNMENT NOTE

ISSUED BY: THE CIVIL AVIATION ADMINISTRATION OF CHINA

BEIJING CHINA

Copies 1, 2 and 3 of this Air Waybill are originals and have the same validity.

Consignee's Name and Address

Consignee's Account Number

It is agreed that the goods described herein are accepted in apparent good order and condition (except as noted) for carriage SUBJECT TO THE CONDITIONS OF CONTRACT ON THE REVERSE HEREOF.THE SHIPPER'S ATTENTION IS DRAWN TO THE NOTICE CONCERNINC CARRIER'S LIMITATION OF LIABILITY.Shipper may increase such limitation of liability by declaring a higher value for carriage and paying a supplemental charge if required.

ISSUING CARRIER MAINTAINS CARGO ACCIDENT LIABILITY INSURANCE

Issuing Carrier's Agent Name and City

Accounting Information

Agent's IATA Code　　Account No.

Airport of Departure(Addr. of First Carrier)and Requested Routing

to | By First Carrier | Routing and Destination | to | by | to | by | Currency | CHGS Code | WT/NAL PPD | WT/NAL COLL | Other PPD | Other COLL | Declared Value for Carriage | Declared Value for Customs

Airport Destination | Flight/Date | For Carrier Use only | Flight/ Date | Amount of Insurance

INSURANCE if carrier offers insurance, and such insurance is requested in accordance with conditions on reverse here of, indicate amount to be insured in figure in box marked amount of insurance.

Handling Information

(for USA only)Those commodities licensed by US for ultimate destination...Diversion contray to US law is prohibited.

No. of Pieces RCP	Gross Weight	Kg Lb	Rate Class Commodity Item No.	Chargeable Weight	Rate Charge	Total	Nature and Quantity of Goods (incl.Dimensions or Volume)

Prepaid　Weight Charge　Collect

Other Charges

Valuation Charge

Tax

Total Other Charges Due Agent

Shipper certifies that the particulars on the face hereof are correct and that insofar as any part of the consignment contains dangerous goods,such part is properly described by name and is in proper condition for carriage by air according to the applicable Dangerous Goods Regulations.

Total Other Charges Due Carrier

Signature of Shipper or his Agent

Total Prepaid　Total Collect

Currency Conversion Rates　CC Charges in Dest. Currency

Executed on (date)　at (place)　Signature of Issuing carrier or its Agent

For Carrier's use only at Destination　Charges at Destination　Total Collect Charges

999—

（二）单据填制二

根据给出的国际货物托运书填制单据。

国际货物托运书（SHIPPER'S LETTER OF INSTRUCTION）

托运人姓名及地址 SHIPPER'S NAME AND ADDRESS GUANGDONG FOREIGN TRADE IMP. & EXP. CORP. 15 – 18/F., GUANGDONG FOREIGN ECONOMIC AND TRADE BUILDING 351 TIANHE ROAD, GUANGZHOU, CHINA	托运人账号 SHIPPER'S ACCOUNT NUMBER	供承运人用 FOR CARRIAGE USE ONLY 班期/日期 FLIGHT/DAY　航班/日期 FLIGHT/DAY CA253/MAY 28, 2004
收货人姓名及地址 CONSIGNEE'S NAME AND ADDRESS ABC COMPANY LIMITED BLUE BIRD STREET, NEW YORK, USA	收货人账号 CONSIGNEE'S ACCOUNT NUMBER	已预留吨位 BOOKED 运费 CHARGES FREIGHT PREPAID
代理人的名称和城市 ISSUING CARRIER'S AGENT NAME AND CITY XYZ SHIPPING CO., LTD.		ALSO NOTIFY
始发站 AIRPORT OF DEPARTURE GUANGZHOU AIRPORT		
到达站 AIRPORT OF DESTINATION JOHN KENNEDY AIRPORT(JEK)		
托运人声明价值 SHIPPER'S DECLARED VALUE 供运输用 FOR CARRIAGE NVD 供海关用 FOR CUSTOMS NCV	保险金额 AMOUNT OF INSURANCE NIL	所附文件 DOCUMENT TO ACCOMPANY AIR WAYBILL 1 COMMERCIAL INVOICE AND 1PACKING LIST

处理情况（包括包装方式、货物标志及号码）
HANDLING INFORMATION (INGL METHOD OF PACKING IDENTIFYING AND NUMBERS)

KEEP UPSIDE

件数 NO. OF PACKAGES	实际毛重 ACTUAL GROSS WEIGHT (K. G.)	运价种类 RATE CLASS	收费重量 CHARGEABLE WEIGHT	费率 RATE/ CHARGE	货物品名及数量（包括体积或尺寸） NATURE AND QUANTITY OF GOODS (INCL. DIMENSION OF VOLUME) 480PCS OF MEN'S SWEATERS
10	100		100	18.00	DIMS: (40×30×25)CM×10

999 | |　　　　999—

Shipper's Name and Address / Shipper's Account Number	NOT NEGOTIABLE 中国民航 CAAC AIR WAYBILL AIR CONSIGNMENT NOTE ISSUED BY: THE CIVIL AVIATION ADMINISTRATION OF CHINA BEIJING CHINA
	Copies 1, 2 and 3 of this Air Waybill are originals and have the same validity.
Consignee's Name and Address / Consignee's Account Number	It is agreed that the goods described herein are accepted in apparent good order and condition (except as noted) for carriage SUBJECT TO THE CONDITIONS OF CONTRACT ON THE REVERSE HEREOF. THE SHIPPER'S ATTENTION IS DRAWN TO THE NOTICE CONCERNINC CARRIER'S LIMITATION OF LIABILITY. Shipper may increase such limitation of liability by declaring a higher value for carriage and paying a supplemental charge if required. ISSUING CARRIER MAINTAINS CARGO ACCIDENT LIABILITY INSURANCE
Issuing Carrier's Agent Name and City Agent's IATA Code / Account No.	Accounting Information
Airport of Departure(Addr. of First Carrier)and Requested Routing	

to	By First Carrier	Routing and Destination	to	by	to	by	Currency	CHGS Code	WT/NAL PPD	WT/NAL COLL	Other PPD	Other COLL	Declared Value for Carriage	Declared Value for Customs

Airport Destination	Flight/Date	For Carrier Use only	Flight/Date	Amount of Insurance	INSURANCE if carrier offers insurance, and such insurance is requested in accordance with conditions on reverse here of, indicate amount to be insured in figure in box marked amount of insurance.

Handling Information

(for USA only)Those commodities licensed by US for ultimate destination...Diversion contray to US law is prohibited.

No. of Pieces RCP	Gross Weight	Kg Lb	Rate Class Commodity Item No.	Chargeable Weight	Rate Charge	Total	Nature and Quantity of Goods (incl.Dimensions or Volume)

Prepaid	Weight Charge	Collect	Other Charges
	Valuation Charge		
	Tax		
	Total Other Charges Due Agent		Shipper certifies that the particulars on the face hereof are correct and that insofar as any part of the consignment contains dangerous goods, such part is properly described by name and is in proper condition for carriage by air according to the applicable Dangerous Goods Regulations. …………………… Signature of Shipper or his Agent
	Total Other Charges Due Carrier		
Total Prepaid		Total Collect	…………………… Executed on (date)　at (place)　Signature of Issuing carrier or its Agent
Currency Conversion Rates		CC Charges in Dest. Currency	
For Carrier's use only at Destination		Charges at Destination	Total Collect Charges　　999—

第四节　装船通知

一、单据填制一

根据有关资料填制装船通知。

A. 信用证资料。

Date of Issue	:	041020
Form of Doc. Credit	:	IRREVOCABLE
Doc. Credit Number	:	M20K2710NS00032
Expiry	:	Date 041115 Place IN BENEFICIARY'S COUNTRY
Applicant	:	SE BANG TRADING CO., LTD. 148 NAMCHEON - 2 DONG, SUYOUNG - KU PUSAN, KOREA
Beneficiary	:	GUANGZHOU ARTS & CRAFTS IMP. & EXP. CORP. 628 GUANGZHOU DADAO ZHONG ROAD, GUANGZHOU, CHINA
Partial Shipments	:	ALLOWED
Transshipment	:	ALLOWED
Loading in Charge	:	GUANGZHOU, CHINA
For Transport to...	:	PUSAN, KOREA
Latest Date of Ship.	:	041105
Descript. of Goods	:	CHINA ORIGIN ARTIFICIAL FLOWERS AB - 06001　5,184DOZ @ USD2.50/DOZ AB - 07049　2,880DOZ @ USD2.80/DOZ AS PER S/C NO. 97A/KF002A DATE OCT. 15, 2004 CIF PUSAN
Documents Required	:	SHIPMENT ADVICE IN FULL DETAILS INCLUDING SHIPPING MARKS, CONTAINER NUMBERS, VESSEL NAME, B/L NUMBER, VALUE AND QUANTITY OF GOODS MUST BE SENT ON THE DATE OF SHIPMENT TO APPLICANT.

B. 其他资料。

INV. NO.: 97KF335　　B/L DATE: OCT. 28, 2004

B/L NO.: DSA97 - 1102　　SHIPPING MARKS: SE BANG/PUSAN

PACKING: AB - 06001　36DOZ/CTN　G. W.: 23KGS/CTN　N. W.: 18KGS/CTN

　　　　AB - 07049　36DOZ/CTN　G. W.: 19KGS/CTN　N. W.: 13KGS/CTN

MEASUREMENT: (40 × 50 × 80) CM/CTN　DATE OF ADVICE: OCT. 29, 2004

CONTAINER NO. MSCU 4097561 (20')　MSCU 4097615 (40')

NAME OF STEAMER: SUI 301/NORASIA V. 49 - 3 W/T HONGKONG

广州工艺进出口公司

GUANGZHOU ARTS & CRAFTS IMP. & EXP. CORP.

628 GUANGZHOU DADAO ZHONG ROAD, GUANGZHOU, CHINA

INVOICE NO.:

To Messrs.:

SHIPPING ADVICE

Name of Commodity:

Quantity:

Invoice Value:

Name of Carrying Steamer:

Date of Shipment:

Shipping Marks:

Credit No.:

Port of Loading:

Port of Discharge::

B/L No.:

Container No.:

二、单据填制二

根据有关资料填制装船通知。

A. 信用证资料。

Credit Number	: LRT9802457
Date of Issue	: 020505
Expiry	: Date 020716 Place CHINA
Applicant	: ABC CORP. AKEKSANTERINK AUTO P. O. BOX 9, FINLAND
Beneficiary	: GUANGDONG RONGHUA TRADE CO., LTD. 168, DEZHENG ROAD SOUTH, GUANGZHOU, CHINA
Amount	: Currency USD Amount 36,480.00 (SAY US DOLLARS THIRTY SIX THOUSAND FOUR HUNDRED AND EIGHTY ONLY.)
Loading in Charge	: GUANGZHOU
For Transport to	: HELSINKI
Shipment Period	: AT THE LATEST JULY 16, 2002
Descrip. of Goods	: 9,600PCS OF WOMEN'S SWEATERS UNIT PRICE: USD3.80/PC, PACKING: 12PCS/CTN OTHER DETAILS AS PER S/C NO. 98SGQ468001 CFR HELSINKI
Documents Required	: ADVICE OF SHIPMENT MUST BE SENT BY FAX TO MARK INSURANCE CO. HELSINKI, FINLAND (FAX NO. 33333) WITH DETAILS OF SHIPMENT INCLUDING VALUE, NAME OF VESSEL, DATE OF SHIPMENT, NAME OF COMMODITY, NUMBER OF PACKAGE; TOTAL NET AND GROSS WEIGHT QUOTING THEIR POLICY NO. 3RT20053. COPY OF THIS FAX TO BE PRESENTED WITH DOCUMENTS UPON NEGOTIATION.
Additional Cond.	: 1. T. T. REIMBURSEMENT IS PROHIBITED. 2. ALL DOCUMENTS MUST BE MARKED THE S/C NO. AND THE L/C NO. 3. SHIPPING MARKS: ABC/HELSINKI/ NO. 1 - UP.

B. 其他资料。

INV. NO.: 2005PCI448

DATE OF SHIPMENT: MAY 20, 2002

B/L NO.: FKK9078533

MEASUREMENT: (40 × 50 × 80) CM/CTN

G. W.: 23KGS/CTN

N. W.: 18KGS/CTN

NAME OF STEAMER: DONGFENG E003 DATE OF ADVICE: MAY 21, 2002

广东荣华贸易有限公司
GUANGDONG RONGHUA TRADE CO., LTD.
168 DEZHENG ROAD SOUTH, GUANGZHOU, CHINA

FAX NO.:

INV. NO.:

To Messrs.:

ADVICE OF SHIPMENT

Name of Commodity:
Quantity:
Invoice Value:
Name of Carrying Steamer:
Date of Shipment:
Shipping Marks:
L/C No.:
Port of Loading:
Port of Discharge:
B/L No.:
S/C No.:
TOTAL NET WEIGHT:
TOTAL GROSS WEIGHT:
POLICY NO.:

第四章
托　运　单

一、中英文术语、短语互译

（一）中译英

（1）托运人________

（2）收货人________

（3）提货单________

（4）分运________

（5）正本提单________

（6）托运单________

（7）运费预付________

（8）场站收据________

（9）运输标志________

（10）运费待付________

（二）英译中

（1）Place of Destination ________

（2）Time of Shipment ________

（3）Booking Note ________

（4）Transshipment ________

（5）Stowage Plan ________

（6）Loading Port ________

（7）Description of Goods ________

（8）Shipping Order ________

（9）Container Load Plan ________

（10）Mate's Receipt ________

二、单项选择题

1. 若货物从广州运往荷兰的鹿特丹港口后，再运至德国一内陆城市 SCHORNDORF，贸易术语为 CIF ROTTERDAM，则托运单的目的港应填(　　)。

A. ROTTERDAM　　B. NETHERLAND

C. SCHORNDORF　　D. GERMANY

2. 开证行 HANGSENG BANK 开来的信用证中，要求 FULL SET OF B/L MADE OUT TO OUR ORDER，则填托运单时在 CONSIGNEE 一栏应填(　　)。

A. TO ORDER　　B. TO OUR ORDER

C. TO ORDER OF HANGSENG BANK　　D. HANGSENG BANK

3. 下面集装箱交接方式中，(　　)是"整箱接，拆箱交"。

A. FCL/FCL　　B. FCL/LCL

C. LCL/FCL　　D. LCL/LCL

4. 托运单 CONSIGNEE 栏目中，若填写为(　　)，则提单必须由托运人背书方可转让。

A. TO ORDER　　B. TO ORDER OF ××× BANK

C. 开证人名称　　D. TO ORDER OF 开证人名称

5. 若信用证同时列明 3 个装运港 XINGANG/QINHUANGDAO/TANGSHAN，在填制托运单时应填(　　)。

A. XINGANG/QINHUANGDAO/TANGSHAN

B. XINGANG

C. 根据 L/C 提供的港口，只填写实际装运港的名称

D. GUANGZHOU

三、多项选择题

1. (　　)是结汇单据，如果缮制错漏、延误等，就会影响安全结汇。

A. 汇票　　B. 发票

C. 托运单　　D. 受益人证明书

2. 托运单收货人栏目填写为(　　)，则其对应的提单可通过背书转让。

A. ABC　CO.　　B. TO ORDER

C. TO ORDER OF SHIPPER　　D. TO ORDER OF××× BANK

3. 下面托运单栏目中，须由船公司填写的是(　　)。

A. 提单编号　　B. 船名

C. 船期　　D. 托运单编号

4. 托运单的运费缴付方式，根据实际情况可填写(　　)。

A. FREIGHT PREPAID　　B. FREIGHT PAID

C. FREIGHT COLLECT　　D. FREIGHT PAYABLE AT DESTINATION

5. 承运人从起运地到目的地都采用整箱交接货物方式的是(　　)。

A. CY TO CY　　B. CY TO CFS

C. DOOR TO CY　　D. CFS TO CY

四、判断题

1. 如来证中要求两个或两个以上的公司为被通知人，若托运单栏内写不下，可只填写一个被通知人。(　　)

2. 货物装船后，大副在收货单上签收。托运人凭已签名的收货单向船公司或船代理换取

全套正本提单。(　)

3. 如在托运单收货人一栏留空，这种表示方法称为空白指示。(　)

4. 被通知人的职责是及时接受船方发出的到货通知并及时提货。(　)

5. 如出口 10 万码花布，分别用粗坯布捆成 100 捆，则填写数目这一栏时应填写 100 捆。(　)

6. 如果买卖合同和信用证都没有规定唛头，则卖方不能自行选择一个合适的唛头。(　)

7. 若一次装运货物中有几种不同的货物，那么在填写毛重这一栏目时，只需填写合计全部的毛重。(　)

8. 若合同或信用证没有特别说明，通常情况下，托运单中的货物说明也必须详细列出货物的型号、规格，不能只写大类名称或统称。(　)

9. 托运单号码一般就是提单号码。(　)

10. 若信用证中规定装运港为 Chinese main port，则在托运单中的装运港应填 Chinese main port，以保持单证一致。(　)

五、单据填制

（一）单据填制一

请根据以下材料填制一份托运单。

A. 信用证条款。

Credit Number	:	SK/25067/2004
Date of Issue	:	DEC. 27, 2004
Expiry	:	Date 050327 Place CHINA
Applicant	:	MAHARAJA DEIRA L. L. C, DUBAI (UAE) P. O. BOX No. 6093, DUBAI (UAE), FAX NO. 263745
Beneficiary	:	GUANGDONG TEXTILES IMP. AND EXP. GRANDTON TRADING CO., LTD., 7/F., GUANGDONG TEXTILES MANSION, NO. 168 XIAOBEI ROAD, GUANGZHOU, CHINA
Amount	:	USD 99,960.00
Partial Shipments	:	Allowed
Transshipment	:	Allowed (AT HONGKONG PORT ONLY)
Shipment Period	:	AT THE LATEST MARCH 27, 2005 (Shipment from CHINA Ports To DUBAI By Steamer)
Covering	:	4,000 DOZEN LADIES LYCRA LONG PANT CIFC2 DUBAI USD25.5 PER DOZEN ALL OTHER DETAILS ARE AS PER S/C No. 2004/2495 PACKING 10DOZ/CTN
Shipping Marks	:	MAHARAJA / 264553/ DUBAI/NO. 1-400
Documents Required	:	* Full set of clean "Shipped on board" ocean Bills of Lading made out to the order of Habib Bank AG Zurich DUBAI. U. A. E. and notify applicant, showing "Freight Prepaid" mentioning L/C NO.
Additional Condition	:	Shipment to be effected by 1×20' container (FCL).

B. 其他资料。

发票号码	GD-TX-9057	托运日期	JAN. 2, 2005
单位毛重	15KGS/CTN	单位净重	12KGS/CTN
单位尺码	(60×20×50) CM/CTN	货物堆存地点	大松岗

中 国 外 运 广 东 公 司
出口货物托运单

提单编号＿＿＿＿＿＿ 托运日期＿＿＿＿＿＿ 托运单位编号＿＿＿＿＿＿

合约编号＿＿＿＿＿＿

船　　名＿＿＿＿＿＿ 船期＿＿＿＿＿＿ 运往地点＿＿＿＿＿＿

托 运 人＿＿＿＿＿＿＿＿＿＿＿＿＿＿＿＿＿＿

受 货 人＿＿＿＿＿＿＿＿＿＿＿＿＿＿＿＿＿＿

通　　知＿＿＿＿＿＿＿＿＿＿＿＿＿＿＿＿＿＿

标记及号码	件　　数	货　　名	重量（公斤）		容积吨
			净	毛	

合计：			共重：			
特约事项						
可否转船				（托运人盖章）		
可否分批		需要提单正本　　份　副本　　份				
货物堆存地点		装船期限		结汇期限		
运费缴付方式			运费账单开送			
信用证号码		货　价	F. O. B.		C. I. F.	
运往香港船名		实际装船日期				
运费吨：		运费率：		运费金额：		

（二）单据填制二

请根据以下资料填制一份托运单。

A. 信用证条款。

DATE AND PLACE OF ISSUE：97/09/28 IN JAPAN

DATE AND PLACE OF EXPIRY：97/11/10 IN GUANGZHOU，CHINA

IRREVOCABLE DOCUMENTARY CREDIT NO.：D－22－P－31209

APPLICANT： SUNNY TRADE ENTERPRISE UNIT A 8/F.，CHINA TRADE CTR 122 WAI YIP ST KWUN TONG KOWLOON，JAPAN	BENEFICIARY： GUANGDONG ARTS AND CRAFTS IMP. AND EXP. CORP.（GROUP） 318 DADE ROAD，GUANGZHOU， CHINA
AMOUNT：USD 30,000.00（US DOLLARS THIRTY THOUSAND ONLY.）	
PARTIAL SHIPMENTS ARE ALLOWED TRANSSHIPMENT IS ALLOWED SHIPMENT FROM GUANGZHOU，CHINA TO TOKYO LATEST 97/10/25	CREDIT AVAILABLE WITH ANY BANK BY NEGOTIATION AGAINST PRESENTATION OF THE DOCS DETAILED HEREIN AND OF THE BENE'S DRAFT（S）AT SIGHT DRAWN ON US FOR FULL INVOICE VALUE

LIST OF DOCUMENTS TO BE PRESENTED：

FULL SET OF ORIGINAL CLEAN "SHIPPED ON BOARD" OCEAN BILLS OF LADING MADE OUT TO ORDER OF THE CHINA AND SOUTH SEA BANK LTD.，MARKED "FREIGHT PREPAID"，NOTIFYING APPLICANT

SHIPPING DOCUMENTS COVERING（AS PER S/C NO. GDF－97－44011128）：

ENERGY SAVING LAMPS LES9W2U

QUANTITY：20,000PCS

UNIT PRICE：@USD1.50/PC，CIF TOKYO，100PCS/CTN

WEIGHT：N. W：8.00KGS/CTN，G. W：10.00KGS/CTN

MEASUREMENT（CTN）：(46×24×38) CM

SPECIAL CONDITION：

THE NAME，ADDRESS，TELEPHONE NUMBER OF SHIPPING AGENT IN TOKYO MUST BE MENTIONED ON B/L.

ALL GOODS MUST BE SHIPPED IN 20' CONTAINER.

B. 其他资料。

发票号码	GDF－97－2503	托运日期	OCT. 20，1997
唛头	SUNNY/TOKYO/NO. 1－200	集装箱号码	1＊20' SOMU2234925
东京货代资料	NAME：ABC SHIPPING CO.，LTD. ADDRESS：222 ROSE STREET，TOKYO，JAPAN TEL：222888		

中国外运广东公司
出口货物托运单

提单编号＿＿＿＿　托运日期＿＿＿＿　托运单位编号＿＿＿＿

合约编号＿＿＿＿

船　　名＿＿＿＿　船期＿＿＿＿　运往地点＿＿＿＿

托 运 人＿＿＿＿

受 货 人＿＿＿＿

通　　知＿＿＿＿

标记及号码	件　数	货　名	重量（公斤）		容积吨
			净	毛	

合计：　　　　共重：

特约事项		
可否转船		（托运人盖章）
可否分批		需要提单正本　　份　副本　　份
货物堆存地点	装船期限	结汇期限
运费缴付方式		运费账单开送
信用证号码		货　价　F. O. B.　　C. I. F.
运往香港船名		实际装船日期

运费吨：　　运费率：　　运费金额：

第五章
报 关 单

一、单项选择题

1. 某进出口公司向某国出口500吨散装小麦，该批小麦分装在一条船的三个船舱内。海关报关单上的“件数”和“包装种类”两个项目填报正确的应是（　　）。

A. 件数为500，包装种类为“吨”　　B. 件数为1，包装种类为“船”

C. 件数为3，包装种类为“船舱”　　D. 件数为1，包装种类为“散装”

2. 海关规定进口货物的进口日期是指(　　)。

A. 申报货物办结海关进口手续的日期

B. 向海关申报货物进口的日期

C. 运载货物的运输工具申报进境的日期

D. 所申报货物进入海关监管场地或仓库的日期

3. 我国某进出口公司从香港购进一批SONY牌电视机，该电视机为日本品牌，其中显像管由韩国生产，集成电路板由新加坡生产，其他零件均由马来西亚生产，最后由韩国组装成整机。该公司向海关申报进口该电视机时，原产地应填报为(　　)。

A. 日本　　B. 韩国　　C. 新加坡　　D. 马来西亚

4. 海关规定对在海关注册登记的企业给予十位数代码编号，称为“经营单位代码”。下列选项中十位数代码的正确组成顺序是(　　)。

A. 地区代码、企业性质代码和顺序代码

B. 企业详细地址代码、特殊地区代码、企业性质代码和顺序代码

C. 企业所在省、直辖市代码，特殊地区代码，企业性质代码和顺序代码

D. 企业所在省、直辖市代码及省辖市、县、计划单列市、沿海开放城市代码，企业性质代码，特殊地区代码和顺序代码

5. 某外资企业出口一批男式全羊毛西服，该批西服分别用约85%的进料加工料件和15%的国产原料加工而成。请问该企业在向海关办理出口申报手续时应填写的报关单是(　　)。

A. 进料加工专用出口货物报关单

B. 一般贸易用出口货物报关单

C. 外商投资企业专用出口货物报关单

D. 来料加工和补偿贸易专用出口货物报关单

6. 某外贸总公司（甲方）与日本某公司（乙方）签订了一项合同。合同规定，由乙方卖给甲方价值4 000美元用于制作服装的辅料，甲方用该辅料和国产主料加工成价值40

万美元的西服返销给乙方。在填制进出口货物报关单贸易方式栏时应填写(　　)。

A. 进口、出口均为“进料对口”

B. 进口为“进料对口”，出口为“一般贸易”

C. 进口、出口均为“一般贸易”

D. 进口为“一般贸易”，出口为“进料对口”

7. 联合国救灾协调员办事处在美国市场采购原产于加拿大的冰雪救灾物资无偿援助我国，该批物资在洛杉矶装船，在日本东京中转后运抵我国，这种情况其报关单“起运国（地区）”栏目应填写为(　　)。

A. 日本　B. 加拿大　C. 美国　D. 联合国

8. 大连某中日合资企业委托辽宁省机械设备进出口公司与日本三菱重工签约进口工程机械，并委托大连外运公司代理报关，在填制进口报关单时，“经营单位”一项应填写(　　)。

A. 该中日合资企业　B. 辽宁省机械设备进出口公司

C. 日本三菱重工　D. 大连外运公司

9. 某服装进出口公司自日本进口一批工作服样装，在向海关申报时，其报关单“贸易方式”栏应填报为(　　)。

A. 一般贸易　B. 货样广告品　C. 货样广告品 A D. 货样广告品 B

10. 报关单“贸易方式”栏应填报为“进料非对口”的是（　　）。

A. 原进料加工项下的成品或半成品，已在海关办理结转手续不直接出口，而是转让给境内其他承接进口料件加工复出口业务的单位进行再加工装配的贸易方式

B. 我方有外贸进出口经营权的企业动用外汇购买进口料件，加工成品或半成品后返销出口的贸易方式

C. 进料加工贸易进口料件，经批准转为内销的贸易方式

D. 特定用途以进料加工形式进口料件加工的成品不返销出境而供应国内市场的贸易方式

二、多项选择题

1. 根据海关对报关单上“运输方式”项目的分类规定，“其他运输”是指下列（　　)运输方式。

A. 管道运输　B. 驮畜运输　C. 自行车装运　D. 人力扛运

2. 下列哪种类型的单位可以作为经营单位进行填报。(　　)

A. 对外签订合同但并非执行合同的单位

B. 非对外签订合同但具体执行合同的单位

C. 委托外贸公司对外签订并执行进口投资设备合同的外商投资企业

D. 接受并办理进口溢卸货物报关纳税手续的单位

3. 在填制报关单时，海关根据进出口商品的不同情况，对商品数量的填报作出了一些规定，请选择下列哪些是符合海关规定的。(　　)

A. 规范的数量和单位，应以海关统计商品目录上规定的数量和单位填写。

B. 与海关规范的数量和单位不一致的实际成交的数量和单位也可填在报关单上。

C. 不能把整机和零件的数量加在一起填报数量。

D. 不能把类似“一卷”、“一箱”、“一捆”等较笼统的数量和单位填在报关单上。

4. 某公司从日本进口联合收割机 10 台及部分附件，分装 30 箱，发票注明每台单价为 CIF Shanghai US＄22,400，总价为 US＄224,000，附件不另计价。进口货物报关单以下栏目正确填报的为(　　)。

A. 成交方式：海运　　B. 件数：30

C. 商品名称：联合收割机及附件　　D. 单价：22 400

5. 进口货物报关单有若干联，请指出下列报关单中的哪几联属于报关单的基本联。(　　)

A. 海关留存联　　B. 企业留存联

C. 海关核销联　　D. 海关统计联

6. 某进出口公司报关员在制作一份进口报关单时，在“标记唛码及备注”栏内填入了以下内容，请选出哪些内容是正确的。(　　)

A. NO MARK 字样　　B. 付汇核销单编号

C. 商检证 1 份及其编号　　D. 进料加工合同共 2 本手册及全部编号

7. 根据海关规定，在填写进出口货物报关单的“贸易方式”时，有未名的贸易方式填写为“其他贸易”。在下列几种贸易方式中，不可填写为“其他贸易”的是(　　)。

A. 溢卸货物　　B. 货样、广告品

C. 暂时进口货物　　D. 对台直接贸易

8. 某合资企业从韩国进口一批作为投资的机器设备，该公司委托 A 进出口公司对外签订进口合同，并代办进口手续。A 进出口公司与外商订货后，随即委托 B 公司具体办理货物运输事宜，同时委托上海 C 报关公司负责办理进口报关手续。请选择下列出现在报关单有关栏目内的单位哪些是填写错误的。(　　)

A. 经营单位：A 进出口公司　　B. 收货单位：某合资企业

C. 申报单位：B 公司　　D. 收货单位：A 进出口公司

9. 某合资企业从英国进口一批作为投资的机器设备，该企业委托 A 进出口公司对外签订进口合同，并代办进口手续，A 进出口公司与外商订货后，随即委托 B 公司具体办理货物运输事宜，下列出现在报关单栏目内的单位，哪些是错误的。(　　)

A. 经营单位：A 进出口公司　　B. 收货单位：某合资企业

C. 申报单位：B 公司　　D. 收货单位：A 进出口公司

10. 请指出下列哪种贸易行为应填写出口货物报关单。(　　)

A. 非保税区运入保税区供加工生产产品用

B. 加工贸易深加工结转

C. 加工贸易成品转内销

D. 保税仓库货物复出口

三、判断题

1. 报关单上的“杂费”指成交价格以外的、应计入完税价格或从完税价格中扣除的

费用，如手续费、佣金、回扣等。(　　)

2. 某进口单位在申报进口租赁期在一年以上的租赁贸易货物时，只填制了一份贸易方式为“租赁贸易”的报关单，海关认为其申报有误。(　　)

3. 报关单上的“收货单位”应为进口货物在境内的最终消费、使用的单位名称，“发货单位”应为出口货物在境内的生产或销售的单位名称。(　　)

4. 某租赁有限公司从事国内租赁业务。该公司委托广州某对外贸易公司从日本进口50台水泥搅拌车，用于租借给国内的建筑公司。由广州某对外贸易公司对外订货，向海关办理进口报关手续时，该批用于租赁货物的贸易方式应填报为“一般贸易”。(　　)

5. 报关单上“商品名称、规格型号”栏，正确的填写内容应有中文商品名称、规格型号，商品的英文名称和品牌，缺一不可。(　　)

6. 某外贸公司与境外贸易商以 FOB 价、即期信用证方式结算订立出口棉麻衬衣的一般贸易出口合同，按规定申报时应填写一式四联报关单，分别是海关留存联、海关统计联、企业留存联、出口退税专用联。(　　)

7. 北京煤炭进出口总公司对巴基斯坦签约出口“水洗炼焦煤”10万吨，由唐山煤炭分公司执行合同，组织货源，并安排出口。在这一情况下报关单“经营单位”栏应填报为“北京煤炭进出口总公司”，11091×××××为北京煤炭进出口总公司的编号。(　　)

8. 经海关批准，从保税仓库内提取一批货物在国际市场上销售，由于该批货物原进入保税仓库时是空运进口的，故该货出仓库时在报关单上“运输方式”栏应填报“航空运输”。(　　)

9. 一批精密仪表在大连机场海关申报出口并转关运输至北京出境，其出口报关单“出口口岸”栏应按实际申请海关所在地填为“大连机场”。(　　)

10. 某仪器出口公司从日本购得分属三个合同的同样规格、不同数量的精密仪器，并同一船同时运达。这些货物品种单一且数量不大，申报时可用一份进口货物报关单，准确、真实、齐全地向海关填报。(　　)

四、单据填制

(一) 单据填制一

根据以下资料填制进口货物报关单。

北京水晶电子进出口公司经北京市机电办批准（批文号码为京机批第00256号），与美国一家公司签订了购买一台400千瓦日本产直流发电机的合同（合同号码为97－Y1－1002），成交价为CIF3 000美元，标记唛码为Y1－1002/BJ，于1997年6月10日装“大东丸”船由东京抵天津新港（0202），提单号为CB－1647，由一个木箱包装，包装重量1 500千克，电机自重1 400千克，经办理转关运输手续后该公司于6月15日向北京海关办理进出口报关手续。

随附单证：发票、装箱单、提单、商检证

总运费：600美元

经营单位代码：1101910077

商品编码：85013300

中华人民共和国海关进口货物报关单

预录入编号：002102133　　　　海关编号：

进口口岸	备案号 ×××	进口日期	申报日期
经营单位	运输方式	运输工具名称	提运单号
收货单位	贸易方式	征免性质 一般征税	征税比例
许可证号	起运国（地区）	装货港	境内目的地

批准文号 0108759	成交方式	运费	保费 502/50/3	杂费 ×××
合同协议号	件数	包装种类	毛重（千克）	净重（千克）

集装箱号 ×××	随附单据	用途 外贸自营内销

标记唛码及备注

项号	商品编码	商品名称、规格型号	数量及单位	原产国（地区）	单价	总价	币制	征免

税费征收情况
×××

录入员　　录入单位	兹声明以上申报无讹并承担法律责任	海关审单批注及放行日期（签章）
报关员 ××× 单位地址 ××× 邮编×××　电话×××	申报单位（签章） 填制日期	审单　　审价 征税　　统计 查验　　放行

（二）单据填制二

下面是一份出口货物报关单，有些项目没有填写，请根据所提供的原始单证，将没有填写的项目按海关规定在报关单上补充填制完整。

RONGHUA TRADE DEVELOPMENT CO., LTD.

厦门荣华贸易发展公司
中国厦门

INVOICE

L/C NO.: 212948

INVOICE NO.: SF732B1397/12　　DATE: DEC. 10, 2003

MESSRS.: J. Y. CONSULTANT CO., LTD.

S/C No.: 03RH88704　ADDRESS: 1-7-20 OTEMON CHUO—FUKUOKA, JAPAN

PER S. S.: SU YUE V. 9801　　DATE OF DEPARTURE: DEC. 30, 2003

FROM SHANGHAI　TO MOJI

MARK	PACKAGE	DESCRIPTION	QUANTITY	UNIT PRICE	AMOUNT
				(USD/KG)	(USD)
N/M	900 CTNS	鲜冬笋 WINTER BAMBOO SHOOTS HS CODE 07099010	9,000KGS 计量单位：千克	1.40	CFR 12,600.00
	3,592 CTNS	鲜香菇 FRESH MUSHROOM HS CODE 07095190	17,960KGS 计量单位：千克	1.80	32,328.00
		外汇核销单编号：35/0591540 经营单位海关注册编号：3502110278 发货单位与经营单位相同 预录入编号：587112114 随附：商检证、动植物检疫证			F: USD 2,250.00

G. W. 29,656KGS

N. W. 26,960KGS

B/L NO.: CSLMJ180180

CONTAINER NO.: CCLU 8505004 (40')

2003 年 12 月 28 日由上海航联报关公司向上海浦江海关（2202）申报，当月 30 日装运出口。

中华人民共和国海关出口货物报关单

预录入编号：　　　　　　　　　海关编号：

<table>
<tr><td colspan="4">出口口岸</td><td colspan="2">备案号
×××</td><td colspan="2">出口日期</td><td colspan="2">申报日期</td></tr>
<tr><td colspan="4">经营单位</td><td colspan="1">运输方式</td><td colspan="3">运输工具名称</td><td colspan="2">提运单号</td></tr>
<tr><td colspan="4">发货单位</td><td colspan="2">贸易方式</td><td colspan="2">征免性质</td><td colspan="2">结汇方式</td></tr>
<tr><td colspan="4">许可证号
×××</td><td colspan="2">运抵国(地区)</td><td colspan="2">指运港</td><td colspan="2">境内货源地
厦门特区</td></tr>
<tr><td colspan="3">批准文号</td><td colspan="1">成交方式</td><td colspan="2">运费
502/5300/3</td><td colspan="2">保费
×××</td><td colspan="2">杂费
×××</td></tr>
<tr><td colspan="3">合同协议号</td><td colspan="1">件数</td><td colspan="2">包装种类</td><td colspan="2">毛重(千克)</td><td colspan="2">净重(千克)</td></tr>
<tr><td colspan="3">集装箱号</td><td colspan="4">随附单据
B. C.</td><td colspan="3">生产厂家
厦门荣华贸易发展公司</td></tr>
<tr><td colspan="10">标记唛码及备注</td></tr>
</table>

项号	商品编码	商品名称、规格型号	数量及单位	最终目的国	单价	总价	币制	征免

<table>
<tr><td colspan="3">税费征收情况</td></tr>
<tr><td>录入员　　录入单位</td><td rowspan="2">兹声明以上申报无讹并承担法律责任

申报单位(签章)

填制日期</td><td>海关审单批注及放行日期(签章)
审单　　审价</td></tr>
<tr><td>报关员
×××
单位地址
×××
邮编×××　电话×××</td><td>征税　　统计

查验　　放行</td></tr>
</table>

第六章
出口收汇核销单

一、单项选择题

1. 出口收汇核销单由(　　)制发。

A. 中国银行　　B. 中国人民银行

C. 国家外汇管理局　　D. 海关

2. 有出口收汇的单位，应到当地外汇管理部门领取外汇管理部门加盖(　　)印章的核销单。

A. 外汇管理　　B. 已核销

C. 验讫章　　D. 监督收汇章

3. 远期出口项下，企业应当在合同规定收汇日起(　　)内到外汇管理局办理核销手续。

A. 10 天　　B. 20 天

C. 30 天　　D. 40 天

4. 国家外汇管理局和海关总署联合开发了电子口岸“出口收汇系统”于(　　)起在全国范围内试行。

A. 2000 年 1 月 1 日　　B. 2001 年 1 月 1 日

C. 2000 年 6 月 1 日　　D. 2001 年 6 月 1 日

5. 即期出口项下，出口单位办理报关后，应当自报关之日起(　　)内，凭核销单及加盖海关“验讫章”的出口报关单等到外汇管理局办理核销手续。

A. 60 天　　B. 30 天

C. 100 天　　D. 90 天

6. 出口单位应当在收到外汇之日起(　　)内凭核销单、银行出具的“出口收汇核销专用联”到外汇管理局办理出口收汇核销。

A. 60 天　　B. 30 天

C. 15 天　　D. 90 天

7. 出口收汇率为 70%（含 70%）至 95% 之间的，评为(　　)。

A. 出口收汇荣誉企业　　B. 出口收汇达标企业

C. 出口收汇风险企业　　D. 出口收汇高风险企业

8. 来料加工项下的出口收汇核销是按照(　　)办理出口收汇核销的。

A. 货物总值　　B. 料件值

C. 工缴费　　D. 外汇局规定的货物总值的百分比

9. 进口单位在外汇指定银行办理付汇手续后，应当将退回的核销单留存联与其他付汇单证一并留存(　　)备查。

A. 3 年　　B. 4 年

C. 5 年　　D. 6 年

10. “口岸电子执法系统”于(　　)起在全国正式运行。

A. 2001 年 6 月 1 日　　B. 2001 年 1 月 1 日

C. 2001 年 9 月 1 日　　D. 2001 年 8 月 1 日

二、多项选择题

1. 进行网上核销后，核销员需将(　　)送交外汇管理部门办理核销手续。

A. 已报关的核销单　　B. 报关单的核销联

C. 银行结汇水单　　D. 出口发票

2. 下列贸易方式无须凭核销单办理报关的是(　　)。

A. 易货贸易　　B. 广告品

C. 援外项目物资　　D. 暂时出口货物

3. 核销单领取后应(　　)，才能办理报关手续。

A. 加盖公章　　B. 进行网上备案

C. 法人代表签名　　D. 加盖报关章

4. 出口收汇核销的单位通常是(　　)。

A. 生产企业　　B. 银行

C. 外商投资企业　　D. 外贸公司

5. 出口单位有(　　)行为的，由外汇管理局给予警告、通报批评、没收违法所得，并处以 5 万元以上 30 万元以下的罚款。

A. 借用、冒用、转让或者买卖核销单的

B. 虚报核销单丢失的

C. 从领单之日起 4 个月内未向外汇管理局送交核销单存根的

D. 重复使用银行出具的出口收汇核销专用联的

三、判断题

1. 货物出口后，无论是哪种方式出口，都必须持海关签章后的核销单、报关单及其他有关单证送银行办理收汇手续。(　　)

2. 某茶叶进出口公司因出货报关急需，向轻工业品进出口公司借了一份核销单向海关申报。(　　)

3. 某企业申领到新版核销单后，无须备案即可到海关报关出口。(　　)

4. 货物出口后，企业应及时将海关签章的核销单、报关单以及银行出具的结汇水单等资料送到外汇管理局办理核销手续。(　　)

5. 核销单遗失后，应当立即自行网上挂失或向外汇管理局申请挂失。(　　)

6. 有进出口经营权的企业如果需要核销单报关出口，无须办理网上申领，即可直接

到外汇管理局申领核销单。( )

7. 代理出口项下的核销手续，应当由委托方领取核销单、办理出口报关及出口收汇核销手续。( )

8. 出口单位遗失报关单的，应当凭银行签发的未核销证明，向海关申请补办。( )

9. 出口单位遗失出口收汇核销专用联的，应当先向外汇管理局提出申请补办，然后凭外汇管理局签发的出口收汇核销专用联补办批准件，到银行补办出口收汇核销专用联。( )

10. 出口收汇考核分为季度考核和年度考核，是指对企业的交单率进行考核。( )

四、案例分析

2004 年 3 月 5 日，达成家具厂有一批家具需出口到迪拜，但该厂没有进出口权，不能向外汇管理局申领核销单，因此向联兴进出口公司买了一份核销单报关出口，货物出口后联兴进出口公司一直对该核销单未能按时收汇核销。请问此例属于什么现象？联兴进出口公司卖出核销单的做法对吗？应如何处理？

五、单据填制

2002 年 4 月 20 日，HT 进出口公司（法人代码：19034346 – 8）与香港资信有限公司通过友好协商，就出口普洱茶事宜在惠州签订了一份出口合同。2002 年 5 月 27 日，HT 进出口公司备好了货物，到惠州海关办理报关出口手续。货物具体情况如下：普洱茶 6 000千克，共 120 箱，用纸箱包装，毛重 6 060 千克，价格为 FOB 深圳每千克 USD1. 22，采用即期 D/P 方式支付。报关单打印出来后的编号为：5162545658。请按照上述资料填写一份核销单。

出口收汇核销单

存根

（粤）编号: 44G288190

出口单位:
单位代码:
出口币种总价:
收汇方式:
预计收款日期:
报关日期:
备注:
此单报关有效期截止到

未经核销此联不得撕开

（出口单位盖章）

出口收汇核销单

（粤）编号:44G288190

出口单位:			
单位代码:			
银行签注栏	类别	币种金额	日期　盖章
海关签注栏:			
外汇局签注栏: 年　月　日（盖章）			

（出口单位盖章）

（海关盖章）

出口收汇核销单

出口退税专用

（粤）编号:44G288190

出口单位:		
单位代码:		
货物名称	数量	币种总价
报关单编号:		
外汇局签注栏: 年　月　日（盖章）		

第七章
出口企业退税及有关单证

一、单项选择题

1. 一般情况下，出口企业应在出口后(　　)内向主管出口退税的税务机关提供“出口收汇已核销证明”。

A. 3 个月　　B. 6 个月

C. 9 个月　　D. 10 个月

2. 对于要求补办出口退税专用联的，在办理出口核销手续后，出口单位应当凭税务部门签发的与该核销单对应的出口未退税证明，向(　　)书面申请办理“出口收汇核销单退税联补办证明”。

A. 外汇管理局　　B. 结汇银行

C. 税务局　　D. 海关

3. 出口申请退税单位在会计核算上作出销售处理后，(　　)向外经贸部门填报“出口货物退（免）税申报表”。

A. 按单　　B. 按月

C. 按年　　D. 可随时

4. 凡经营出口产品的企业，均应填具(　　)，报经所在地主管出口退税的税务机关审核后批准执行。

A. 出口货物报关单　　B. 出口产品退税鉴定表

C. 出口货物退（免）税申报表　　D. 出口收汇已核销证明

5. 凡属于工业企业直接出口或委托代理出口的出口发票，应审核产品的(　　)，确定退税的计税依据。

A. FOB 价　　B. CIF 价

C. CFR 价　　D. FCA 价

二、多项选择题

1. 以下不能申请退税的是(　　)。

A. 来料加工厂出口一批服装　　B. 易货贸易下出口一批小麦

C. 捐赠一批速食面给泰国　　D. 没有出口经营权的某企业出口一批货物

2. 外贸公司向当地税务局申请退税，应提供的证明资料有(　　)。

A. 盖有海关验讫章的出口货物报关单

B. 出口销售发票

C. 进货发票

D. 银行结汇水单

3. 属于生产企业直接出口的自制产品，凡以CIF价结算的，除了两单两票外，还需提供(　　)。

A. 银行结汇水单　　B. 代理出口协议书

C. 出口货物货运单　　D. 出口保险单

三、判断题

1. 红星食品厂生产一批食品，并直接出口，则该商品出口前应缴纳增值税和消费税，并在出口后集齐所有单据向税务部门申请退税。(　　)

2. 办理出口退税时，须提供的两单两票是指出口货物报关单出口退税专用联、出口结汇水单、出口发票、出口产品增值税发票。(　　)

3. 报关单位如需申请退税的，应增填一份“出口货物报关单”，并在右上角盖上“申请出口产品退税专用联”。(　　)

4. 凡属于转关出口产品要求退税的，可在出境地海关办理出口手续后，直接在“出口货物报关单”上批注，以便办理退税。(　　)

5. 当企业将不同税率的出口产品放在一起核算时，由企业将不同的产品按适用的税目、税率计算，划分不清的，退税税率一律按从高的原则办理。(　　)

6. 根据《国家税务总局关于出口货物退（免）税管理有关问题的通知》规定：出口企业应在货物报关出口之日起90日内，向退税部门申报办理出口货物退（免）税手续。(　　)

第八章 信用证申请书

一、中英文术语、短语互译

（一）中译英

（1）议付__________

（2）延期付款__________

（3）开证人__________

（4）受益人__________

（5）转运__________

（6）分运__________

（7）空运单__________

（8）账号__________

（9）通知行__________

（10）到期日__________

（二）英译中

（1）Airmail __________

（2）Acceptance __________

（3）Sight Payment __________

（4）Price Term __________

（5）Tolerance of Amount __________

（6）Latest Date of Shipment __________

（7）Express Delivery __________

（8）Banking Charges __________

（9）For Beneficiary's Account __________

（10）Transacted By __________

二、单项选择题

1. 若在信用证申请书中的金额前加上 about、approximately、circa 等词语，根据《UCP600》，允许有（　　）的金额增减幅度。

A. 3%　　B. 5%

C. 10%　　D. 15%

2. 若规定货物装船后 30 天内付款，则在信用证申请书中汇票的付款期限应填为(　　)。

A. AT 30 DAYS SIGHT　　B. AT 30 DAYS AFTER B/L DATE

C. AT 30 DAYS FROM INVOICE DATE　　D. AT * * * SIGHT

3. 若信用证的申请书中，要求到期日为 5 月 30 日，但未规定在装运日后必须交单的期限。则当受益人 5 月 8 日取得提单后，其最迟应于(　　)前向银行交单。

A. 5 月 9 日　　B. 5 月 23 日

C. 5 月 29 日　　D. 5 月 30 日

4. 开证时要注意(　　)一致。

A. 证同　　B. 单证

C. 单单　　D. 证货

5. 在信用证申请书中汇票的付款人应填为(　　)。

A. 开证人　　B. 开证行或指定付款行

C. 通知行　　D. 受益人

6. 某公司从英国的纽卡斯尔进口一批货物到广州，则申请书中的 LOADING ON BOARD FROM 后应填为(　　)。

A. GUANGZHOU　　B. ENGLAND

C. NEWCASTLE　　D. NEWCASTLE ENGLAND

7. 下列说法不正确的是(　　)。

A. 开立信用证时，进口人应向银行交付保证金

B. 开证行根据合同开立信用证

C. 开证后，银行的权利和义务只限于信用证的规定，只对信用证负责

D. 开证后，银行的权利和义务还要受到合同的约束

8. 下列关于信用证修改的说法错误的是(　　)。

A. 修改应由开证人办理

B. 经开证行、受益人同意，才能生效

C. 受益人可对一份修改通知书中的内容有选择地接受

D. 原证的条款，在受益人向通知行发出接受修改前仍对受益人有效

三、多项选择题

1. 若在信用证申请书中无明确规定，根据《UCP600》的规定，应视为允许的有(　　)。

A. 分运　　B. 转运

C. 接受第三者装运单据　　D. 可撤销信用证

2. 信用证申请书上常见的付款方式有(　　)。

A. 即期支付　　B. 承兑支付

C. 议付　　D. 延期支付

3. 申请开立信用证的具体手续有(　　)。

A. 递交有关合同的副本及附件　　B. 填写开证申请书

C. 缴付保证金　　D. 递交发票

4. 信用证申请书中，下列(　　)不是由开证人填写。

A. 开证日　　B. 到期日

C. L/C 号码　　D. 通知行

5. 如使用(　　)术语时，应在信用证申请书中的保单条款前的括号中打“×”。

A. CIF　　B. FOB

C. CFR　　D. CIP

四、判断题

1. 信用证申请书已印好常见单据要求，如不需要某些单据，则在其前面的括号中打“×”。(　　)

2. 若合同中有装运期的起止日期，则最迟必须让卖方在装运期的最后一天就能收到信用证。(　　)

3. 合同中规定要在信用证上明确条款，如内容较多，可使用“参阅第×××号合同”或“第×××号合同项下货物”等条款，或将有关合同作为信用证附件附在信用证后。(　　)

4. 进口人对卖方的要求，在申请开证时，应按合同有关规定转化成有关单据，具体规定在信用证中。(　　)

5. 如在信用证申请书中采用延期付款方式，则卖方一般将使货价比采用承兑支付方式高。(　　)

6. 一般情况下，为避免风险，买卖双方都不应轻易接受“提交 2/3 套的正本提单，另一份正本提单径寄给买方”。(　　)

7. 如合同规定该笔货款由信用证和托收两种方式各付 50%，则应在信用证申请书中“汇票金额”中填写“50% of invoice value”。(　　)

8. 如在信用证申请书中没注明是否允许转让，则开证行将视为申请可转让的信用证。(　　)

9. 如要求受益人提交两份正本发票，可在发票条款份数中注明“DUPLICATE”。(　　)

10. 在信用证申请书的装运期中，开证人可通过使用诸如“迅速”、“立即”、“尽快”之类的词语，促使受益人尽快完成装运。(　　)

五、单据填制

（一）单据填制一

请根据以下材料填制信用证申请书（申请开证时间为1998年4月26日）。

售 货 合 同
SALES CONTRACT

卖　方：

Sellers：ABC CORP.　　Contract No.：98SGQ468001

Date：APR. 22，1998

地址：　　Signed at：GUANGZHOU

Address：AKEDSANTERINK AUTO P. O. BOX. 9，FINLAND　　Telex：0835

Fax：83556688

Buyers：GUANGDONG LIGHT ELECTRICAL APPLIANCES CO.，LTD.

Address：52，DEZHENG ROAD SOUTH，GUANGZHOU，CHINA.　　Telex：

Fax：

This Sales Contract is made by and between the Sellers and the Buyers，whereby the sellers agree to sell and the Buyers agree to buy the under-mentioned goods according to the terms and conditions stipulated below：

（1）货号、品名及规格 Name of Commodity and Specifications	（2）数量 Quantity	（3）单位 Unit	（4）单价 Unit Price	（5）金额 Amount
HALOGEN FITTING W500	9，600PCS	PC	CIF GUANGZHOU USD3. 80/PC	USD36，480. 00
5% more or less both in amount and quantity allowed		Total Amount		USD 36，480. 00

（6）Packing：30PCS/CARTON　　（7）Delivery from HELSINKI to GUANGZHOU

（8）Time of Shipment：Within 30 days after receipt of L/C，allowing transshipment and partial shipment.

（9）Terms of Payment：By irrevocable Letter of Credit in favor of the Sellers to be available by sight draft to be opened and to reach FINLAND before MAY 15，1998and to remain valid for negotiation in FINLAND until the 15th days after the foresaid Time of Shipment.
L/C must mention this contract number. All banking Charges outside China（the mainland of China）are for account of the Beneficiary.

（10）Insurance：To be effected by Sellers for 110% of full invoice value covering F. P. A. up to GUANGZHOU
~~To effected by buyers~~

（11）Arbitration：All dispute arising from the execution of or in connection with this contract shall be settled admittedly by negotiation. In case of settlement can be reached through negotiation the case shall then be submitted to China International Economic & Trade Arbitration Commision. In Shenzhen（or in Beijing）for arbitration in act with its sure of procedures. The arbitral award is final and binding upon both parties.

The Seller ABC CORP.　　The Buyer GUANGDONG LIGHT ELECTRICAL APPLIANCES CO.，LTD.

IRREVOCABLE DOCUMENTARY CREDIT APPLICATION

TO:　　　　　　　　　　　　　　　　　　　　**Date:**

Beneficiary (full name and address)

L/C NO.
Ex-Card No.
Contract No.

Date and place of expiry of the credit

Partial shipments
☐ allowed ☐ not allowed

Transshipment
☐ allowed ☐ not allowed

☐ Issue by airmail　☐ With brief advice by teletransmission
☐ Issue by express delivery
☐ Issue by teletransmission (which shall be the operative instrument)

Loading on board/ dispatch/ taking in charge at/ from

not later than
for transportation to

Amount (both in figures and words)

Description of goods:

Packing:

Credit available with
☐ by sight payment　☐ by acceptance　☐ by negotiation
☐ by deferred payment at
against the documents detailed herein
☐ and beneficiary's draft for　　% of the invoice value
at
on

☐ FOB　☐ C&F　☐ CIF
☐ or other terms

Documents required: (marked with ×)

1. (　) Signed Commercial Invoice in　　copies indicating L/C No. and Contract No.
2. (　) Full set of clean on board ocean Bills of Lading made out to order and blank endorsed, marked "freight[ ] to collect/[ ] prepaid[ ] showing freight amount" notifying applicant.
3. (　) Air Waybills showing "freight[ ] to collect/[ ] prepaid[ ] indicating freight amount" and consigned to
4. (　) Memorandum issued by　　　　consigned to
5. (　) Insurance Policy/Certificate in　　copies for　　% of the invoice value showing claims payable in China in currency of the draft, blank endorsed, covering([ ] Ocean Marine Transportation /[ ] Air Transportation/ [ ] Over Land Transportation) All Risks, War Risks.
6. (　) Packing List/ Weight Memo in　　copies issued by quantity/ gross and net weights of each package and packing conditions as called for by the L/C.
7. (　) Certificate of Quantity /Weight in　copies issued by an independent surveyor at the loading port, indicating the actual surveyed quantity/ weight of shipped goods as well as the packing condition.
8. (　) Certificate of Quantity in　　copies issued by [ ] manufacturer /[ ] public recognized surveyor /[ ]
9. (　) Beneficiary's certified copy of cable/ telex dispatched to the accountee within　　hours after shipment advising[ ] name of vessel/[ ] flight No. /[ ] wagon No., date, quantity, weight and value of shipment.
10. (　) Beneficiary's Certificate certifying that extra copies of the documents have been dispatched according to the contract terms.
11. (　) Shipping Co.'s Certificate attesting that the carrying vessel is chartered or booked by accountee or their shipping agents.
12. (　) Other documents, if any:

Additional instructions:

1. (　) All banking charges outside the opening bank are for beneficiary's account.
2. (　) Documents must be presented within　　days after the date of issuance of the transport documents but within the validity of this credit.
3. (　) Third party as shipper is not acceptable. Short Form/ Blank Back B/L is not acceptable.
4. (　) Both quantity and amount　　% more or less are allowed.
5. (　) Prepaid freight drawn in excess of L/C amount is acceptable against presentation of original charges voucher issued by shipping Co. / Air Line/ or it's agent.
6. (　) All documents to be forwarded in one cover, unless otherwise stated above.
7. (　) Other terms, if any:

Account No.:　　　　with ________________ (name of bank)

Transacted by:　　　　(Applicant: name, signature of authorized person)

Telephone No.:　　　　(with seal)

(二)单据填制二

请根据以下材料填制信用证申请书(申请开证时间为2001年3月1日)。

售　货　合　同

SALES CONTRACT

卖　方:
Sellers: ABC CORPORATION

Contract No.: 2001－107
Date: JAN. 5, 2001

地址:
Address: OSAKA, JAPAN OSACY SECTION.

Signed at: SHANGHAI
Telex: 0835
Fax: 83556688

买　方:
Buyers: SHANGHAI TEXTILES IMP. AND EXP. CORP.
Address: 27 ZHONGSHAN ROAD, SHANGHAI, CHINA.

Telex: 44371
Fax: (020)82673475

WE HEREBY THE SELLERS AGREE TO SELL AND THE BUYERS TO BUY THE COMMODITY/IES MENTIONED IN THIS CONTRACT SUBJECT TO THE TERMS AND CONDITIONS STIPULATED AS FOLLOWS:

NAME OF COMMODITY & SPECIFICATION, PACKING AND SHIPPING MARK	QUANTITY (PCS.)	UNIT PRICE	AMOUNT
100% PURE COTTON TOWEL		CIF SHANGHAI	
ART. NO. 49394 (014428)	3,000	USD1.00	USD3,000.00
ART. NO. 49393 (014428)	3,000	USD1.00	USD3,000.00
ART. NO. 55306 (014429)	2,000	USD1.25	USD2,500.00
REMARKS: 1) EACH IN PLASTIC BAGS, 10 BAGS TO A CARTON TOTAL 800 CARTONS 2) SHIPPING MARK: ITOCHU SHANGHAI NO. 1－800		TOTAL:	USD8,500.00
TOTAL VALUE: SAY US DOLLARS EIGHT THOUSAND FIVE HUNDRED ONLY.			

TIME OF SHIPMENT: Within 45 days of receipt of letter of credit and not later than the month of MAY 2001 with partial shipments and transshipment allowed.

PORT OF LOADING: OSAKA JAPAN

PORT OF DESTINATION: SHANGHAI

TERMS OF PAYMENT: By 100% Irrevocable Sight Letter of Credit Opened by the Buyer to reach the Seller not later than APRIL 15th, 2001 and to be available for negotiation in JAPAN until the 15th day after the date of shipment. In case of late arrival of the L/C, the Seller shall not be liable for any delay in shipment and shall have the right to rescind the contract and /or claim for damages.

INSURANCE: To be effected by the Seller for 110% of the CIF invoice value covering ALL RISKS AND WAR RISK only as per China Insurance Clauses.

TERMS OF SHIPMENT: To be governed by "INCOTERMS 2000". For transactions concluded on CFR or CIF terms, all surcharges including port congestion surcharges, etc. levied by the shipping company, in addition to freight, shall be for the Buyer's account.

The Buyer
SHANGHAI TEXTILES IMP.
AND EXP. CORPORATION
(签名)

The Seller
ABC CORPORATION
(签名)

IRREVOCABLE DOCUMENTARY CREDIT APPLICATION

TO: Date:

<table>
<tr><td colspan="2">Beneficiary(full name and address)</td><td>L/C NO.
Ex-Card No.
Contract No.</td></tr>
<tr><td colspan="2"></td><td>Date and place of expiry of the credit</td></tr>
<tr><td>Partial shipments
□ allowed □ not allowed</td><td>Transshipment
□ allowed □ not allowed</td><td rowspan="2">□ Issue by airmail □ With brief advice by teletransmission
□ Issue by express delivery
□ Issue by teletransmission(which shall be the operative instrument)</td></tr>
<tr><td colspan="2" rowspan="2">Loading on board/ dispatch/ taking in charge at/ from

not later than
for transportation to</td></tr>
<tr><td>Amount (both in figures and words)</td></tr>
<tr><td colspan="2" rowspan="2">Description of goods:

Packing:</td><td>Credit available with
□ by sight payment □ by acceptance □ by negotiation
□ by deferred payment at
against the documents detailed herein
□ and beneficiary's draft for % of the invoice value
at
on</td></tr>
<tr><td>□ FOB □ C&F □ CIF
□or other terms</td></tr>
</table>

Documents required:(marked with ×)

1. ( ) Signed Commercial Invoice in copies indicating L/C No. and Contract No.
2. ( ) Full set of clean on board ocean Bills of Lading made out to order and blank endorsed, marked "freight[ ]to collect/[ ]prepaid[ ]showing freight amount" notifying applicant.
3. ( ) Air Waybills showing "freight[ ]to collect/[ ]prepaid[ ]indicating freight amount" and consigned to
4. ( ) Memorandum issued by consigned to
5. ( ) Insurance Policy/Certificate in copies for % of the invoice value showing claims payable in China in currency of the draft, blank endorsed, covering([ ]Ocean Marine Transportation /[ ]Air Transportation/ [ ]Over Land Transportation) All Risks, War Risks.
6. ( ) Packing List/ Weight Memo in copies issued by quantity/ gross and net weights of each package and packing conditions as called for by the L/C.
7. ( ) Certificate of Quantity /Weight in copies issued by an independent surveyor at the loading port, indicating the actual surveyed quantity/ weight of shipped goods as well as the packing condition.
8. ( ) Certificate of Quantity in copies issued by [ ] manufacturer /[ ]public recognized surveyor /[ ]
9. ( ) Beneficiary's certified copy of cable/ telex dispatched to the accountee within hours after shipment advising[ ]name of vessel/[ ]flight No. /[ ]wagon No. , date, quantity, weight and value of shipment.
10. ( ) Beneficiary's Certificate certifying that extra copies of the documents have been dispatched according to the contract terms.
11. ( ) Shipping Co. 's Certificate attesting that the carrying vessel is chartered or booked by accountee or their shipping agents.
12. ( ) Other documents, if any:

Additional instructions:

1. ( ) All banking charges outside the opening bank are for beneficiary's account.
2. ( ) Documents must be presented within days after the date of issuance of the transport documents but within the validity of this credit.
3. ( ) Third party as shipper is not acceptable. Short Form/ Blank Back B/L is not acceptable.
4. ( ) Both quantity and amount % more or less are allowed.
5. ( ) Prepaid freight drawn in excess of L/C amount is acceptable against presentation of original charges voucher issued by shipping Co. / Air Line/ or it's agent.
6. ( ) All documents to be forwarded in one cover, unless otherwise stated above.
7. ( ) Other terms, if any:

Account No. : with ______________________ (name of bank)

Transacted by: (Applicant: name, signature of authorized person)

Telephone No. : (with seal)

第九章
综合制单练习

按下列信用证的要求和给定的资料填制各套结汇单据。

综合制单练习一

Output Message Type : ISSUE OF A DOCUMENTARY CREDIT
Sent by : HNBNKRSEA ××× HANA BANK, SEOUL
Output Date/Time : 050106/1617
Priority : NORMAL
HUR : 050106DJOS00179

---

27 : Sequence of Total
1/1

40A : Form of Documentary Credit
IRREVOCABLE

20 : Documentary Credit Number
M12CL601ES00032

31C : Date of Issue
050105 05-JAN-2005

31D : Date and Place of Expiry
050215 AT YOUR COUNTRY 15-FEB-2005

50 : Applicant
STORY SHARP CO., LTD.
NO. 502 GL PLAZA, 713-1
HEANGSHIN-DONG, DUCKYANG-GU,
GOYANG-SI, GYEONGGI-DO, KOREA

59 : Beneficiary—Name & Address
GUANGDONG FOREIGN TRADE IMP. & EXP. CORP.
15-18/F., GUANGDONG FOREIGN ECONOMIC AND
TRADE BUILDING 351 TIANHE ROAD
GUANGZHOU, CHINA

32B : Currency Code, Amount
USD43, 200.00 US DOLLAR 43, 200.00

39A : Percentage Credit Amt Tolerance
10/10

41D : Available With... By... —Name & Addr.

ANY BANK BY NEGOTIATION

42C : Drafts at...

BENEFICIARY DRAFTS AT SIGHT

FOR 100 PCT OF THE INVOICE VALUE

42A : Drawee-BIC

HNBNCNSH × × ×   HANA BANK SHANGHAI BRANCH

SHANGHAI

43P : Partial Shipments

ALLOWED

43T : Transshipment

ALLOWED

44A : On Board/Disp/Taking Charge at/F

HONGKONG

44B : For Transportation to...

BUSAN, KOREA

44C : Latest Date of Shipment

050130   30-JAN-2005

45A : Description of Goods &/or Services

ORIGIN CHINA

FOB HONGKONG

80G COLOUR PAPER LENGTH: 9,500M   30MT @ USD1,440.00

WIDTH: 1,000MM

INSIDE ROLL DIA.: 75MM

OUTSIDE ROLL DIA.: 100CM-120CM

46A : Documents Required

1) FULL SET OF CLEAN ON BOARD OCEAN BILLS OF LADING MADE OUT TO THE ORDER OF HANA BANK, SEOUL MARKED FREIGHT COLLECT AND NOTIFY ACCOUNTEE

2) SIGNED COMMERCIAL INVOICE IN THREE FOLDS

3) PACKING LIST IN THREE FOLDS

4) INSPECTION CERTIFICATE ISSUED BY STORY SHARP CO., LTD. STATING THE GOODS ARE COMPLETELY CONFORM TO THE BENEFICIARY'S ORDER

47A : Additional Conditions

+CONFIRMATION CHGS, IF ANY, ARE FOR ACCOUNT OF BENEFICIARY.

+10PCT MORE OR LESS IN Q'TY AND AMOUNT ALLOWED.

+EXCEPT SO FAR AS OTHERWISE EXPRESSLY STIPULATED HEREIN, ALL DOCUMENTS SHOULD BE INDICATED L/C NUMBER AND MUST BE FORWARDED DIRECTLY TO US IN ONE LOT BY COURIER SERVICES.

+ADDRESS OF THE ISSUING BANK

9-10, EULJIRD, 2-KA, JUNG-GU, SEOUL, KOREA

ZIP CODE: 100-720

ATTN: INTERNATIONAL BUSINESS OPERATION CENTER

71B : Charges

+ALL BANKING CHARGES OUTSIDE KOREA AND REMITTANCE CHARGES

ARE FOR ACCOUNT OF BENEFICIARY.

48 : Period for Presentation
DOCUMENTS MUST BE PRESENTED WITHIN 10 DAYS AFTER THE DATE OF SHIPMENT BUT WITHIN EXPIRY DATE

49 : Confirmation Instructions
CONFIRM

53A : Reimbursing Bank – BIC
HANA BANK SHANGHAI BRANCH
SHANGHAI

78 : Instr to Payg/Accptg/Negotg Bank
BENEFICIARY DRAFT SHOULD BE FORWARED TO DRAWEE BANK.
+IF DOCUMENTS ARE PRESENTED WITH DISCREPANCIES, A DISCREPANCY FEE OF USD60.00 (JPY7,000.00 OR EUR60.00) OR EQUIVALENT SHOULD BE DEDUCTED TO BENEFICIARY.
+THE NEGOTIATING BANK/PRESENTING BANK MUST SENT AN ADDITIONAL SET OF EACH DOCUMENT TO US FOR OUT FILES ALONG WITH THE ORIGINAL DOCUMENTS. IF NOT, USD10.00 WILL BE DEDUCTED FROM PAYMENT.

57D : "Advise Through" Bank—Name & Addr.
DONGSHAN SUB-BRANCH

72 : Sender to Receiver Information
+U.C.P. (1993 REVISION) I.C.C. PUBLICATION NO. 500

此证分两批装运，销货合同号码为：CPU04SC140。

第一批制单资料：

发票号：CPU04SC140A	发票日期：JAN. 18, 2005
提单号：50100289BUS	提单日期：JAN. 21, 2005
船名：KMTC ULSAN V. 501N	装船标记：N/M
集装箱号：KMTU7045319/846421/20'	
商品数量：14.188MTS	合计：21 ROLLS
毛重：14.188MTS	净重：14.188MTS
尺码：1 000×1 050 (MM) /ROLL	总尺码：19.950 CBMS

第二批制单资料：

发票号：CPU04SC140B	发票日期：JAN. 21, 2005
提单号：50200389BUS	提单日期：JAN. 28, 2005
船名：HONG KONG STAR V. 036N	装船标记：N/M
集装箱号：KMTU7311070/846360/20'	
商品数量：14.227MTS	合计：23 ROLLS
毛重：14.227MTS	净重：14.227MTS
尺码：1 000×936 (MM) /ROLL	总尺码：21.528CBMS

第一次装运全套单据

F14

1

凭
Drawn under ______________________________

信用证 第 号
L/C No. ______________________________

日期 年 月 日
dated ______________________________

按 息 付 款
Payable with interest @ ____________ %per annum

号码 汇票金额 中国 广州 年 月 日
No. ____________ **Exchange** for Guangzhou,China ________ 20 ________

见票 日 后（本 汇 票 之 副 本 未 付）付
At ____________ sight of this **FIRST** of Exchange (Second of exchange being unpaid)

pay to the order of ______________________________ 或其指定人

金 额
the sum of

此致
To: ______________________________

____

广东省对外贸易进出口公司

Guangdong Foreign Trade Imp. & Exp. Corp.

15 – 18/F., Guangdong Foreign Economic and Trade Building

351 Tianhe Road, Guangzhou, China

商业发票

COMMERCIAL INVOICE

Messrs.:

INVOICE NO. :
INVOICE DATE :
L/C NO. :
L/C DATE :
S/C NO. :

Exporter:

Transport details:

Terms of payment:

Marks & Numbers	Description of Goods	Quantity	Unit Price	Amount

广东省对外贸易进出口公司

Guangdong Foreign Trade Imp. & Exp. Corp.

15 - 18/F., Guangdong Foreign Economic and Trade Building

351 Tianhe Road, Guangzhou, China

装箱单

PACKING LIST

ORIGINAL

Exporter:

INV. DATE :

INVOICE NO. :

B/L NO. :

S/C NO. :

L/C NO. :

Transport details:

标记 Marks & Numbers	件数 Quantity	货名 Description of Goods	净重 Net Weight	毛重 Gross Weight	尺码 Measurement

BILL OF LADING

Shipper	B/L No.
Consignee	**Combined Transport BILL OF LADING** RECEIVED in apparent good order and condition except as otherwise noted the total number of containers or other packages or units enumerated below for transportation from the place of receipt to the place of delivery subject to the terms and conditions hereof. One of the Bills of Lading must be surrendered duly endorsed to the Carrier by or on behalf of the Holder of the Bill of Lading, the rights and liabilities arising in accordance with the terms and conditions hereof shall, without prejudice to any rule of common law or statute rendering them binding on the Merchant, become binding in all respects between the Carrier and the Holder of the Bill of Lading as though the contract evidenced hereby had been made between them. IN WITNESS whereof the number of original Bills of Lading stated under have been signed. All of this tenor and date, one of which being accomplished, the other (s) to be void.
Notify Address	

Pre-carriage by	Place of Receipt	For delivery of goods please apply to :
Ocean Vessel　Voy. No.	Port of Loading	
Port of Discharge	Place of Delivery	Final Destination for the Merchant's Reference only

Particulars Furnished by Merchants

Container, Seal No. & Marks & Nos.	No. of Package & Description of Goods	Gross Weight Kgs	Measurement m^3

FREIGHT & CHARGES	Revenue Tons.	Rate　Per	Prepaid	Collect

Prepaid at	Payable at	Place and date of issue
Total Prepaid	No. of Original B(s)/L	Stamp & Signature

LADEN ON BOARD THE VESSEL

Date

By.................................

第二次装运全套单据

F14

凭
Drawn under --

信用证　　　　　　第　　　　　　　　号
L/C　　　　　　No. --

日期　　　　　　年　　　　月　　　　日
dated --

按　　　　息　　　　　　　　付　款
Payable with interest @ ------------------ %per annum

号码　　　　汇票金额　　　　　　　　中国　广州　　　　年　　月　　日
No. ---------------- **Exchange** *for*　　　　　　Guangzhou,China ------------ 20 ------------

见票　　　　　　　　　　　　　　　　日　后（本　汇　票　之　副　本　未　付）付
At ---------------------- sight of this **FIRST** of Exchange (Second of exchange being unpaid)

pay to the order of -- 或其指定人

金　额
the sum of

此致
TO: ---

广东省对外贸易进出口公司

Guangdong Foreign Trade Imp. & Exp. Corp.

15 – 18/F., Guangdong Foreign Economic and Trade Building

351 Tianhe Road, Guangzhou, China

商业发票

COMMERCIAL INVOICE

Messrs.:

INVOICE NO. :
INVOICE DATE :
L/C NO. :
L/C DATE :
S/C NO. :

Exporter:

Transport details:

Terms of payment:

Marks & Numbers	Description of Goods	Quantity	Unit Price	Amount

广东省对外贸易进出口公司

Guangdong Foreign Trade Imp. & Exp. Corp.

15－18/F., Guangdong Foreign Economic and Trade Building

351 Tianhe Road, Guangzhou, China

装箱单

PACKING LIST

ORIGINAL

Exporter:

INV. DATE :

INVOICE NO. :

B/L NO. :

S/C NO. :

L/C NO. :

Transport details:

标记 Marks & Numbers	件数 Quantity	货名 Description of Goods	净重 Net Weight	毛重 Gross Weight	尺码 Measurement

BILL OF LADING

<table>
<tr><td colspan="2">Shipper</td><td colspan="3">B/L No.</td></tr>
<tr><td colspan="2">Consignee</td><td colspan="3" rowspan="2">Combined Transport BILL OF LADING
RECEIVED in apparent good order and condition except as otherwise noted the total number of containers or other packages or units enumerated below for transportation from the place of receipt to the place of delivery subject to the terms and conditions hereof. One of the Bills of Lading must be surrendered duly endorsed to the Carrier by or on behalf of the Holder of the Bill of Lading, the rights and liabilities arising in accordance with the terms and conditions hereof shall, without prejudice to any rule of common law or statute rendering them binding on the Merchant, become binding in all respects between the Carrier and the Holder of the Bill of Lading as though the contract evidenced hereby had been made between them. IN WITNESS whereof the number of original Bills of Lading stated under have been signed. All of this tenor and date, one of which being accomplished, the other (s) to be void.</td></tr>
<tr><td colspan="2">Notify Address</td></tr>
<tr><td>Pre-carriage by</td><td>Place of Receipt</td><td colspan="3" rowspan="2">For delivery of goods please apply to:</td></tr>
<tr><td>Ocean Vessel　　Voy. No.</td><td>Port of Loading</td></tr>
<tr><td>Port of Discharge</td><td colspan="2">Place of Delivery</td><td colspan="2">Final Destination for the Merchant's Reference only</td></tr>
<tr><td>Container, Seal No. & Marks & Nos.</td><td colspan="2">No. of Package & Description of Goods</td><td>Gross Weight Kgs</td><td>Measurement m^3</td></tr>
<tr><td colspan="5">Particulars Furnished by Merchants</td></tr>
</table>

FREIGHT & CHARGES	Revenue Tons.	Rate　　Per	Prepaid	Collect

Prepaid at	Payable at	Place and date of issue
Total Prepaid	No. of Original B(s) /L	Stamp & Signature

LADEN ON BOARD THE VESSEL

Date

By. ....

综合制单练习二

MT 700 **ISSUE OF A DOCUMENTARY CREDIT**

Basic Header	F 01 BKCHCNVJA400 1202 869809
Application Header	700 041126ICRAITMMA0506567177837 2004 - 11 - 27 N * BANCA DI CREDITO COOPERATIVO DI * SORISOLE E LEPRENO * SORISOLE
Sequence of Total	1/1
Form of Cec. Credit	IRREVOCABLE
Doc. Credit Number	088696000825
Date of Issue	2004 - 11 - 15
Expiry	DATE 2005 - 01 - 24 PLACE CHINA
Applicant	SPIL BERG DI YONG KEE FUI VIA A. DE GASPERI 4 24018 VILLA D' ALME' (BG) ITALY
Beneficiary	CHINA PACKAGING UNION GUANGZHOU CO., LTD. 7/F., NO. 753 DONGFENGDONG RD., GUANGZHOU, CHINA
Amount	CURRENCY USD AMOUNT 32,016.00
Pos. /Neg. Tol (%)	10/10
Available with/by	ANY BANK BY NEGOTIATION AGAINST THE DOCUMENTS DETAILED HEREIN AND BENEFICIARY'S DRAFTS AT SIGHT DRAWN ON US FOR FULL INVOICE VALUE.
Partial Shipments	NOT ALLOWED
Transshipment	ALLOWED
Loading in Charge	GUANGZHOU CHINA
For Transport to ...	GENOA ITALY
Latest Date of Ship.	2005 - 01 - 15
Descript. of Goods	MYANMAR TEAK GRADE A (UNFINISHED) SP. 16MM MYANMAR TEAK INDUSTRIAL PARQUET SP. 14MM AS PROFORMA INV. RGCI/PI004 (SPL - 001) DD NOV. 904 PRICE CFR GENOA
Documents Required	1) EIGHT COMMERCIAL INVOICES IN ORIGINAL. 2) EIGHT PACKING LIST IN ORIGINAL. 3) FULL SET CLEAN ON BOARD OCEAN BILL OF LADING ISSUED TO ORDER AND BLANK ENDODRSED MARKED FREIGHT PREPAID NOTIFY APPLICANT. 4) EIGHT CERTIFICATES OF ORIGIN FORM A ISSUED AND LEGALIZED BY COMPETENT AUTHORITY.
Additional Cond.	1) REFERENCE TO THIS CREDIT NUMBER MUST BE SHOWN ON ALL DOCUMENTS. 2) DOCUMENTS MUST BE SENT BY SPECIAL COURIER AT THE FOLLOWING ADDRESS U. P. F. — VIA DALWAZIA, 2—24047 TREVGLIO

(BG) ATT. NE MAR AMATO ADRIANA.

3) IF DOCUMENTS DON'T COMPLY WITH THE TERMS AND CONDITIONS OF PRESENT L/C, SERVICE CHARGES OF USD50.00 WILL BE DEDUCTED FROM ANY REMITTANCE MADE UNDER THIS CREDIT.

Details of Charges	ALL CHARGES AND COMMS OUTSIDE ITALY ARE FOR BENEFICIARY'S ACCOUNT.
Presentation Period	WITHIN 7 DAYS AFTER B/L DATE BUT WITHIN THE CREDIT VALIDITY
Confirmation	WITHOUT
Advise through	BANK OF COMMUNICATION GUANGZHOU BRANCH, CHINA
Send. to Rec. Info.	THIS IS THE OPERATIVE INSTRUMENTS NO MAIL CONFIRMATION WILL FOLLOW THIS CREDIT IS SUBJECT TO UCP REVISION 1993 ICC PUBLICATION N0. 500.

有关资料：

INV. NO.: RGCL2584

INV. DATE: JAN. 7, 2005

B/L NO.: 100397

B/L DATE: JAN. 12, 2005

S/C NO.: RGCL/PI004 (SPL-001)

FORM A NO.: GZ081/205/086

NAME OF STEAMER: HUI YUE 11 HAO V. 5112S

SHIPPING MARKS: N/M

CONTAINER & SEAL NO.: TELU2390424 (20'GP) /5429086

GOODS:

MYANMAR TEAK GRADE A (UNFINISHED) SP. 16MM 860m^2 @USD32.10/m^2

PACKING: 2.5m^2/BAG N. W. 30KGS/BAG G. W. 31KGS/BAG

MYANMAR TEAK INDUSTRIAL PARQUET SP. 14MM 300m^2 @USD14.7/m^2

PACKING: 1.5m^2/BAG N. W. 22KGS/BAG G. W. 23KGS/BAG

TOTAL MEASUREMENT: 18.022 CBMS

该货物是完全自产品

F14

1

凭
Drawn under --

信用证　　第　　号
L/C　　*No.* --

日期　　年　　月　　日
dated --

按　　息　　付款
Payable with interest @ ------------------ *%per annum*

号码　　汇票金额　　中国　广州　　年　　月　　日
No. --------------- **Exchange** *for*　　*Guangzhou,China* ------------ 20 ------------

见票　　日后（本汇票之副本未付）付
At -------------------- *sight of this* **FIRST** *of Exchange*（*Second of exchange being unpaid*）

pay to the order of -- 或其指定人

金　额
the sum of

此致
TO : --

广州中包联外经实业有限公司
China Packaging Union Guangzhou Co., Ltd.

7/F., No. 753 Dongfeng Rd., Guangzhou, China

商业发票
COMMERCIAL INVOICE

Messrs.:

INVOICE NO.　:

INVOICE DATE :

L/C NO.　:

L/C DATE　:

S/C NO.　:

Exporter:

Transport details:

Terms of payment:

Marks & Numbers	Description of Goods	Quantity	Unit Price	Amount

Consignor		**FBL**	No. / Country Code. HK
		HKNEGOTIABLE FIATA MULTIMODAL TRANSPORT BILL OF LADING Issued subject to UNCTAD/ICC Rules for Multimodal Transport Documents (ICC publication 481)	
Consigned to order of		INTERGROUP SHIPPING (ASIA) LTD.	
Notify address		3 Floor, Block 2 Tien Chu Centre. 1E Mok Cheong Street, Tokwawan, KowLoon, Hong Kong Tel: (852) 2760 8872 P. O. Box 20445 Hennessy Road Post Office Fax: (852) 2760 8442 Telex: 43429 INGRO HX Cable Address: HKINGROUP	
Place of receipt			
Ocean vessel	Port of loading		
Port of discharge	Place of delivery	LICENCE NO.	

Marks and numbers	Number and kind of packages	Description of goods	Gross weight	Measurement

according to the declaration of the consignor

ORIGINAL

Declaration of Interest the consignor in timely delivery (Clause 6. 2).	Declared value for ad valorem rate according to the declaration of the consignor(Clauses 7 and 8).

The goods and instructions are accepted and dealt with subject to the Standard Conditions printed overleaf. Taken in charge in apparent good order and condition, unless otherwise noted herein, at the place of receipt for transport and delivery as mentioned above. One of these Multimodal Transport Bills of Lading must be surrendered duly endorsed in exchange for the goods. In witness whereof the original Multimodal Transport Bills of Lading all of this tenor and date have been signed in the number stated below, one of which being accomplished the other (s) to be void.

Freight amount	Freight payable at	Place and date of issue
Cargo Insurance through the undersigned ☐ not covered ☐ Covered according to attached Policy	Number of Original FBL's	Stamp and signature

提单背书：

广州中包联外经实业有限公司
China Packaging Union Guangzhou Co. , Ltd.
7/F. , No. 753 Dongfeng Rd. , Guangzhou, China

装箱单
PACKING LIST

ORIGINAL

Exporter:

INV. DATE :
INVOICE NO. :
B/L NO. :
S/C NO. :
L/C NO. :

Transport details:

标记 Marks & Numbers	件数 Quantity	货名 Description of Goods	净重 Net Weight	毛重 Gross Weight	尺码 Measurement

ORIGINAL

1. Goods consigned from (Exporter's business name, address, country)	Reference No. GENERALIZED SYSTEM OF PREFERENCES CERTIFICATE OF ORIGIN (Combined declaration and certificate) FORM A issued in THE PEOPLE'S REPUBLIC OF CHINA (COUNTRY) See Notes overleaf
2. Goods consigned to (Consignee's name, address, country)	
3. Means of transport and route (as far as known)	4. For official use

5. Item number	6. Marks and numbers of packages	7. Number and kind of packages; description of goods	8. Origin criterion (see Notes overleaf)	9. Gross weight or other quantity	10. Number and date of invoices

11. Certification It is hereby certified, on the basis of control carried out, that the declaration by the exporter is correct. -- Place and date, signature and stamp of certifying authority	12. Declaration by the exporter The undersigned hereby declares that the above details and statements are correct; that all the goods were produced in -- (country) and that they comply with the origin requirements specified for those goods in the Generalized System of Preferences for goods exported to -- (importing country) -- Place and date, signature of authorized signatory

综合制单练习三

ISSUE OF A DOCUMENTARY CREDIT

Sender　: IBSPITTM414
　　* SANPAOLO IMI S. P. A
　　* PAVIA ITALY
Receiver : SOGECN22 × × ×
　　* SOCIETE GENERALE
　　* （GUANGZHOU BRANCH）
　　* GUANGZHOU, CHINA

= Message Text = = = = = = = = = = = = = = = =

27　: Sequence of Total
1/1

40A　: Form of Documentary Credit
IRREVOCABLE

20　: Documentary Credit Number
3109/1065

31C　: Date of Issue
050206　FEB. 6, 2005

31D　: Date and Place of Expiry
050406　CHINA　APR. 6, 2005

50　: Applicant
ARELLA AND C. SPA
PIAZZA COLLEGIO CAIROLI N. 3
27100 PAVIA, ITALY

59　: Beneficiary
GUANGDONG TEA IMP. & EXP. CORP.
26 – 30/F., GUANGDONG FOREIGN ECONOMICS & TRADE BUILDING
351 TIANHE ROAD, GUANGZHOU, CHINA

32B　: Currency Code, Amount
USD (US DOLLAR)
USD37,636.00 (US DOLLARS THIRTY SEVEN THOUSAND SIX HUNDRED AND THIRTY SIX ONLY.)

39A　: Percentage Credit Amt Tolerance
10/10

41A　: Available with... by...
ANY BANK BY NEGOTIATION AGAINST THE DOCUMENTS DETAILED HEREIN AND BENEFICIARY'S DRAFTS AT 60 DAYS SIGHT DRAWN ON US FOR 100 PCT OF THE INVOICE VALUE.

43P　: Partial Shipment
NOT ALLOWED

43T　: Transshipment
ALLOWED

44A　: Loading in Charge
CHINESE PORT

44B　: For Transportation to
LA SPEZIA PORT
44C　: Latest Date of Shipment
050320　MAR. 20, 2005
45A　: Descript. of Goods
4538 CHINA BLACK TEA ABT. 4,000 KGS. @ USD4.50/KG
5380 CHINA GREEN TEA ABT. 4,000 KGS. @ USD5.20/KG
CIFC3% LA SPEZIA PORT (1 × 20' FCL/200 PAPERSACKS)
PACKED IN PAPERSACKS, PALLETIZED AND CONTAINERIZED AS PER THE SALES CONFIRMATION NO. BTS78905.
THE PRICE IS TO BE UNDERSTOOD PER KILO NET SHIPPED WEIGHT CIF LA SPEZIA LESS 3 PERCENT COMMISSION, INCLUDING PACKING.
46A　: Documents Required
1) SIGNED COMMERCIAL INVOICE, ORIGINAL PLUS TWO COPIES, EVIDENCING THAT THE GOODS SHIPPED COMPLY WITH THE S/C NO. BTS78905 DATED 050112
2) 3/3 CLEAN ON BOARD BILLS OF LADING MADE OUT TO THE ORDER OF ARELLA AND C. SPA MARKED FREIGHT PREPAID AND NOTIFY TO CASASCO AND NARDI - VIA DON GIOVANNI CALABRIA, 30 - 20132 MILANO PHONE 02 - 2729241
3) CERTIFICATE OF WEIGHT
4) CERTIFICATE OF ORIGIN FORM A ISSUED BY THE COMPETENT LOCAL AUTHORITY IN TWO COPIES
5) MARINE INSURANCE POLICY/CERTIFICATE COVERING ALL RISKS AND WAR RISK FOR 110 PERCENT OF THE CIF INVOICE VALUE
47A　: Additional Conditions
+/- 10 PCT IN AMOUNT, QUANTITY AND WEIGHT IS ALLOWED
ALL DOCUMENTS MUST INDICATE THIS CREDIT NUMBER
PLEASE SEND DOCUMENTS TO:
SANPAOLO IMI SPA
VIA FABIO FILZI N. 2 - 27100 PAVIA (ITALY)
71B　: Charges
ALL BANKING CHARGES AND COMMISSIONS OUTSIDE OF ITALY ARE FOR BENEFICIARY'S ACCOUNT
49　: Confirmation Instructions
WITHOUT
78　: Instr to Payg/Accptg/Negotg Bank
AT RECEIPT OF DOCUMENTS IN CONFORMITY WITH CREDIT TERMS, WE SHALL CREDIT YOU AS PER YOUR INSTRUCTIONS AT MATURITY DATE.
57D　: "Advise Through" Bank-Name & Addr.
SOCIETE GENERALS—GUANGZHOU BRANCH
21ST FLOOR PEACE WORLD PLAZA
362 - 366 HUANSHI EAST RD., GUANGZHOU
72　: Sender to Receiver Information
SUBJECT TO ICC PUS 500, 1993 REVISION AND SUBJECT TO THE

UNIFORM RULES FOR BANK TO BANK REIMBURSEMENT UNDER DOC. CREDIT ICC PUB 525.

有关资料：

INVOICE NO. : TAR20057149
INVOICE DATE: MAR. 2, 2005
B/L NO. : GSG05 - 723
B/L DATE: MAR. 15, 2005
FORM A NO. : GZ7/80067/0589
POLICY NO. : TES3478921
SHIPPING MARK: N/M
PACKED IN 200 PAPERSACKS
CONTAINER, SEAL NO. : TEXU3730336/KHS487605/20'
NAME OF STEAMER: PUDONG SENATOR V. 743
WEIGHT: N. W. : @40 KGS　　G. W. : @40. 7 KGS
PORT OF LOADING: GUANGZHOU
该货物是完全自产品

F14

1

凭
Drawn under ....

信用证　　　　第　　　　号
L/C　　　　No. ....

日期　　　　年　　　　月　　　　日
dated ....

按　　　　息　　　　付款
Payable with interest @ .... %per annum

号码　　　　汇票金额　　　　中国　广州　　年　月　日
No. .... **Exchange** for 　　　　Guangzhou,China .... 20 ....

见票　　　　日后（本汇票之副本未付）付
At .... sight of this **SECOND** of Exchange (Second of exchange being unpaid)

pay to the order of .... 或其指定人

金　额
the sum of

此致
To: ....
....

....

广 东 茶 叶 进 出 口 公 司

Guangdong Tea Imp. & Exp. Corp.

26 - 30/F. , Guangdong Foreign Economics & Trade Building

351 Tianhe Road, Guangzhou, China

商业发票

COMMERCIAL INVOICE

Messrs. :

INVOICE NO. :
INVOICE DATE :
L/C NO. :
L/C DATE :
S/C NO. :

Exporter:

Transport details:

Terms of payment:

Marks & Numbers	Description of Goods	Quantity	Unit Price	Amount

广 东 茶 叶 进 出 口 公 司

Guangdong Tea Imp. & Exp. Corp.

26 – 30/F., Guangdong Foreign Economics & Trade Building

351 Tianhe Road, Guangzhou, China

CERTIFICATE OF WEIGHT

ORIGINAL

No. :　　　　Date:

Shipping Marks	Quantities & Descriptions of Goods	Net Weight	Gross Weight

ORIGINAL

<table>
<tr><td colspan="4">1. Goods consigned from (Exporter's business name, address, country)</td><td colspan="3" rowspan="2">Reference No.

GENERALIZED SYSTEM OF PREFERENCES
CERTIFICATE OF ORIGIN
(Combined declaration and certificate)
FORM A
issued in THE PEOPLE'S REPUBLIC OF CHINA
(COUNTRY)

See Notes overleaf</td></tr>
<tr><td colspan="4">2. Goods consigned to (Consignee's name, address, country)</td></tr>
<tr><td colspan="4">3. Means of transport and route (as far as known)</td><td colspan="3">4. For official use</td></tr>
<tr><td>5. Item number</td><td>6. Marks and numbers of packages</td><td colspan="2">7. Number and kind of packages; description of goods</td><td>8. Origin criterion (see Notes overleaf)</td><td>9. Gross weight or other quantity</td><td>10. Number and date of invoices</td></tr>
<tr><td colspan="3">11. Certification
It is hereby certified, on the basis of control carried out, that the declaration by the exporter is correct.

Place and date, signature and stamp of certifying authority</td><td colspan="4">12. Declaration by the exporter
The undersigned hereby declares that the above details and statements are correct; that all the goods were produced in
----
(country)
and that they comply with the origin requirements specified for those goods in the Generalized System of Preferences for goods exported to
----
(importing country)

Place and date, signature of authorized signatory</td></tr>
</table>

PICC PROPERTY

中保财产保险有限公司

The people's insurance（Property）Company of China，Ltd.

发票号码　　　　　　　　　　　　　　　　保险单号次
Invoice No.　　　　　　　　　　　　　　　Policy No.

海 洋 货 物 运 输 保 险 单
MARINE CARGO TRANSPORTATION INSURANCE POLICY

被保险人：
Insured：

中保财产保险有限公司（以下简称本公司）根据被保险人的要求，及其所缴付约定的保险费，按照本保险单承担险别和背面所载条款与下列特别条款承保下列货物运输保险，特签发本保险单。

This policy of Insurance witnesses that the People's Insurance（Property）Company of China，Ltd.（hereinafter called "the Company"），at the request of the Insured and in consideration of the agreed premium paid by the Insured，undertakes to insure the undermentioned goods in transportation subject to the conditions of this Policy as per the Clauses printed overleaf and other special clauses attached hereon.

保险货物项目 Descriptions of Goods	包装　单位　数量 Packing Unit Quantity	保险金额 Amount Insured

承 保 险 别　　　　　　　　　　　　　　　货 物 标 记
Conditions　　　　　　　　　　　　　　　Marks of Goods

总保险金额：
Total Amount Insured：

保费　　　　　　　载运输工具　　　　　　　　　　开航日期
Premium　as arranged　Per conveyance S. S.　　　　Slg. on or abt.

起运港　　　　　　　　　目的港
From　　　　　　　　　　to

所保货物，如发生本保险单项下可能引起索赔的损失或损坏，应立即通知本公司下述代理人查勘。如有索赔，应向本公司提交保险单正本（本保险单共有　　份正本）及有关文件。如一份正本已用于索赔，其余正本则自动失效。

In the event of loss or damage which may result in a claim under this Policy，immediate notice must be given to the Company's Agent as mentioned hereunder. Claims，if any，one of the Original Policy which has been issued in Original（s）together with the relevant documents shall be surrendered to the Company. If one of the Original Policy has been accomplished，the others to be void.

中保财产保险有限公司
THE PEOPLE'S INSURANCE（PROPERTY）COMPANY OF CHINA，LTD.

赔款偿付地点
Claim payable at

日期　　　　　　　在
Date　　　　　　　at

地址：
Address：

BILL OF LADING

Shipper	B/L No.
Consignee	**Combined Transport BILL OF LADING** RECEIVED in apparent good order and condition except as otherwise noted the total number of containers or other packages or units enumerated below for transportation from the place of receipt to the place of delivery subject to the terms and conditions hereof. One of the Bills of Lading must be surrendered duly endorsed to the Carrier by or on behalf of the Holder of the Bill of Lading, the rights and liabilities arising in accordance with the terms and conditions hereof shall, without prejudice to any rule of common law or statute rendering them binding on the Merchant, become binding in all respects between the Carrier and the Holder of the Bill of Lading as though the contract evidenced hereby had been made between them. IN WITNESS whereof the number of original Bills of Lading stated under have been signed. All of this tenor and date, one of which being accomplished, the other (s) to be void.
Notify Address	

Pre-carriage by	Place of Receipt	For delivery of goods please apply to:
Ocean Vessel Voy. No.	Port of Loading	
Port of Discharge	Place of Delivery	Final Destination for the Merchant's Reference only

Particulars Furnished by Merchants

Container, Seal No. & Marks & Nos.	No. of Package & Description of Goods	Gross Weight Kgs	Measurement m^3

FREIGHT & CHARGES	Revenue Tons.	Rate Per	Prepaid	Collect

Prepaid at	Payable at	Place and date of issue
Total Prepaid	No. of Original B(s)/L	Stamp & Signature

LADEN ON BOARD THE VESSEL

Date

By ______________________

综合制单练习四

ISSUE OF A DOCUMENTARY CREDIT

Application Header	JANBBDDHAJBD 2189 045834 040529 2009 N * JANATA BANK * DHAKA * (LOCAL OFFICE)
User Header	Service Code 103: Bank Priority 113: Msg. User. Ref. 108: ABUL Info. From CI. 115:
Sequence of Total	1/1
Form of Coc. Credit	IRREVOCABLE
Doc. Credit Number	0093040600308
Date of Issue	040525
Expiry	Date 040615 Place IN CHINA
Applicant Bank	JANBBDDHJBD * JANATA BANK * DHAKA * (LOCAL OFFICE)
Applicant	M/S. SPEEDWELL LIMITED PLOT NO. M-4/2, ROAD NO. -7, SECTION-7, MIRPUR, DHAKA-1216, BANGLADESH
Beneficiary	GUANGDONG TEXTILES IMPORT & EXPORT COTTON, YARN & PIECE-GOODS COMPANY LTD. 8/F., GUANGDONG TEXTILES MANSION, 168 XIAOBEI ROAD, GUANGZHOU, CHINA
Amount	Currency USD Amount 7,650.00
Available with/by	ANY BANK IN CHINA BY NEGOTIATION
Drafts at...	120 DAYS SIGHT FROM THE DATE OF NEGOTIATION
Drawee	JANBBDDHJBD * JANATA BANK * DHAKA * (LOCAL OFFICE)
Partial Shipments	ALLOWED
Transshipment	ALLOWED
Loading in Charge	ANY SEA PORT OF CHINA
For Transport to...	CHITTAGONG, BANGLADESH
Descript. of Goods	

FABRICS FOR 100PCT EXPORT ORIENTED READYMADE GARMENTS INDUSTRY
4,500YDS 98/2 COTTON/SPANDE × CANVAS CONST: 21 + 12 × 16 + 16 + 70D 140 × 62
WIDTH 50/52INCH AT THE RATE OF USD1. 70/YD AS PER PROFORMA INVOICE
NO. 2004CTHS02008 DATED 01-05-2004 OF THE BENEFICIARY.
TERMS OF DELIVERY: C N F CHITTAGONG

Documents Required

A) ORIGINAL SIGNED INVOICE IN QUINTUPLICATE CERTIFYING MERCHANDISE TO BE OF CHINA ORIGIN.

B) FULL SET OF ORIGINAL CLEAN SHIPPED ON BOARD OCEAN BILL OF LADING DRAWN OR ENDORSED TO THE ORDER OF JANATA BANK, LOCAL OFFICE, DHAKA MARKED FREIGHT PREPAID NOTIFY OPENERS AND US GIVING FULL NAME AND ADDRESS.

C) CERTIFICATE OF ORIGIN ISSUED BY BENEFICIARY CERTIFYING MERCHANDISE OF CHINA ORIGIN.

D) BENEFICIARY'S CERTIFICATE TO THE EFFECT THAT THEY HAVE COMPLIED ALL TERMS AND CONDITIONS OF THEIR PROFORMA INVOICE NO. 2004CTHS02008 DT. 01-05-2004.

E) DETAILS PACKING, WEIGHT AND MEASUREMENT LIST REQUIRED IN TRIPLICATE.

Additional Cond.

1) L/C AUTHORISATION FORM NO. 129306 AND H. S. CODE NO. 5208.5200 TO APPEAR IN ALL INVOICES.

2) DOCUMENTS EVIDENCING SHIPMENTS MUST NOT BEFORE THE DATE OF OPENING OF THIS CREDIT.

3) SHIPMENT/TRANSSHIPMENT BY ISRAIL, MONTENIGRO AND SERBIA FLAG/VESSEL STRICTLY PROHIBITED.

4) THIRD PARTY, SHORT FORM, BLANK BACKED BILL OF LADING NOT ACCEPTABLE.

5) BILL OF LADING TO INDICATE GROSS AND NET WEIGHT AND CONTAINER NUMBER OF MERCHANDISE.

6) INTEREST WILL BE PAID BY OPENER USANCE PERIOD AT LIBOR FROM THE DATE OF NEGOTIATION.

7) EXCEPT OTHERWISE EXPRESSLY STATED, THIS CREDIT IS SUBJECT TO UNIFORM CUSTONS AND PRACTICE FOR DOCUMENTARY CREDIT (1993 REVISION) ICC PUBLICATION NO. 500.

8) L/C NO. 0093040600308 SHOULD APPEAR ON ALL DOCUMENTS.

9) THIS L/C IS OPENED AGAINST EXPORT L/C NO. 253011372706-B DATED 10-06-2003 TO APPEAR ALL DOCUMENTS.

10) ALL EVIDENCING SHIPMENT UNDER THIS CREDIT MUST BE ADVISED BY THE BENEFICIARY IMMEDIATELY AFTER SHIPMENT DIRECT TO M/S. CITY GENERAL INSURANCE CO., LTD. LOCAL OFFICE, BAITUL HOSSATN BUILDING 3RD. FLOOR, 27, DILKUSHA C/A, DHAKA-1000, BANGLADESH AND THE APPLICANT REFERRING TO INSURANCE COVER NOTE NO. CGIC/LO/MC-191/05/04 DATED 25-05-2004 GIVING FULL DETAILS OF SHIPMENT AND A COPY TO THIS ADVICE ACCOMPANY EACH SET OF DOCUMENTS.

Details of Charges ALL BANKING CHARGES OUTSIDE BANGLADESH ARE FOR THE BENEFICIARY'S ACCOUNT.

A FEE OF USD50.00 WILL BE CHARGED IN CASE OF DISCRIPANT DOCUMENT.

REIMBURSEMENT CHARGE USD50.00 WILL BE DEDUCTED AT THE TIME OF PAYMENT.

Presentation Period WITHIN 15 DAYS OF SHIPEMNT BUT WITHIN THE VALIDITY OF CREDIT.

Confirmation WITHOUT

Instructions

1) ORIGINAL AND DUPLICATE SET OF DOCUMENTS TO BE SENT BY SUCCESSIVE REGD. AIRMAIL/COURIER SERVICE IMMEDIATELY AFTER NEGOTIATION/PRESENTATION.

2) AMOUNT OF DRAFT (S) NEGOTIATED/PRESENTED SHOULD BE ENDORSED ON REVERSE OF THIS CREDIT.

3) WE SHALL ARRANGE REMITTANCE OF THE PROCEEDS ON RECEIPT OF DOCUMENTS COMPLYING WITH THE TERMS OF THE CREDIT.

Send. To Rec. Info. DRAFT TO BE DRAWN ON US AT 120 DAYS SIGHT FOR 100PCT INVOICE VALUE.
DOCS TO BE FORWARDED TO: JANATA BANK
LOCAL OFFICE, 1 - DILKUSHA C/A,
DHAKA - 1000, BANGLADESH.

有关资料：

INV. NO.: 24HS024018　　INV. DATE: MAY 28, 2004

B/L NO.: FYPX0403335CHI　　B/L DATE: MAY 31, 2004

PORT OF LOADING: SHANGHAI PORT　　NAME OF VESSEL: MOL MAAS V. 571W

CONTAINER & SEAL NO.: APZU3028274/4014710

WEIGHT: N. W.: 75.0KGS/BALE　　G. W.: 77.3KGS/BALE

TOTAL MEASUREMENT: 3CBMS　　TOTAL QUANTITY: 4,491.4 YDS

MARKS & NUMBERS: SIRETCH CANVAS
COLOR:
BALS NO.:
MADE IN CHINA

PACKING: 22BALES								
COLOUR: KHAKI			COLOUR: BROWN			COLOUR: GREY		
B/NO.	LOT NO.	QTY. (Y.)	B/NO.	LOT NO.	QTY. (Y.)	B/NO.	LOT NO.	QTY. (Y.)
1	A	183.7	1	B	213.3	1	B	246.0
2	A	199.1	2	B	270.1	2	B	206.7
3	A	203.4	3	A	214.4	3	B	222.0
4	A	231.9	4	A	202.3	4	A	302.9
5	A	146.6	5	A	121.3	5	A	227.5
6	A	194.6				6	A	201.2
						7	B	188.1
						8	A	108.3
						9	A	247.1
						10	A	247.1
						11	A	212.2

F14

1

凭
Drawn under ....

信用证　　　　第　　　　号
L/C　　　　*No.* ....

日期　　　　年　　　　月　　　　日
dated ....

按　　　　息　　　　　　　　付款
Payable with interest @ .... *%per annum*

号码　　　　汇票金额　　　　　　中国　　广州　　　年　　月　　日
No. .... **Exchange** *for* 　　　　*Guangzhou,China* .... 20..............

见票　　　　　　　　　　　　　　日后（本汇票之副本未付）付
At .... *sight of this* **FIRST** *of Exchange (Second of exchange being unpaid)*

pay to the order of .... 或其指定人

金　额
the sum of

此致
To: ....
....

....

广东省纺织品进出口花纱布有限公司

GUANGDONG TEXTILES IMPORT & EXPORT COTTON, YARN & PIECE-GOODS COMPANY LTD. 8/F., GUANGDONG TEXTILES MANSION, 168 XIAOBEI ROAD, GUANGZHOU, CHINA

商业发票

COMMERCIAL INVOICE

Messrs.:

INVOICE NO. :
INVOICE DATE :
L/C NO. :
L/C DATE :
S/C NO. :

Exporter:

Transport details:

Terms of payment:

Marks & Numbers	Description of Goods	Quantity	Unit Price	Amount

BILL OF LADING

Shipper	B/L No.
	Combined Transport BILL OF LADING RECEIVED in apparent good order and condition except as otherwise noted the total number of containers or other packages or units enumerated below for transportation from the place of receipt to the place of delivery subject to the terms and conditions hereof. One of the Bills of Lading must be surrendered duly endorsed to the Carrier by or on behalf of the Holder of the Bill of Lading, the rights and liabilities arising in accordance with the terms and conditions hereof shall, without prejudice to any rule of common law or statute rendering them binding on the Merchant, become binding in all respects between the Carrier and the Holder of the Bill of Lading as though the contract evidenced hereby had been made between them. IN WITNESS whereof the number of original Bills of Lading stated under have been signed. All of this tenor and date, one of which being accomplished, the other (s) to be void.
Consignee	
Notify Address	

Pre-carriage by	Place of receipt	For delivery of goods please apply to :
Ocean Vessel　Voy. No.	Port of Loading	
Port of Discharge	Place of Delivery	Final Destination for the Merchant's Reference only

Particulars Furnished by Merchants

Container, Seal No. & Marks & Nos.	No. of Package & Description of Goods	Gross Weight Kgs	Measurement m^3

FREIGHT & CHARGES	Revenue Tons.	Rate　Per	Prepaid	Collect

Prepaid at	Payable at	Place and date of issue
Total Prepaid	No. of Original B (s) /L	Stamp & Signature

LADEN ON BOARD THE VESSEL

Date

By.................................

广东省纺织品进出口花纱布有限公司
GUANGDONG TEXTILES IMPORT & EXPORT COTTON, YARN & PIECE-GOODS COMPANY LTD.
产地证明书
CERTIFICATE OF ORIGIN

发票号（INV. NO.）:

L/C NO.:

日期（DATE）:

兹证明下列商品系中华人民共和国生产／制造

(This is to certify that the undermentioned commodities were produced/manufactured in the People's Republic of China)

标记及号码（Mark & No.）	品名（Commodity）	数量（Quantity）	重量（Weight）

广东省纺织品进出口花纱布有限公司

GUANGDONG TEXTILES IMPORT & EXPORT COTTON, YARN & PIECE-GOODS COMPANY LTD. 8/F., GUANGDONG TEXTILES MANSION, 168 XIAOBEI ROAD, GUANGZHOU, CHINA

装船通知

SHIPPING ADVICE

To:

Inv. No. :
Inv. Date :
Inv. Value :
L/C No. :
S/C No. :

Port of Shipment:
Port of Destination:
Date of Shipment:
Vessel's Name:
Commodity:
Quantity:
Weight:

广东省纺织品进出口花纱布有限公司

GUANGDONG TEXTILES IMPORT & EXPORT COTTON, YARN & PIECE-GOODS COMPANY LTD. 8/F., GUANGDONG TEXTILES MANSION, 168 XIAOBEI ROAD, GUANGZHOU, CHINA

BENEFICIARY'S CERTIFICATE

Date:

RE: INV. NO.:　　　　　　L/C NO.:

广东省纺织品进出口花纱布有限公司

GUANGDONG TEXTILES IMPORT & EXPORT COTTON, YARN & PIECE-GOODS COMPANY LTD. 8/F., GUANGDONG TEXTILES MANSION, 168 XIAOBEI ROAD, GUANGZHOU, CHINA

DETAILS PACKING, WEIGHT AND MEASUREMENT LIST

NO. :
DATE :

COLOUR:

B/NO.	LOT NO.	QTY. （Y.）

TTL. :

COLOUR:

B/NO.	LOT NO.	QTY. （Y.）

TTL. :

DETAILS PACKING, WEIGHT AND MEASUREMENT LIST

NO. :

DATE :

COLOUR:

B/NO.	LOT NO.	QTY. (Y.)

TTL. :

TOTAL :

G. WT.:

N. WT.:

MEAST.:

综合制单练习五

```
2012FEB08 17:15:32                                          Logical Terminal GDPF
MT S700                  Issue of a Documentary Credit             Page 00001
                                                                   Func JSRVPRI
MSGACK  DWS7651 Auth OK, key B1010715763B19FC, BKCHCNBJ KRTHTHBK record784564
Basic Header           F  01 BKCHCNBJA400 0583 459182
Application Header     O 700 1554 120208 KRTHTHBKAXXX 3533 377148 120208 1657 N
                                         *KRUNG THAI BANK PUBLIC COMPANY
                                         *LIMITED
                                         *BANGKOK
User Header            Service Code      103:
                       Bank. Priority    113:
                       Msg User Ref.     108:
                       Info. from CI     115:
Sequence of Total      *27    : 1 / 1
Form of Doc. Credit    *40 A  : IRREVOCABLE
Doc. Credit Number     *20    : BL 210390
Date of Issue           31 C  : 120208
Expiry                 *31 D  : Date 120430 Place CHINA
Applicant              *50    : WATANA TOOL COMPANY LIMITED
                                277-279 BORIPAT ROAD,POMPRAB,
                                BANGKOK 10100,THAILAND.
Beneficiary            *59    : GUANGDONG TEXTILES IMP AND EXP
                                MEIFENG GARMENTS CO.,LTD.
                                6/F,GUANGDONG TEXTILES MANSION
                                168 XIAO BEI RD.,GUANGZHOU,CHINA
Amount                 *32 B  :          Currency USD Amount 22,876,34
Available with/by      *41 D  : KRUNG THAI BANK PCL.,SUANMALI IBC.
                                BY PAYMENT
Drafts at ...           42 C  : 60  DAYS AFTER SIGHT
Drawee                  42 D  : KRUNG THAI BANK PCL.,SUANMALI IBC.
Partial Shipments       43 P  : ALLOWED
Transshipment           43 T  : ALLOWED
Loading in Charge       44 A  :
           GUANGZHOU,CHINA
For Transport to ...    44 B  :
           BANGKOK,THAILAND
Latest Date of Ship.    44 C  : 120415
Descript. of Goods      45 A  :
           906 PCS.'SHUANG GE' CHAIN BLOCKS HS-C TYPE.
           DETAILS AS PER P/INV. NO.2012GMBS05019.
           C.I.F.C2  BANGKOK,THAILAND
Documents required      46 A  :
           + SIGNED COMMERCIAL INVOICE IN 10 COPIES SHOWING
           SEPARATELY F.O.B.VALUE,FREIGHT CHARGE,INSURANCE PREMIUM AND
           C.I.F.VALUE.
           + FULL SET PLUS TWO N/N COPIES OF CLEAN ON BOARD OCEAN
           BILLS OF LADING MADE OUT TO ORDER OF KRUNG THAI BANK PUBLIC
           COMPANY LIMITED MARKED FREIGHT PREPAID NOTIFY : APPLICANT.
           + MARINE INSURANCE POLICY OR CERTIFICATE IN DUPLICATE,ENDORSED
           IN BLANK,FOR FULL INVOICE VALUE PLUS 10 PERCENT STATING CLAIMS
           PAYABLE IN THAILAND COVERING OCEAN MARINE CARGO CLAUSES(A)
           AS PER CIC CLAUSE.NAMING SETTLING AGENT IN THAILAND
           + PACKING LIST IN 6 COPIES.
Additional Cond.        47 A  :
           + ALL DOCUMENTS MENTIONING THIS L/C NO.
           + IN THE EVENT THAT DOCUMENTS PRESENTED UNDER THIS L/C
           ARE FOUND TO BE DISCREPANT, WE SHALL GIVE ITS NOTICE OF
           REFUSAL AND SHALL HOLD DOCUMENTS AT YOUR DISPOSAL SUBJECT TO
           THE FOLLOWING CONDITION IF WE HAS NOT RECEIVED YOUR DISPOSAL
           INSTRUCTIONS FOR THE DISCREPANT DOCUMENTS PRIOR TO RECEIPT OF
           THE APPLICANT'S WAIVER OF DISCREPANCIES WE SHALL RELEASE
           THE DOCUMENTS TO THE APPLICANT WITHOUT NOTICE TO YOU AND
           DISC.FEE USD50.00 SHALL BE DEDUCTED FROM THE PROCEEDS.
           + SHIPPING MARK:WTT/BANGKOK.
```

2012FEB08 17:15:37　　　　　　　　　　　　　Logical Terminal GDPF
MT S700　　　　　　Issue of a Documentary Credit　　　　Page 00002
　　　　　　　　　　　　　　　　　　　　　　　　　　　Func JSRVPRI

Details of Charges　71 B : ALL BANK CHARGES OUTSIDE
　THAILAND INCLUDING COST OF WIRE,
　AND REIM.CHARGE ARE FOR
　APPLICANT'S ACCOUNT AND INTEREST
　IS FOR BENEFICIARY'S ACCOUNT.
Confirmation　*49 : WITHOUT
Instructions　78 :
+ AT MATURITY DATE WE SHALL REIMBURSE YOU
AS YOUR INSTRUCTION PROVIDED ALL TERMS AND CONDITIONS
HAVE BEEN COMPLIED WITH L/C TERMS.
+ DRAFT(S) AND DOCUMENTS TO BE SENT TO US BY COURIER SERVICE
MAILING ADDRESS SUANMALI IBC.,20 YUKHON 2 RD.,POMPRAB,BANGKOK
10100,THAILAND.
+ THIS ADVICE IS OPERATIVE WITH NO CONFIRMATION TO FOLLOW AND
SUBJECT TO ICC 2007 REVISION PUB 600.
Send. to Rec. Info.　72 : KINDLY ACKNOWLEDGE RECEIPT THIS
　CREDIT BY RETURN SWIFT WILL BE
　MUCH APPRECIATED.
Trailer　Order is <MAC:> <PAC:> <ENC:> <CHK:> <TNG:> <PDE:>
　MAC:50D5BCB8
　CHK:8D5509CE772F

15 APR 2012

S.W.IFT 中国银行

有关资料：

出口公司名称	广东省纺织品进出口美丰服装有限公司 出口公司单证签署人：刘山峰		
发票号码	201205019GMBS	发票日期	2012 年 4 月 9 日
提单号码	CAN2006789	提单日期	2012 年 4 月 11 日
货运代理人	CHANG HONG SHIPPING CO. LTD.		
货代提单签发人	张三贵	运　费	USD819.00
保单号码	20402014902010052	保单日期	2012 年 4 月 10 日
泰国理赔代理	BANGKOK INSURANCE CO., LTD. 302 BANGKOK UNSURANCE BUILDING SILOM ROAD, BANGKOK 10500, THAILAND		
保　费	USD114.72	集装箱号	YMLU2958162/MF0102813
承运人	PAC OCEAN LINES S. A.	船　名	MING CONTAINER V65S

实际装船货物	'SHUANG GE' CHAIN BLOCK HS-C TYPE					
	SPEC.	QUANTITY (PCS)	U. PRICE (PC)	N. W. (CTN)	G. W. (CTN)	MEAS. (CTN)
			CIFC2 BANGKOK, THAILAND			
	1T*2.5M	300PCS	USD17.70	14KGS	16KGS	(30*25*20) CM
	1.5T*2.5M	250PCS	USD22.60	15KGS	17KGS	(35*25*20) CM
	2T*2.5M	150PCS	USD24.88	16KGS	18KGS	(35*25*20) CM
	3T*3M	120PCS	USD30.85	18KGS	20KGS	(45*25*20) CM
	5T*3M	80PCS	USD44.24	20KGS	22KGS	(60*40*35) CM
	20T*5M	6PCS	USD235.00	26KGS	28KGS	(80*50*40) CM

综合制单练习六

SANWJPJSXXXX 2993 836916 110125 1422 N
*THE SANWA BANK, LTD.,
*OSAKA

User **Header** Service Code 103:
Bank. Priority 113:
Msg Ref. 108:
Info. from CI 115:

Sequence of Total *27 : 1 / 1
Form of Doc. Credit *40 A : IRREVOCABLE
Doc. Credit Number *20 : 41-1463961-052
Expiry *31 D : Date 110320 Place IN THE COUNTRY OF BENEFICIARY
Applicant *50 : KONDOTEC INC.
2-90, SAKAIGAWA, 2-CHOME, NISHI-KU,
OSAKA 5500024, JAPAN
Beneficiary *59 : SINOCHEM GUANGDONG IMPORT AND
EXPORT CORPORATION
58, ZHAN QIAN ROAD, GUANGZHOU,
CHINA
Amount *32 B : Currency USD Amount 22.311,89
Available with/by *41 D : ANY BANK
BY NEGOTIATION
Drafts at ... 42 C : SIGHT
Drawee 42 D : THE SANWA BANK LTD OSAKA
Partial Shipments 43 P : NOT ALLOWED
Transhipment 43 T : NOT ALLOWED
Loading in Charge 44 A :
CHINESE PORT
For Transport to ... 44 B :
OSAKA, JAPAN
Latest Date of Ship. 44 C : 110310
Descript. of Goods 45 A :
+PVC LAYFLAT WATER DISCHARGE HOSE, BLUE COLOR.
AS PER P.O.A09553 DATED 11/22/2010

CIFD5 OSAKA, JAPAN
Documents required 46 A :
+SIGNED COMMERCIAL INVOICE IN DUPLICATE INDICATING VESSEL NAME AND P.O.NO.
+FULL SET LESS ONE ORIGINAL OF CLEAN ON BOARD OCEAN B/L MADE OUT TO ORDER OF SHIPPER AND BLANK ENDORSED MARKED FREIGHT PREPAID NOTIFY APPLICANT
+INSURANCE POLICY OR CERTIFICATE IN DUPLICATE ENDORSED IN BLANK FOR 110 PERCENT OF THE INVOICE VALUE INCLUDING:
INSTITUTE CARGO CLAUSES (ALL RISKS)
CLAIMS TO BE PAYABLE IN JAPAN IN THE CURRENCY OF THE DRAFT
+G.S.P. CERTIFICATE OF ORIGIN FORM'A' IN ONE PHOTO COPY
+PACKING LIST IN TWO
+BENEFICIARY'S CERTIFICATE STATING THAT ONE SET OF NEGOTIABLE DOCUMENTS INCLUDING 1/3 ORIGINAL B/L AND ORIGINAL GSP CERT EXCEPT INSURANCE POLICY HAVE BEEN FACSIMILED TO APPLICANT AND THEN SENT BY COURIER SERVICE WITHIN 3 DAYS AFTER B/L DATE.
Additional Cond. 47 A :
+THE VESSEL NAME MUST BE CLEARLY SHOWN ON INVOICE AND PACKING LIST
+SHIPMENT EFFECTED BY CONTAINER.

```
XIUANo1  08:28:29                                          Logical Terminal CD
MT:S700                 Issue of a Documentary Credit      Page 00
                                                           Func JSi
Details of Charges     71 B : ALL BANKING CHARGES OUTSIDE JAPAN
                              ARE FOR ACCOUNT OF
                              BENEFICIARY
Presentation Period    48   : DOCUMENTS MUST BE PRESENTED WITHIN
                              10 DAYS AFTER THE DATE OF SHIPMENT
                              BUT WITHIN THE CREDIT EXPIRY
Confirmation          *49   : WITHOUT
Instructions           78   :
                SPECIAL INSTRUCTIONS TO NEGOTIATING BANK:
                REIMBURSEMENT BY TELETRANSMISSION IS UNACCEPTABLE
                ALL DOCUMENTS MUST BE SENT TO OUR ADDRESS:1-1 KAWARAMACHI 2
                CHUO-KU OSAKA 541-0048 JAPAN IN ONE LOT BY COURIER SERVICE

                IN REIMBURSEMENT, WE SHALL COVER YOU AS REQUESTED.
                A DISCREPANCY FEE OF USD50.00
                WILL BE DEDUCTED FROM THE PROCEEDS IF DOCUMENTS CONTAINING
                DISCREPANCIES ARE PRESENTED TO US UNDER THIS CREDIT.
                A REMITTANCE CHARGE OF USD68.00 WILL ALSO BE DEDUCTED FROM
                PROCEEDS IF SETTLEMENT IS MADE BY T.T. REMITTANCE.
Send. to Rec. Info.  72   : UCP 600 SHALL APPLY TO THE CREDIT
                              CONCERNED
Trailer                       Order is <MAC:> <PAC:> <ENC:> <CHK:> <TNG:> <
                              MAC:E1BECEA2
                              CHK:F70664CAA51D
```

有关资料：

出口公司	中化广东进出口公司 出口公司单据签署人：李明天		
发票号码	01AG0525 - 074	发票日期	2011 年 2 月 21 日
总净重	17 100 千克	总毛重	18 000 千克
集装箱交接	FCL　　CY/CY	总尺码	26 立方米
提单号码	JA93200017	提单日期	2011 年 2 月 26 日
船　　名	CAPE COOK V. 0109E	装运港	广州港
承运人	SINOTRANS GUANGDONG COMPANY 承运人提单签发人：刘丽娟		
保单号码	PEXP20014401AG - 074	投保日期	2011 年 2 月 25 日
集装箱号	SITU2982898/1267471（20’）	合同号码	44GD125AG - 074
FORM A 申请日	2011 年 2 月 23 日	FORM A 号	GZ1/80330/0064
货物包装情况	WRAPED WITH PLASTIC FILM AND WITH CORRUGATED BONED ED AND BOTTOM AND SIDE, TOTAL IN 23 PALLETS.		
实际装船货物	PVC 扁平管 2IN * 10M　50ROLLS　USD4. 85/ROLL 2IN * 20M　90ROLLS　USD9. 70/ROLL 2IN * 30M　118ROLLS　USD14. 45/ROLL 2IN * 50M　496ROLLS　USD24. 10/ROLL 2IN * 100M　180ROLLS　USD48. 40/ROLL	唛头： KIW A09553 OSAKA NO. 1-UP MADE IN CHINA	

综合制单练习七

恒 生 銀 行
HANG SENG BANK

SUCCESS DEVELOPMENT TRADING LTD　　　　Date : 15-Jan-2011
39 /FL. BLOCK 3. FLAT F. NAM FUNG
PLAZA. TSEUNG KWAN O.N.T.
HONG KONG

Dear Sir,

Documentary Credit No.	667-01-3042855
Amount	USD 26,330.40
LC issuing bank	NORDEA BANK DANMARK A/S COPENHAGEN DENMARK
Applicant	YYSK ABC TRADING LTD.
In favour of	SUCCESS DEVELOPMENT TRADING LTD.
Our Ref :	DCAGZU030021

In accordance with the terms of Article 9(a) of UCP 600 we advise having received the captioned Documentary Credit in your favour.

Please Check the terms and conditions of this credit immediately and note that we are unable to make any changes without the issuing bank's authority. Accordingly, should any of its terms/conditions be unacceptable to you, please contact the applicant directly with a view to obtaining a suitable amendment without delay to be advised to us. You are not entitled to rely on any communications or any discussions at any time with us, the issuing bank or applicant as in any way amending this credit, save to the extent that the credit has been amended in writing under an advice signed by our authorised signatories. Your attention is also drawn to articles 4 and 5 of UCP600.

Please attach the original of this form to the documentary credit when presenting documents for negotiation.

Attached please find the documentary credit.

We have debited your account 502-002819-055 As follows:

DC Advising Comm.	**USD** 26.00
Total	**USD** 26.00

Yours faithfully,
Hang Seng Bank Limited

Authorized Signature(s)

恒生銀行有限公司广州分行 **Hang Seng Bank Limited, Guangzhou Branch**
于香港特別行政区成立 Incorporated in HKSAR with Limited Liability
广州市天河北路233号中信广场商场首层 邮政编码510613 G/F Shopping Arcade CITIC Plaza, 233 Tian He North Road Guangzhou Postal Code 510613 PRC
电话 Tel (8620) 8752 0008　图文传真 Fax (8620) 8752 0606

15287

恒生銀行
HANG SENG BANK

Branch

SUCCESS DEVELOPMENT TRADING LTD.　　Our ref.: DCAGZU030021

USD TWENTY SIX THOUSAND THREE HUNDRED THIRTY AND CENTS FORTY ONLY

Dear Sirs,

Without any responsibility or engagement on the part of this Bank, we advise having received the following SWIFT message dated 14-Jan-2011

From NORDEA BANK DANMARK A/S COPENHAGEN DENMARK

40A	FORM OF DC	IRREVOCABLE TRANSFERABLE
20	DC NO	667-01-3042855
31C	DATE OF ISSUE	14JAN2011
31D	EXPIRY DATE AND PLACE	
	DATE OF EXPIRY	15MAR2011
	PLACE OF EXPIRY	IN CHINA
50	APPLICANT	YYSK ABC TRADING LTD OEKONOMIAFDELINGEN FOERETAGSVAEGEN 685 S-23855 ARLOEV SWEDEN
59	BENEFICIARY	
	FULL N/A	SUCCESS DEVELOPMENT TRADING LTD 39/FL BLOCK 3 FLAT F, NAM FUNG PLAZA TSEUNG KWAN O.N.T. HONGKONG
32B	DC AMT	
	CCY/AMT	USD26,330.40
39A	PCT CR AMT TOLERANCE	
	PCT CR AMT TOLERANCE	10/10
41D	AVAILABLE WITH/BY	
	AVAILABLE WITH	ANY BANK BY NEGOTIATION
42C	DRAFTS AT	AT SIGHT
42D	DRAWEE	
	FULL N/A	ISSUING BANK
43P	PARTIAL SHIPMENTS	PROHIBITED
43T	TRANSHIPMENT	ALLOWED
44A	LOADING/DISPATCH AT/FM CHINA	
44B	FOR TRANSPORTATION TO GOTHENBURG, SWEDEN	
44C	LATEST DATE OF SHIPMENT	28FEB2011

..........TO BE CONTINUED ON PAGE 2..........

For HANG SENG BANK LTD.

....
AUTHORIZED SIGNATURE(S)

1528

恒生銀行 Branch
HANG SENG BANK

SUCCESS DEVELOPMENT TRADING LTD Our ref.: DCAGZU030021

DC No. 667-01-3042855 of NORDEA BANK DANMARK A/S COPENHAGEN DENMARK

45A GOODS
+AS PE S/C NO 2011KG02350 AND JYSK ORDER 4500341081:
8400 PCS OF GARMENTS ART 3900300 USD 1,25/PC, 40 PCS/CTN
15520 PCS OF GARMENTS ART 3901400 USD.1,02/PC,40 PCS/CTN
+ C F R GOTHENBURG, SWEDEN

46A DOCUMENTS REQUIRED
+ INVOICES IN 1 FOLD, SHOWING THE NAME OF AGENT IN DENMARK
+ COPIES OF INVOICES IN 4 FOLD
+ PACKING LIST IN 1 FOLD
+ COPIES OF PACKING LISTS IN 3 FOLD
+ FULL SET ON BOARD MARINE BILLS OF LADING ISSUED TO ORDER OF APPLICANT MARKED FREIGHT PREPAID
+ CERTIFICATE OF ORIGIN IN 1 FOLD
+ COPY OF CERTIFICATE OF ORIGIN IN 1 FOLD

47A ADDITIONAL CONDITIONS
+ WE ARE INFORMED THAT INSURANCE IS COVERED BY APPLICANT.
+ 10,00 PERCENT MORE OR LESS IN QUANTITY ALLOWED
+ ALL DOCUMENTS MUST BE ISSUED IN ENGLISH
+ MULTIMODAL TRANSPORT DOCUMENTS ACCEPTABLE EVIDENCING SHIPMENT CLEAN ON BOARD ON A NAMED VESSEL
+ PLEASE NOTE THAT A FEE OF DKK 500,00 OR EQUIVALENT WILL BE DEDUCTED FROM THE AMOUNT PAID, IF WE HAVE TO CONTACT APPLICANT IN ORDER TO WAIVE DISCREPANCIES IN THE PRESENTED DOCUMENTS.
+ AGENT:
SCHOU ISENKRAM A/S
INDUSTRIVEJ 36
6580 VAMDRUP
DENMARK
CREDIT AMOUNT INCLUDES 5 PER CENT AGENTS COMMISSION FOR ABOVE MENTIONED AGENT.
THE AMOUNT WILL BE DEDUCTED AT THE TIME OF PAYMENT.
+ BILL OF LADING MUST SHOW CONTAINER NUMBER.
+ BARCODE HAS TO BE MARKED ON EACH SET OR PICE AND BARCODE ON EACH OUTHER COLLIE.
+ P/L MUST BE SPECIFIED PER ART NUMBER AND CONTAINER NUMBER.

71B	DETAILS OF CHARGES	ALL COMMISSION AND CHARGES ARE FOR BENEFICIARIES ACCOUNT. OUR CHARGES WILL BE DEDUCTED/CLAIMED AT THE TIME OF PAYMENT, NEGOTIATION OR EXPIRY.
48	PERIOD FOR PRESENTATION	15 DAYS
49	CONFIRMATION INSTRUCTIONS	WITHOUT
78	INFO TO PRESENTING BK ON RECEIPT OF MAIL ADVICE OF NEGOTIATION WE SHALL COVER AS PER INSTRUCTIONS RECEIVED	
57D	ADVISE THRU FULL N/A	HANG SENG BANK LTD GUANGZHOU BRANCH HONG KONG
72	BK TO BK INFO	PLEASE FORWARD DOCS. IN ONE LOT BY COURIER TO NORDEA BANK AS, CHRISTIANSBRO, STRANDGADE 3, 0900 COPENHAGEN C, DENMARK PHONE BENEFICIARY

FOR HANG SENG BANK LT

AUTHORIZED SIGNATURE(S)

HERE ENDS THE FOREGOING MESSAGE. THIS ADVICE CONSTITUTES A DOCUMENTARY CREDIT ISSUED BY THE ABOVE BANK AND MUST BE PRESENTED WITH THE DOCUMENTS/DRAFTS FOR NEGOTIATION/PAYMENT. THE AMOUNT OF EACH DRAWING MUST BE ENDORSED BY THE NEGOTIATING BANK ON THE REVERSE HEREOF. EXCEPT SO FAR AS OTHERWISE EXPRESSLY STATED IN THE CREDIT, THIS DOCUMENTARY CREDIT IS SUBJECT TO UNIFORM CUSTOMS AND PRACTICE FOR DOCUMENTARY CREDITS (2007 REVISION), INTERNATIONAL CHAMBER OF COMMERCE PUBLICATION NO.600.

有关资料：

出口公司名称	成功发展贸易有限公司 出口公司单据签署人：马明龙		
发票号码	201101020SDT	发票日期	2011年1月20日
提单号码	CNHUA01439	提单日期	2011年1月26日
船　　名	YANG CHENG 9　V. 0303		
运　　费	USD1300. 00		
集装箱号	1 * 20'　CAXU6136359/073593		
承运人	KENWA SHIPPING CO. , LTD.		
货运代理人	CHINA OCEAN SHIPPING AGENCY GUANGZHOU 货代提单签发人：陈锋		
装运港	广州港		
商品编码	52095100. 92		
产地证号码	CCPIT440106323		
产地证申报日	2011年1月22日		
装箱情况	PACKING：40PCS/CTN		

		QUANTITY (PC)	N. W. (CTN)	G. W. (CTN)	MEAS. (CTN)
实际装船货物	GARMENTS				
	ART 3900300	8400PCS	@6KGS	@6. 5KGS	@（40 * 35 * 32）CM
	ART 3901400	15600 PCS	@6KGS	@6. 5KGS	@（40 * 35 * 332）CM
唛头	唛头1：ABC/ 3900300/ NO. 1 - 210 唛头2：ABC/ART 3901400/NO. 1 - 390				

综合制单练习八

2011JUL13　08：55：30　　Logical Terminal G5A7

IT　S700　　**Issue of a Documentary Credit**　　Page　00001

Fune　GZPRQ

MSGACK　DWS7651 Auth OK,　key　03,　BKCHCNBJ　MITKJPJT　record 564785

Basic Header	F　01 BKCHCNBJA400 8493　103614		
Application Header	0　700　1223　980113　MITKJPJTAXXX 2237 199654 110713 1123 ＊SAKURA　BANK, LTD., THE (FORMERLY ＊MITSUI TAIYO KOBE) ＊TOKYO		
User Header	Service Code		103:
	Bank Priority		113:
	Msg User Ref.		108:
	Info. From CI		115:
Sequence of Total	*27	:	1 / 1
Form of　Doc. Credit	*40 A	:	IRREVOCABLE
Doc.　Credit　Number	*20	:	645-3000598
Date　of　Issue	31 C	:	110713
Expiry	*31 D	:	Date 110825 Place IN THE COUNTRY OF BENEFICIARY
Applicant	*50	:	ABC CO., LTD. 7-CHOME UENO TAITO-KU TOKYO, JAPAN
Beneficiary	*59	:	GUANGDONG MACHINERY IMPORT AND EXPORT CORP. (GROUP) 726 DONG FENG ROAD EAST, GUANGZHOU, CHINA
Amount	*32 B	:	Currency　USD　Amount　15960,00
Available with/by	*41 D	:	ANY BANK IN CHINA BY NEGOTIATION
Drafts at . . .	42 C	:	DRAFT(S) AT 30 DAYS SIGHT INDUPLICATE TO ORDER OF OURSELVE
Drawee	42 A	:	MITKJPJT ＊SAKURA　BANK, LTD., THE (FORMERLY ＊MITSUI TAIYO KOBE) ＊TOKYO
Partial Shipments	43 P	:	PARTIAL SHIPMENTS ARE NOT ALLOWED
Transshipment	43 T	:	TRANSIHIPMENT IS NOT ALLOWED
Loading in Charge	44 A	:	GUANGZHOU PORT
For Transport to . .	44 B	:	YOKOHAMA
Latest Date of Ship.	44 C	:	111010
Descript. Of Goods	45 A	:	

"RABBIT" BRAND SHOVEL WITH METAL HANDLE, S501MH 400DOZ FOR
20FT CONTAINER. AS PER S/C NO. A98JP19900006,
TRADE TERM: CIFD5% YOKOHAMA

Documents required　　46 B　　:

＊SIGNED INVOICE IN 2 COPIES, 5% DISCOUNT SHOULD BE DEDUCTED FROM TOTAL INVOICE VALUE, CERTIFYING MERCHANDISE TO BE OF CHINESE ORIGIN.

＊PACKING LIST IN 2 COPIES.

＊FULL SET OF CLEAN ON BOARD OCEAN BILLS OF LADING MADE OUT TO ORDER OF SHIPPER AND BLANK ENDORSED, MARKED "FREIGHT PREPAID" AND NOTIFY APPLICANT, SHOWING SHIPPING AGENT AT YOKOHAMA.

2011JUL11　08：55：31　　　　Logical Terminal G5A7
IT　S700

Issue of a Documentary Credit

Page　00001
Fune　GZPRQ

＊INSURANCE POLICY OR CERTIFICATE IN DUPLICATE, ENDORSED IN BLANK FOR 110 PER CENT OF THE CIF INCOICE VALUE.
INSURANCE MUST INCLUDE:
OCEAN MARINE CARGO CLAUSES (ALL RISKS) AND OCEAN MARINE CARGO WAR RISK CLAUSES OF THE PEOPLE'S INSURANCE CO. OF CHINA.
CLAIMS PAYABLE IN JAPAN IN CURRENCY OF DRAFT(S).
＊CERTIFICATE OF ORIGIN G.S.P. 'FORM A', ORIGINAL AND ONE COPY, EVIDENCING CHINA AS ORIGIN OF GOODS

Additional Cond.　47 A　:
*ALL DOCUMENTS MENTIONING THIS L/C NO.
*T.T. REIMBURSEMENT IS NOT ACCEPTABLE.
*AMOUNT AND QUANTITY 5PCT MORE OR LESS ALLOWED.
*IF ANY DISCREPANCY, WE SHALL DEDUCT USD50.00 BEING OUR FEE FROM THE PROCESS

Details of Charges　71 B　: ALL BANKING CHARGES OUTSIDE JAPAN ARE FOR ACCOUNT OF THE BENEFICIARY

Presentation Period　48　DOCUMENTS MUST BE PRESENTED WITHIN 15 DAYS AFTER THE DATE OF SHIPMENT

Confirmation　*49　WITHOUT

Instructions　78　:
NEGOTIATING BANK SHOULD FORWARD THE DOCUMENTS DIRECT TO THE SAKURA BANK, LTD., TOKYO INT'L OPERATIONS CENTER
C.P.O. BOX 766, TOKYO, JAPAN
BY REGISTERED AIRMAIL IN ONE LOT.
ON RECEIPT OF THE REQUIRED DOCUMENTS WHICH COMPLY WITH THE TERMS OF THIS CREDIT, WE WILL COVER TO THEM IN ACCORDANCE WITH THEIR INSTRUCTION.

Trailer　Order is <MAC:> <PAC:> <ENC:> <CHK:> <TNG:> <PDE:>
MAC:5CA83538
CHK:A35474D30747

有关资料：

出口公司	广东省机械进出口（集团）公司 出口公司单据签署人：吴天贵		
发票号码	2011－199－2030	发票日期	2011年9月2日
提单号码	COSO299120029	提单日期	2011年9月12日
FORM A 号码	GZ5/80706/6658	FORM A 申请日期	2011年9月6日
货　　物 原材料情况	完全中国产，不含任何进口成分		
保单号码	KC2011－02151	投保日期	2011年9月11日
承运人	COSCO CONTAINER LINES		
货运代理人	CHINA OCEAN SHIPPING AGENCY GUANGZHOU 货代提单签发人：陈锋		
承运人 横滨代理	SEIWA CO., LTD.（SUB－AGENT OF COSCO－SEIWA）		
集装箱号	1＊20' FCL FBZU0205688　SEAL154345		
船　　名	JING AN CHENG V. 0224E		
净　　重	24KGS/BUN	毛　　重	25KGS/BUN
货物装箱情况	1DOZ/BUN	尺　　码	（80＊35＊23）CM/BUN
单　　价	USD40.00/DOZ		
实际装船货物	420 DOZ		
唛　　头	A98JP1990006 YOKOHAMA NO.1－UP		
议付行	中国银行广东分行 票据签署人：李黎明		

综合制单练习九

2G084

Wachovia Bank, National Association
Shanghai Branch
Unit 1604, Aurora Plaza, 99 Fucheng Road, Shanghai, P.R.C.
美国美联银行有限公司
上海市富城路 99 号震旦国际大楼 1604 单元

Phone: 86-021-68599928
Fax: 86-021-68596882
SWIFT: PNBPCNSH
TELEX: 83030 WACH HX

WACHOVIA

DATE 05/31/2012 ADVISED L/C OUR REF. NO. EA099334

ADVISING BANK	CORRESPONDENT/ISSUING BANK LEBANESE CANADIAN BANK S.A.L. GHANTOUS BLDG.: DORA BOULEVARD POB 11-2520 BEIRUT LEBANON
BENEFICIARY GUANGDONG LIGHT HOUSEWARE CO.,LTD. 52 DEZHENG RD SOUTH GUANGZHOU-CHINA	REF. NO. OF CORR/ISSUING BANK 207/21/09/000038 AMOUNT : 10,154.70USD EXPIRY DATE : 07/20/2012 ISSUE DATE : 05/28/2012
APPLICANT : THE SONS OF FAYSAL HAMDOUN S.A.R.L	

-We have been requested to advise to you the attached letter of credit. Our advice of this letter of credit conveys no obligation on the part of our bank. (We draw your attention to Article 12a of UCP600)
-Documents must conform strictly with the terms of the attached letter of credit. If you are unable to comply with same, please communicate directly with the applicant in order to have the issuing bank amend the relevant condition(s).
-When presenting of documents, please include the original advice of credit, original advice of amendment, if any. If no original advice of credit is presented along with the documents, the presenting bank is required to indicate on their cover schedule certifying that they had endorsed the credit for the drawing amount.
-All documents must be presented to Wachovia Bank, National Association, Shanghai at the address as indicated above.
-Should you choose to present documents directly to us, please fill out the attached Collection Order. If we pay, we will pay in the L/C currency to your account with your banker. Please note we are unable to pay in CNY. To defray the cost of sending documents to us, we will refund your courier cost up to USD2.50. For more information on Wachovia Bank N.A., visit our Head Office's Web site at www.wachovia.com.
-We reserve the right to refuse to become a party to any transaction that may violate such U.S. sanctions, and act in accordance with the guidelines of such sanctions.
-All inquiries regarding this credit should be directed to Trade operations at Tel: 021-6859-9928 by select 1 for Chinese language and then select 4 for Customer Care Unit.
-Please send your inquiries to our Customer Service. E-mail Address: customercaretrade.shanghai@wachovia.com
-Please let us have your payment of CNY 324.00 being the advising fee.
- Notwithstanding the confirmation request from the issuing bank, Wachovia Bank, N.A. as the advising bank has not confirmed the LC at the request of the beneficiary.

```
5/28/2012 20:15:04
     GSMOS Ref # CNHG20120528SDS7840          - OSN # 0477113207
-------------------------------------------------------------------------
              Authentication Result: Correct with current key
---------------------- Instance Type and Transmission ------------------
   Original received from SWIFT
   Priority                       : Normal
   Message Output Reference       : 0800 120528PNBPCNSHCXXX0477113207
   Correspondent Input Reference  : 1431 120528LECALBBEAXXX6866399973
------------------------------- Message Header --------------------------
 Swift Output   : 700 ISSUE OF A DOCUMENTARY CREDIT
 Sender         : LECALBBEAXXX
                  LEBANESE CANADIAN BANK S.A.L.
                  GHANTOUS BLDG.
                  DORA BOULEVARD
                  BEIRUT, LEBANON LB
 Receiver       : PNBPCNSHCXXX
                  WACHOVIA BANK, NA
                  UNIT 1604
                  99 FUCHENG ROAD, PUDONG
                  SHANGHAI, CHINA
-------------------------------- Message Text ---------------------------
 27 : Sequence of Total
      1/1
 40A: Form of Documentary Credit
      IRREVOCABLE
 20 : Documentary Credit Number
      207/21/09/000038
 31C: Date of Issue
      120528
 40E: Applicable Rules
      UCPURR LATEST VERSION
 31D: Date and Place of Expiry
      120720 AT YOUR COUNTERS
 50 : Applicant
      THE SONS OF FAYSAL HAMDOUN S.A.R.L
      BEIRUT - LEBANON
 59 : Beneficiary
      GUANGDONG LIGHT HOUSEWARE CO.,LTD.
      52 DEZHENG RD SOUTH GUANGZHOU-CHINA
      TEL:86-20-83519457/86-20-83850292
      FAX:86-20-83355241/86-20-83332622
 32B: Currency Code, Amount
      USD10154,70
 39B: Maximum Credit Amount
      NOT EXCEEDING
 41A: Available With... By... (BIC)
      PNBPCNSH
      WACHOVIA BANK, NA
      UNIT 1604
      99 FUCHENG ROAD, PUDONG
      SHANGHAI, CHINA
      BY PAYMENT
 43P: Partial Shipments
      NOT PERMITTED
 43T: Transhipment
      PERMITTED
 44E: Port of Loading/Airport of Departure
      GUANGZHOU PORT - CHINA
```

5/28/2012 20:15:04 2
GSMOS Ref # CNHG20120528SDS7840 - OSN # 0477113207 (Continued)

44F: Port of Discharge/Airport of Destination
BEIRUT PORT - LEBANON
44C: Latest Date of Shipment
120705
45A: Description of Goods and/or Services
ALUMINIUM LADDER 1.0 MM.

DESCRIPTION	QUANTITY	U. PRICE	TOTAL AMOUNT
.			
GHH3 3 STEPS	40 PCS	USD. 9.28	USD. 371.20
GHH4 4 STEPS	50 PCS	USD.10.54	USD. 527.00
GHH5 5 STEPS	100 PCS	USD.12.44	USD.1,244.00
GHH6 6 STEPS	150 PCS	USD.14.16	USD.2,124.00
GHH7 7 STEPS	200 PCS	USD.16.13	USD.3,226.00
GHH8 8 STEPS	150 PCS	USD.17,75	USD.2,662.50

.
PACKING : IN NYLON SACS
.
SHIPMENT : IN 1 X 40 FEET HQ CONTAINER
.
AS PER PROFORMA INVOICE NO.09RQA2G084 DATED MAY 18,2012.
.
TOTAL AMOUNT OF L/C NOT EXCEEDING USD. 10,154.70 (U.S.DOLLARS TEN THOUSAND ONE HUNDRED FIFTY FOUR AND 70/100 ONLY)
.
F.O.B. GUANGZHOU PORT - CHINA (AS PER INCOTERMS 2010) AT THE PRICE OF F.C.A. CONTAINER LOADED ONTO VESSEL AT GUANGZHOU PORT - CHINA AT BENEFICIARIES RISK AND EXPENSES

46A: Documents Required
1- SIGNED COMMERCIAL INVOICE IN THREE COPIES, BEARING THE FOLLOWING STATEMENTS: '' WE HEREBY CERTIFY THAT THIS INVOICE IS AUTHENTIC, (ITS CONTENTS ARE TRUE), PRICES MENTIONED HEREIN ARE CORRECT AND CURRENT WITHOUT DEDUCTION OF ANY ADVANCE PAYMENT MADE ON ACCOUNT, AND THAT THE ORIGIN OF THE GOODS IS EXCLUSIVELY CHINESE AND THAT IT IS THE ONLY INVOICE ISSUED BY US FOR THE MERCHANDISE DESCRIBED THEREIN''.
''WE CONFIRM THAT THE GOODS SHIPPED ARE CONFORM TO THOSE LISTED ON PROFORMA INVOICE NO. 09RQA2G084 DATED MAY 18,2012''.
COMMERCIAL INVOICE SHOULD SHOW THE NUMBER OF PACKAGES, THE GROSS WEIGHT AND THE NET WEIGHT.
THREE COPIES MUST BE CERTIFIED BY THE CHAMBER OF COMMERCE.
2- COMPLETE SET OF CLEAN MARINE OCEAN BILL OF LADING CONSIGNED TO THE ORDER OF LEBANESE CANADIAN BANK SAL
MARKED: CONTAINER ACTUALLY LOADED ON BOARD ON (ON BOARD DATE) (WHICH MUST BE SIGNED AND STAMPED BY THE SAME SIGNOR OF THE BILL OF LADING)
AND FREIGHT PAYABLE AT DESTINATION
NOTIFY: THE SONS OF FAYSAL HAMDOUN SARL.
BEIRUT - LEBANON
(SHORT FORM OR BLANK BACK DOCUMENTS NOT ACCEPTABLE)
BILL OF LADING SHOULD SHOW THAT THE SHIP DOES NOT SAIL UNDER AN ISRAELI FLAG AND WILL NOT CALL AT ANY ISRAELI PORT (A SEPARATE CERTIFICATE IN THIS CONCERN IS ACCEPTABLE)
IN CASE BILL OF LADING PRESENTED IN MULTIPLE PAGES, ALL THE PAGES SHOULD REFER TO THE DATE AND NUMBER OF THE BILL OF LADING AND SIGNED BY THE CARRIER OR ITS AGENT OR BY THE MASTER OR ITS AGENT.
3- IACS CERTIFICATE ISSUED AND SIGNED BY THE CARRIER OR HIS AGENT

5/28/2012 20:15:04 3
GSMOS Ref # CNHG20120528SDS7840 - OSN # 0477113207 (Continued)

46A: Documents Required
STATING THAT:''THE CARRYING VESSEL IS A REGULAR LINER VESSEL, IS CLASSIFIED 100 A1 OR EQUIVALENT, AND IS OF STEEL CONSTRUCTION CLASSED WITH A MEMBER OR ASSOCIATE MEMBER OF THE INTERNATIONAL ASSOCIATION OF CLASSIFICATION SOCIETY (IACS)''.
4- ISM CERTIFICATE ISSUED AND SIGNED BY THE OWNER OR HIS AGENT IN ONE ORIGINAL AND ONE COPY STATING AS FOLLOWS:'' WE CERTIFY THAT AT THE TIME OF LOADING THE CARRYING VESSEL NAMED (INDICATE THE NAME) IS ISM CODE CERTIFIED AND HOLDS A VALID INTERNATIONAL SAFETY MANAGEMENT CERTIFICATE AS WELL AS A VALID ISM CODE DOCUMENT OF COMPLIANCE AS REQUIRED BY THE SOLAS CONVENTION 1974 AS AMENDED''.
5- CERTIFICATE OF ORIGIN ISSUED OR CERTIFIED BY THE CHAMBER OF COMMERCE IN THREE COPIES CERTIFYING THAT THE GOODS ARE OF CHINESE ORIGIN .
6- PACKING LIST IN THREE COPIES.
7- WEIGHT NOTE AND SPECIFICATION LIST IN THREE COPIES.

47A: Additional Conditions
1- ALL DOCUMENTS REQUIRED MUST BEAR L/C NO. 207/21/09/000038
2- ALL OF ORIGINALS AND COPIES MUST BE SIGNED BY HANDWRITING OVER THE RUBBER STAMP OF THE COMPANY NOTWITHSTANDING THAT THE DOCUMENTS ARE ISSUED ON THE HEADING PAPER OF THAT COMPANY.
3- ALL THE DOCUMENTS MUST BE ISSUED IN ENGLISH LANGUAGE BESIDES ANY OTHER LANGUAGE USED IN THE DOCUMENTS.
4- ALL THE DOCUMENTS MUST BE DATED.
5- DOCUMENTS ISSUED AND/OR DATED BEFORE THE DATE OF ISSUANCE OF THE CREDIT ARE NOT ACCEPTABLE.
6- TRANSPORT DOCUMENTS SHOWING NAME OF A THIRD PARTY AS SHIPPER OR CONSIGNOR NOT ACCEPTABLE. ARTICLE 14 k OF UCP 600 NOT APPLICABLE.
7- IF DISCREPANT DOCUMENTS ARE PRESENTED, ADDITIONAL HANDLING CHARGES I.E USD. 50.00 WILL BE INCURRED AND WILL BE ON BENEFICIARIES ACCOUNT WHETHER THE DISCREPANCIES ARE ADVISED OR NOT.
8- APPLICANTS AND BENEFICIARIES ADDRESS MUST BE THE SAME AS STIPULATED IN THE CREDIT.
9- CHARGES: ALL BANKING CHARGES AND COMMISSIONS OUTSIDE LEBANON INCLUDING CONFIRMATION CHARGES (IF ANY) AND REIMBURSING BANK CHARGES ARE ON BENEFICIARIES ACCOUNT AND CANNOT BE CLAIMED FROM US EVEN IF THE L/C CANCELLED OR UNUTILIZED.
10- COMMERCIAL INVOICE ISSUED FOR AN AMOUNT EXCEEDING THE LIMIT PERMITTED BY THE CREDIT IS NOT ACCEPTABLE.ART 18b NOT APPLICABLE.
11- ALL ORIGINAL TRANSPORT DOCUMENTS REQUIRED UNDER THIS CREDIT MUST BE PREPRINTED WITH THE WORD ''ORIGINAL''.
12- TRANSPORT DOCUMENTS BEARING REFERENCE BY STAMP OR OTHERWISE TO CHARGES ADDITIONAL TO THE FREIGHT IS NOT ACCEPTABLE.
13- THE MARINE BILL OF LADING MUST CLEARLY INDICATE THE NAME OF THE CARRIER AND CLEARLY STATES ITS FUNCTION/QUALITY IN THE FOLLOWING STRICT MANNER:''THE CARRIER'' AND NOT ''AS CARRIER''.

71B: Charges
SEE FIELD 47A: ADDITIONAL CONDITIONS.

48 : Period of Presentation
15 DAYS AFTER DATE OF SHIPMENT

49 : Confirmation Instructions
MAY ADD

5/28/2012 20:15:04 4
GSMOS Ref # CNHG20120528SDS7840 - OSN # 0477112207 (Continued)

53A: Reimbursing Bank (BIC)
PNBPUS3NNYC
WACHOVIA BANK, NA
375 PARK AVENUE
NY 4080
NEW YORK,NY, UNITED STATES

78 : Instructions to Paying/Acpting/Nego Bank
+ AFTER COMPLYING PRESENTATION AT YOUR COUNTERS, YOU ARE AUTHORIZED TO NEGOTIATE DOCUMENTS PRESENTED UNDER THE ABOVE MENTIONED L/C SPECIFYING ITS AMOUNT UNDER SWIFT CONFIRMATION TO US.
IN COVER OF YOUR PAYMENT WE AUTHORIZE YOU TO REIMBURSE YOURSELVES ON OUR USD.A/C NO. 2000193003242 HELD WITH WACHOVIA BANK N.A - NEW YORK VALUE FIVE WORKING DAYS UNDER SWIFT CONFIRMATION TO US.
+ PLEASE CONSIDER THE PRESENT MESSAGE AS CONTAINING FULL DETAILS THUS THE OPERATIVE INSTRUMENT OF CREDIT.
WACHOVIA BANK HOLDS SPECIAL INSTRUCTIONS REGARDING DOCUMENT DISPOSAL AND REIMBURSEMENT OF THIS LETTER OF CREDIT.

72 : Sender to Receiver Information
+ PLEASE SEND DOCUMENTS BY DHL
SPECIAL COURIER TO OUR ADDRESS
IN BEIRUT: LEBANESE CANADIAN BANK
SAL. DORA BLVD. GHANTOUS BLDG.
BEIRUT - LEBANON

------------------------------ Message Trailer ------------------------------

{MAC:00000000}
{CHK:9810B18AEED1}
END

有关资料：

出口公司	广东轻出百货有限公司 出口公司单据签署人：周国通		
发票号码	2012HQA2G084	发票日期	2012年6月13日
提单号码	CHIBEY90734	提单日期	2012年6月17日
船　　名	DANDELINE　V. AMS－1152W		
集装箱号	1＊40’ HQ　FCL/ FCL　CY/CY SBAU5161475/297788		
目的港	贝鲁特港（BEIRUT）		
承运人	SINO－LINE SHIPPING LIMITED		
货运代理人	GLOBAL AIM TRADING AND SHIPPING（G. A. T. S） 货代提单签发人：吴茂君		
CO 号码	CCPIT088587360	CO 申报日期	2012年6月15日
商品编码	761699	ISM 日期	2012年6月17日
唛　　头	N/M	IACS 日期	2012年6月17日

实际装船货物：

	QUANTITY (PCS)	PACKAGE (CTNS)	N. W (KGS/CTN)	G. W. (KGS/CTN)	MEAS. (CBMS/CTN)
ALUMINIUM LADDER	1.0MM				
GHH3　3STEPS	40	8	8.50	9.00	1.60＊0.30＊0.34
GHH4　4STEPS	50	10	9.50	10.00	1.60＊0.30＊0.34
GHH5　5STEPS	99	33	11.50	12.00	1.81＊0.39＊0.34
GHH5　5STEPS	1	1	11.50	12.00	1.81＊0.39＊0.34
GHH6　6STEPS	150	50	12.50	13.00	1.81＊0.39＊0.34
GHH7　7STEPS	198	66	13.50	14.20	2.00＊0.41＊0.34
GHH7　7STEPS	2	1	13.50	14.20	2.00＊0.41＊0.34
GHH8　8STEPS	150	50	14.80	15.50	2.00＊0.41＊0.34
PACKING：IN NYLON SACS					

综合制单练习十

OFFICE: AGRICULTURAL BANK OF CHINA HENGSHUI BRANCH
ADDRESS: 358 EAST SHENGLI ROAD HENG SHUI CITY 053000 HEBEI CHINA

信 用 证 通 知 书

NOTIFICATION OF DOCUMENTARY CREDIT

DATE 日期 Sep 22, 2011

TO: 致 DONGFENG FOOD CO. LTD.	Our Ref No. 我行编号 030EX09041O287
	Amount 金额 USD33,894.00
Issuing Bank 开证行 MIZRAHI TEFAHOT BANK LTD. 17, LINCOLN STREET	Transmitted to us through 转递行
L/C No. 信用证号 TA/055/56765/1	Issuing Date 开证日期 Sep 21, 2011

Dear Sirs, 迳启者:
We have pleasure in advising you that we have received from the A / M bank a(n)
兹 通 知 贵 公 司 , 我 行 收 自 上 述 银 行

(X) SWIFT ISSUING	SWIFT开立	(　) MAIL CONFIRMATION OF	证实书
(　) TELEX ISSUING	电传开立	(　) UNEFFECTIVE	未生效
(　) MAIL ISSUING	邮寄开立	(X) ORIGINAL	正本
(　) PRE-ADVISING OF	预先通知	(　) DUPLICATE	副本

Letter of Credit, contents of which are as per attached sheet(s).
This advice and the attached sheet(s) must accompany the relative documents when presented.
信 用 证 一 份 , 现 随 附 通 知 。 贵 公 司 交 单 时 , 请 将 本 通 知 书 及 信 用 证 一 并 提 示 。

Remarks 备注:

-PLEASE NOTE THAT THIS ADVICE DOES NOT CONSTITUTE OUR CONFIRMATION OF THE ABOVE L/C NOR DOES IT CONVEY ANY ENGAGEMENT OR OBLIGATION ON OUR PART.
本通知书不构成我行对此信用证之保兑及其他任何责任.

This L / C consists of　　　　sheet(s), including the covering letter and attachment(s).
本信用证连同面函及附件共　　　　页。

If you find any terms and conditions in the L / C which you are unable to comply with and / or any error(s), It is suggested that you contact applicant directly for necessary amendment(s) so as to avoid any difficulties which may arise when documents are presented.
如 本 信 用 证 中 有 无 法 办 到 的 条 款 及 / 或 错 误 , 请 迳 与 开 证 申 请 人 联 系 进 行 必 要 的 修 改 , 以 排 除 交 单 时 可 能 发 生 的 问 题。

Please credit ____________ as advising fee to our A / C
No. ____________ with ____________.
本通知费 ____________ 请划入我行 ____________ 账户,
账号 ____________ 。

负责人签收:

SAFE Reference :023049080190921
Received from :MIZBILIT
MIZRAHI TEFAHOT BANK LTD.
Message Type :MT 700 ISSUE OF A DOCUMENTARY
Date :Sep 22 2011
:27:Sequence of Total
1/2
:40A:Form of Documentary Credit
IRREVOCABLE
:20:Documentary Credit Number
TA/055/56765/1
:40E:
UCP LATEST VERSION
:31D:Date and Place of Expiry
111105 ISRAEL
:50:Applicant
G.WILLI-FOOD INTERNATIONAL LTD
NAHAL SNIR STREET 3
YAVNE ISRAEL
:59:Beneficiary
DONGFENG FOOD CO. LTD
DATUN INDUSTRIAL ZONE,
SHENZHOU CITY, HEBEI PROVINCE,
CHINA 053873
:32B:Currency Code, Amount
USD33894,
:41A:Available With ... By ...
MIZBILIT
BY PAYMENT
:43P:Partial Shipments
NOT ALLOWED
:43T:Transshipment
ALLOWED
:44E:
TIANJIN PORT
:44F:
ASHDOD PORT
:44C:Latest Date of Shipment
111015
:45A:Description of Goods and/or Services
2 X 40 FT FCLS TO CONTAIN THE FOLLOWING:
1. 1 X 40 FT FCL CONTAINING 1050 STRONG EXPORT CARTONS,
EACH CARTON TO CONTAIN 72 BAGS (12 X 6) OF
22 GR BAGS OF APPLE CHIPS NATURAL FLAVOUR WITHOUT PEEL,
PACKED IN 6 UNITS PACKAGE, AT USD 0.218/22 GR BAG.
BARCODE FOR 22 GR BAG: 6928740700544,
BARCODE FOR THE 6 UNITS PACKAGE: 7290011615314

2. 1 X 40 FT FCL TO CONTAIN:
A. 525 STRONG EXPORT CARTONS, EACH CARTON TO CONTAIN 76 BAGS OF
APPLE CHIPS ORIGINAL FLAVOUR WITHOUT PEEL IN 22 GR BAGS
AT USD 0.218/BAG
BARCODE: 6928740700544

SAFE Reference :023049080190921
Received from :MIZBILIT
MIZRAHI TEFAHOT BANK LTD.
Message Type :MT 700 ISSUE OF A DOCUMENTARY
Date :Sep 22 2011

B. 525 STRONG EXPORT CARTONS.EACH CARTON TO CONTAIN 40 BAGS OF APPLE CHIPS ORIGINAL FLAVOUR WITHOUT PEEL IN 43 GR BAGS, AT USD 0.415/BAG.
BARCODE: 6928740700643.
PRICE BASIS: FOB
TIANJIN PORT
:47A:Additional Conditions
+ALL DOCUMENTS MUST INDICATE OUR ABOVE CREDIT NUMBER
+IF L/C SHOULD EXPIRE UNUTILIZED AT ADVISING BANK'S OR THROUGH BANK'S COUNTERS ANY CHARGES FOR NON - UTILIZATION TO BE BORNE BY BENEFICIARY
:71B:Charges
ALL BANK CHARGES OUTSIDE OF ISRAEL ARE FOR BENEFICIARY'S ACCOUNT
:49:Confirmation Instructions
WITHOUT
:78:Instruction to the Paying/Accepting/Negotiating Back
+ON PRESENTATION OF DOCUMENTS IN STRICT CONFORMITY WITH L/C TERMS AND CONDITIONS, PLS SEND SAME TO US BY SPECIAL COURIER TO : 105 ALLENBY ST. TEL AVIV. AND WE SHALL COVER YOU AS PER YOUR INSTRUCTIONS 5 WORKING DAYS AFTER RECEIPT OF DOCUMENTS AT OUR COUNTERS, DATE OF WHICH WE SHALL ADVISE YOU.
+DEBITS/REIMBURSEMENTS FOR DISCREPANT DOCUMENTS ARE NOT PERMITTED
+IF DISCREPANT DOCUMENTS ARE PRESENTED. ISSUING BANK'S HANDLING CHARGES OF 0.1 PCT (MIN USD 25.00) PLUS TELECOMMUNICATION CHARGES WILL BE APPLIED
:72:Sender to Receiver Information
/ACCT/6550-1-90024

SAFE Reference :023049080290921
Received from :MIZBILIT
MIZRAHI TEFAHOT BANK LTD.
Message Type :MT 701 ISSUE OF A DOCUMENTARY
Date :Sep 22 2011
:27:Sequence of Total
2/2
:20:Documentary Credit Number
TA/055/56765/1
:46B:Documents Required
+ 6 MANUALLY SIGNED ORIGINAL INVOICES IN NAME OF APPLICANT STATING THAT GOODS ARE OF CHINA ORIGIN
+ BILLS OF LADING FULL SET CLEAN ON BOARD MARKED FREIGHT PAYABLE AT DESTINATION MENTIONING FULL WORDING OF THE ARAB UNLOADING PROHIBITION CLAUSE AS FOLLOWS:IN VIEW OF DANGER OF CONFISCATION WARRANTED VESSEL/AIRCRAFT IS NOT TO CALL AT PORTS/ AIRPORTS AND NOT TO ENTER THE TERRITORIAL WATERS/AIRSPACE OF SYRIA, LEBANON, JORDAN, IRAQ, SAUDI ARABIA, YEMEN, SUDAN, LYBIA OR ANY OTHER ARAB COUNTRY EXCEPT EGYPT PRIOR TO UNLOADING IN ISRAEL UNLESS IN DISTRESS OR SUBJECT TO FORCE MAJEURE, AND NOTIFY APPLICANT MADE OUT TO THE ORDER OF MIZRAHI TEFAHOT BANK LTD TEL AVIV.
BILL OF LADING STATING THAT THE CARRIER RESERVES ITS RIGHT TO RELEASE GOODS WITHOUT RECEIVING THE ORIGINAL BILL OF LADING WILL NOT BE ACCEPTED.
B/L(S) MUST BE ISSUED BY
ZIM INTEGRATED SHIPPING SERVICES LTD AND MUST EVIDENCE SHIPPING IN 2 X 40 FT FCLS AND LOADING THE CONTAINERS
UNDER THE WATERLINE.
B/L MUST STATE THE FULL NAME AND THE VAT REGISTRATION NUMBER OF THE IMPORTER 520043209 ,WHICH MUST APPEAR
BELOW NOTIFY PARTY DETAILS (IN SAME FIELD), AND VAT REGISTRATION NUMBER OF THE FOREIGN SUPPLIER IN HIS COUNTRY, WHICH MUST APPEAR IN FIELD OF SHIPPER
BELOW SUPPLIER'S DETAILS AND AN UNEQUIVOCAL DESCRIPTION OF THE IMPORTED GOODS INCLUDING THE FIRST FOUR DIGITS OF THE IMPORTED GOODS, H.S.CLASSIFICATION NO. 2006
WHICH MUST APPEAR AFTER DESCRIPTION OF GOODS(IN SAME FIELD).
+ PACKING LIST IN 03 COPIES
+ BNF'S WRITTEN, GUARANTEED AND SIGNED DECLARATION STATING THAT: A. GOODS ARE PACKED IN STRONG EXPORT CARTONS. B. GOODS ARE PACKED IN SUCH A WAY THAT THEY WILL NOT BE DAMAGED DURING TRANSPORTATION. C. EACH ITEM BEARS ENGLISH - HEBREW TEXT STICKER WITH COMPLETE PACKAGING DESIGN WITH WILLI FOOD LOGO WITH PRODUCT'S NAMES, INGREDIENTS, KOSHER INDICATIONS AND NUTRITIONAL VALUES PER 100GR AND PER UNIT, AS PER APPLICANT'S INSTRUCTIONS AND CONFIRMATION DATED MAY 10TH 2009. D. EACH BAG BEARS THE OU KOSHER LOGO + CHATAM SOFER BNEI BERAQ KOSHER LOGO. E. EACH 22 GR BAG, 6 UNITS PACKAGE AND 43 GR BAG BEARS EXPIRY DATE, WHICH IS 16 MONTHS FROM PRODUCTION DATE. F. THE 6 UNITS PACKAGE IS PRINTED ACCORDING TO APPLICANT'S DESIGN AND INSTRUCTIONS, INCLUDING APPLICANT'S BARCODE, LOGO, KOSHER LOGO, PRODUCT'S NAME AND 5+1 FREE OF CHARGE TEXT AND WEIGHT. G. EACH CARTON BEARS CARTON MARKS AS PER APPLICANT'S INSTRUCTIONS AND

```
SAFE Reference          :023049080290921
Received from           :MIZBILIT
                         MIZRAHI TEFAHOT BANK LTD.
Message Type            :MT 701 ISSUE OF A DOCUMENTARY
Date                    :Sep 22 2011
```

EXPIRY DATE. H. SHELF LIFE OF THE PRODUCT IS 16 MONTHS FROM PRODUCTION DATE. I. PRODUCTION DATE IS NOT PRINTED, ONLY EXPIRY DATE IS PRINTED ON EACH 22 GR BAG, THE 5+1 PACKAGING AND EACH 43 GR BAG. J. GOODS ARE FRESH PRODUCTION. K. INSIDE THE CONTAINER THERE ARE ALSO LOADED 2 PCT EMPTY CARTONS OF EACH PRODUCT.

+ LABORATORY ANALYSIS RELATED TO THIS SHIPMENT, MENTIONING L/C AND INVOICE NUMBERS.
+ PHYTOSANITARY CERTIFICATE ISSUED BY CIQ.
+ BEN'S WRITTEN DECLARATION THAT ONE ORIGINAL OF EACH DOCUMENT REQUIRED HAS BEEN FAXED TO APPLICANT AND THEN ONE COPY OF EACH DOCUMENT REQUIRED HAS BEEN SENT TO HIM BY SPECIAL COURIER WITHIN 10 DAYS FROM B/L DATE.
+ QUALITY CERTIFICATE ISSUED BY CIQ.
+ COPY OF BENEFICIARY'S INSTRUCTIONS TO THE SHIPPING LINE, SHOWING BNF'S INSTRUCTIONS TO THE SHIPPING LINE FOR LOADING THE CONTAINER IN THE VESSEL UNDER THE WATERLINE.

有关资料：

出口公司	东风食品有限公司 出口公司单据签署人：龙德生			
发票号码	HBGF2011 - 2548		发票日期	2011 年 10 月 15 日
提单号码	ZIMUXNG1161647		提单日期	2011 年 10 月 26 日
船　名	MERKUR CLOUD V. 941S		唛　头	N/M
集装箱号	1 * 40'　CY/CY　ZCSU2694750/D - 452149			
承运人	ZIM INTEGRATED SHIPPING SERVICES LTD 承运人提单签发人：林东生			
货物装箱情况		净重	毛重	尺码
	72 BAGS/CTN：	1. 584KGS/CTN	2. 584KGS/CTN	（55 * 40 * 256）CM/CTN
	76 BAGS/CTN：	1. 672KGS/CTN	2. 824KGS/CTN	（55 * 40 * 266）CM/CTN
	40 BAGS/CTN：	1. 72KGS/CTN	2. 568KGS/CTN	（55 * 40 * 244）CM/CTN

参考文献

1. 余世明．国际商务单证实务．广州：暨南大学出版社，2008.
2. 余世明．报关员资格考试辅导．广州：暨南大学出版社，2002.
3. 余世明．全国外销员资格考试辅导．广州：暨南大学出版社，2002.
4. 余世明．国际贸易实务练习题及分析解答．广州：暨南大学出版社，2004.
5. 余世明，冼燕华．国际商务模拟实习教程．广州：暨南大学出版社，2004.
6. 余世明．国际货运代理资格考试辅导．广州：暨南大学出版社，2004.
7. 全国国际商务专业人员职业资格考试指定用书编委会．国际商务基础理论与实务．北京：中国对外经济贸易出版社，2003.
8. 中国国际货运代理协会．国际航空货运代理理论与实务．北京：中国商务出版社，2005.
9. 周树玲．外贸单证实务．北京：对外经济贸易大学出版社，2004.
10. 刘启萍，周树玲．外贸英文制单．北京：对外经济贸易大学出版社，2002.
11. 顾　民．外贸制单与结汇．北京：对外经济贸易大学出版社，2001.
12. 梅清豪．外贸信用证实务．上海：东方出版中心，1997.
13. 姚大伟．国际贸易单证实务．北京：中国对外经济贸易出版社，2002.
14. 黎孝先．国际贸易实务．北京：对外经济贸易大学出版社，1994.
15. 吴百福．进出口贸易实务教程．上海：上海人民出版社，2004.
16. 罗来仪，李乃军．对外贸易业务问题集解．北京：对外经济贸易大学出版社，2000.
17. 吴小平．保险原理与实务．北京：中国金融出版社，2003.
18. 陈海联等．报关员考试习题精解．北京：中国海关出版社，2002.

参考文献